Courts, Corrections, and the Constitution

Courts, Corrections, and the Constitution

The Impact of Judicial Intervention on Prisons and Jails

Edited by
JOHN J. DiIULIO, JR.

New York   Oxford
OXFORD UNIVERSITY PRESS
1990

Oxford University Press

Oxford   New York   Toronto
Delhi   Bombay   Calcutta   Madras   Karachi
Petaling Jaya   Singapore   Hong Kong   Tokyo
Nairobi   Dar es Salaam   Cape Town
Melbourne   Auckland

and associated companies in
Berlin   Ibadan

Published by Oxford University Press, Inc.,
200 Madison Avenue, New York, New York 10016

Oxford is a registered trademark of Oxford University Press

Library of Congress Cataloging-in-Publication Data
Courts, corrections, and the Constitution :
the impact of judicial intervention
on prisons and jails
edited by John J. DiIulio, Jr.
p.   cm.   ISBN 0-19-506141-1
1. Prisons—Law and legislation—United States.
2. Correctional law—United States.
3. Judicial process—United States.
I. DiIulio, John J.   KF9730.C68   1990   344.73′035—dc20
[347.30435]   89-70946

9 8 7 6 5 4 3 2 1

Printed in the United States of America
on acid-free paper

Acknowledgments

On behalf of the authors of this volume, I would like to thank the many colleagues who read all or most of the draft manuscript, especially Jameson W. Doig, Mark Alan Hughes, and Ethan Nadelmann. I would also like to thank the Smith Richardson Foundation for its generous support of this project. Last but not least, let me thank Valerie Aubry and her staff at Oxford, and Princeton's Valerie Kanka, Jayne Bialkowski, and Nan Nash for their help with this volume.

Contents

Contributors

ROBERT C. BRADLEY is an assistant professor in the Department of Political Science at Illinois State University. He is currently involved in examining the attributes of the federal district judges who have directly intervened in the operation of prisons and jails through the use of structural reform decrees. In addition, he is researching the implications of structural reform decrees on the correctional, economic, judicial, and political systems.

BRADLEY STEWART CHILTON is assistant professor of political science at Washington State University in Pullman. He received his B.A. in sociology and economics from Milton College, his M.A. in political science from the University of Wisconsin–Madison, and his Ph.D. in political science from the University of Georgia. His dissertation on prison reform litigation in Georgia was awarded the 1988 National Association of Schools of Public Affairs and Administration (NASPAA) Annual Dissertation Award. He teaches jurisprudence, public administration, law and public affairs, and administration of justice.

CLAIR A. CRIPE is general counsel of the Federal Bureau of Prisons in Washington, D.C. He has been an attorney for the Bureau of Prisons for twenty-seven years, the past fourteen as general counsel. He is also a professorial lecturer in corrections law at the National Law Center in George Washington University. Besides his involvement in hundreds of lower court cases, he has directly supported the government's position in several Supreme

Court cases, such as *Bell v. Wolfish, Washington Post v. Saxbe*, and *Abbott v. Meese*. For several years he has been a member of the Public Correctional Policy Committee of the American Correctional Association, which has produced policy guidelines for corrections professionals nationwide.

BEN M. CROUCH has been a professor of sociology at Texas A & M University for the past eighteen years. In addition to a number of papers dealing with corrections and deviance, he has published a book entitled *The Keepers: Prison Guards and Contemporary Corrections* (1980). In 1989 he and James Marquart published *An Appeal to Justice: Litigated Reform of Texas Prisons*. He is currently researching the relationship between drugs and crime and is initiating, with Dr. Marquart, a study of prison gangs.

JOHN J. DIIULIO, JR. is associate professor of politics and public affairs at Princeton University. He spent the 1988–89 academic year as a John M. Olin Faculty Fellow and Guest Scholar at the Brookings Institution. At Princeton he teaches in the Woodrow Wilson School of Public and International Affairs and in the department of politics. He chairs the Woodrow Wilson School's domestic and urban policy graduate program. He received his Ph.D. in political science from Harvard University. A winner of the American Political Science Association's Leonard D. White Award in Public Administration, he is the author of *Governing Prisons: A Comparative Study of Correctional Management* (1987), as well as other books and articles, including *Barbed Wire Bureaucracy: Administration in the Federal Bureau of Prisons, 1930–1990*, forthcoming from Oxford University Press. He has done consulting work for the National Institute of Justice, the National Institute of Corrections, the New York City Board of Corrections, and other agencies.

SHELDON EKLAND-OLSON is professor of sociology at the University of Texas at Austin and is currently special assistant to the chancellor of the University of Texas system. He has recently published *Texas Prisons* (1987) and a number of articles on capital punishment.

MALCOLM M. FEELEY is professor of law and chair of the Center for the Study of Law and Society at the University of California at Berkeley. He is the author of numerous books and articles, including *The Process is the Punishment* (1979), winner of the ABA's Silver Gavel Award, *Court Reform on Trial* (1983), and coauthor of *The Policy Dilemma* (1980). He is currently writing a book on the impact of court orders on prison conditions, as well as completing several studies on the transformation of the criminal process in the eighteenth and nineteenth centuries.

ROGER A. HANSON is senior staff associate of the National Center for State Courts in Williamsburg, Virginia. He holds a degree from the University of Minnesota. In 1984 and 1985 he was a visiting fellow at the National Institute of Justice, and in the first half of 1988 he was a visiting scholar at the National Center for State Courts. His current research interests are alternative dispute resolution, managing civil and criminal appeals, and postconviction actions. He is the author of "Contending Perspectives on Federal Court Efforts to Reform State Institutions" (*University of Colorado Law Review*, Spring 1988).

JAMES W. MARQUART is associate professor of criminal justice at Sam Houston State University. He has recently coauthored a book with Ben M. Crouch entitled *An Appeal to Justice: Litigated Reform of Texas Prisons* (1989) and is currently engaged in conducting research on the death penalty in Texas. He has published several articles on this topic in academic journals.

STEVE J. MARTIN is in private practice and is actively involved with prison litigation at Walla Walla, San Quentin, Attica, and a number of other sites. He received his B.S. and M.A. in correctional administration from Sam Houston State University and his J.D. from the University of Tulsa School of Law. He has been a member of the Texas Council on Offenders with Mental Impairments (1988–89), a special assistant attorney general in Austin, Texas (1985–86), a visiting faculty member at the University of Texas School of Law (1985–86), a general counsel to the Texas Department of Corrections (1981–85), a U.S. probation and parole officer in Tulsa, Oklahoma, and McAllen, Texas (1975–80), and a Texas prison guard.

EDWARD E. RHINE is an assistant chief in the Probation Services Division, Administrative Office of the Courts, in Trenton, New Jersey. He received his B.A. in sociology from Ohio University and his M.A. and Ph.D., also in sociology, from Rutgers University. He is currently coauthoring a book on parole in the United States and Canada, and is coeditor of *Observations on Parole: A Collection of Readings from Western Europe, Canada and the United States* (1987). He has worked for the Department of Corrections and the State Parole Board in New Jersey.

TED STOREY received a B.A. in American studies from Columbia University in 1983. At the University of California at Berkeley he received an M.A. from the Jurisprudence and Social Policy Program in 1987 and a J.D. from the Boalt Hall School of Law in 1989. He is currently practicing in San Francisco.

SUSETTE M. TALARICO is professor of political science and director of criminal justice studies at the University of Georgia. She is the author of *The Social Contexts of Criminal Sentencing* (1987) and a variety of other books, monographs, and articles. Currently she is working on a study of rape shield and tort law reforms.

BERT USEEM is currently a senior scientist at the Urban Research Institute at the University of Louisville and is on leave from the University of Illinois at Chicago, where he is an associate professor of sociology. He has published (with Peter Kimball) *States of Siege: U.S. Prison Riots, 1971–1986* (Oxford, 1989).

Courts, Corrections, and the Constitution

Introduction:
Enhancing Judicial Capacity

JOHN J. DiIULIO, JR.

> Judges are not wardens, but we must act as wardens to the
> limited extent that unconstitutional prison conditions force us
> to intervene when those responsible for the conditions have
> failed to act.
> —*Harris v. Flemming*, 839 F.2d 1232 (7th Cir. 1988)

As late as 1970, judges played a negligible role in the administration
of prisons. For most of the previous two centuries, prisoners were
"slaves of the state." A prisoner was beaten for minor rule infractions, worked mercilessly, starved, forced to live in filth, and made
to suffer cruelties and hardships. Little or no help could be expected
from the bench. Wardens were the sovereigns of the cellblocks, free
to do pretty much as they wished with the incarcerated citizens in
their charge. For prisoners, the Constitution was a locked door, and
the protections of the Bill of Rights were hidden from sight.

During the past several decades, things began to change as the
"slave of the state" doctrine metamorphased into the "hands-off"

doctrine. In the 1954 case of *Banning v. Looney*, a federal circuit court ruled that judges do not have "the power to supervise prison administration or to interfere with ordinary prison rules and regulations." If prisoners happened to be in the hands of caring officials and lived under decent conditions, that was just fine; but if they happened to be in the charge of abusive officials and existed under wretched conditions, that was just too bad. An impenetrable constitutional wall separated the judge's chambers from the warden's cellblocks.

Over the last two decades, that wall has crumbled. Today, in dozens of jurisdictions, all or part of the correctional system is under judicial orders to change and improve. Some thirty correctional agencies are operating under "conditions of confinement" court orders; many have class action suits in progress and population limits set by the courts; many also have court-appointed special masters, monitors, and compliance coordinators. Judges have issued directives on a wide range of prison issues, including health care services, staff training practices, sanitation standards, food services, inmate grievance procedures, and the constitutionality of prison conditions "in their totality." In some prison systems, texts of court orders and consent decrees are now used as staff training manuals and inmate handbooks.

Judicial intervention in prisons and jails has sparked a great deal of controversy. Broadly speaking, there are two main schools of thought. Proponents of "judicial activism" maintain that the judges' intervention has been both constitutionally proper and highly effective. When other responsible government officials, both elected and appointed, fail to provide for safe and humane conditions behind bars, judges must act to uphold inmates' legal and constitutional rights. Such action is consistent with the principle of "checks and balances." Through special masters and other agents, judges can fashion enlightened penal policies and oversee their implementation. Where judges have intervened, prison conditions have improved.

Proponents of "judicial restraint" argue that the judges' intervention has been both constitutionally irresponsible and largely ineffective. Judges are authorized to interpret the law, not to make and administer it. Activist judges are guilty of violating the principle of "separation of powers." Judges are democratically unaccountable "generalists" lacking the expertise and resources to determine appropriate correctional policies and practices. Where judges have intervened, costs, prison violence, and other problems have mounted.

The contributors to this volume comprise a diverse group of political scientists, sociologists, legal scholars, justice professionals, and attorneys who have stood at the intersection of courts, corrections, and the Constitution. To us, the constitutional and moral status of judges' writ to intervene is an interesting, important, and unresolved question of public philosophy. In ways simple and subtle, we disagree among ourselves over how best to resolve it. But we are united in the view that philosophical disputes over the *right* of judges to intervene ought not to be conflated, as they so often are, with empirical disputes over the *capacity* of judges to intervene in ways that make prisons and jails more safe, civilized, and cost-effective. Even those of us who, like me, are inclined philosophically toward judicial restraint recognize that judges have become a permanent and, in some instances, clearly positive feature of America's correctional landscape. And even those of us who are inclined philosophically toward judicial activism recognize that the results of judicial intervention in this area have been mixed.

This volume is an exploratory work aimed at identifying, in a preliminary way, the political, administrative, budgetary, and other conditions that may increase or diminish the capacity of judges to intervene in ways that improve (or at least do not worsen) the quality of life behind bars. Under what conditions, if any, can judicial capacity be enhanced, and how, if at all, can we foster those conditions?

This book is addressed to elected officials, corrections commissioners, prison and jail managers, union representatives, prisoners' rights activists, criminal justice scholars, and other citizens who may need to wrestle with this issue in an honest way. It is also addressed to political scientists, sociologists, public administration scholars, and legal theorists who, though they may have no professional interest in the topic, will find in these pages much that is relevant to their more general concerns. Last but by no means least, it is addressed to the nation's federal, state, and local judges and to court-appointed special masters, monitors, and compliance coordinators. As we shall see, judges and their agents may largely determine whether the intersection of courts, corrections, and the Constitution is the scene of smooth traffic or tragic accidents.

In chapter 1 Malcolm H. Feeley and Roger A. Hanson offer a critical review of the literature on judicial intervention into prisons and jails. As they suggest, the impact of judicial intervention in this area has been hotly debated rather than closely analyzed, but there is a small and growing body of work that raises important and researchable questions.

Chapters 2 through 4 present analyses of the causes and consequences of judicial intervention in the nationally publicized case of *Ruiz v. Estelle*. Begun in 1972 and brought to a virtual close in 1986, the *Ruiz* litigation eventuated in sweeping changes in the Texas Department of Corrections. In chapter 2 I offer a mostly negative assessment of the impact of judicial intervention on Texas prisons. In chapter 3 Sheldon Ekland-Olson and Steve J. Martin offer a mostly positive assessment of the impact of judicial intervention on Texas prisons. And in chapter 4 Ben M. Crouch and James W. Marquart offer a more mixed assessment of this instance of judicial intervention.

Among other things, these "three faces of *Ruiz*" illustrate how near and yet how far we are from ways of analyzing court intervention that yield reliable generalizations about judicial capacity. Each analysis moves from the same basic facts, but the "facts" do not speak for themselves. To some extent, the three interpretations reflect the different disciplinary, experiential, and ideological outlooks of their respective authors. But after sifting through these differences, one is left with an abundance of similarities, both explicit and underlying. For example, each essay considers the impact of judicial intervention on both the formal and informal elements of Texas prison administration, demonstrating in each case how efficacious the bench can be in changing these elements. Indeed, the seemingly disparate "three faces of *Ruiz*" pose strikingly similar lessons about how to enhance judicial capacity in this area.

Though not as widely publicized as *Ruiz*, the recent case of *Guthrie v. Evans* in Georgia is fascinating in its own right and, in the hands of Bradley S. Chilton and Susette M. Talarico, even more revealing as a source of clues about how to bolster judicial capacity.

In chapter 5 Chilton and Talarico analyze judicial intervention and its effects on prison conditions as they relate to *Guthrie*.

In chapter 6 we leave state prison systems and the South for Ted S. Storey's study of court intervention in New York City jails. New York City has one of the nation's largest, most politically complicated, and most distressed jail systems. Storey focuses on the role of one federal judge in effecting major reforms in that system, including the establishment of the new Manhattan Tombs jail. This is one instance of judicial intervention that can be pronounced an almost unqualified success. As we shall argue, this success, and the more limited successes documented in our other cases, seems strongly related to the quality of the interventionist judge's understanding of the system's problems and to his or her manner of dealing with the elected and appointed officials responsible for translating the court's orders into administrative action.

In chapter 7 Edward E. Rhine analyzes how court decisions concerning prisoners' rights to due process have affected the administration of Rahway State Prison, a maximum security facility in New Jersey. Rhine's assessment of the impact of judicial intervention on formal disciplinary procedures and other aspects of prison management is pregnant with concrete suggestions about how to enhance judicial capacity.

In chapter 8 Bert Useem analyzes judicial intervention in the West Virginia case of *Crain v. Bordenkircher*. Like many other instances of judicial intervention in prisons, this one came on the heels of a major prison riot. But unlike most others, this intervention was shaped by a state constitutional provision, which the judge sought to define and enforce, mandating that corrections officials not only provide basic amenities and services behind bars but rehabilitate prisoners as well. Among other important lessons, Useem's analysis of *Crain* may be read to highlight the limits of judicial capacity.

As was true of the judge in *Ruiz*, the judge in *Crain* was known as a "liberal activist," having intervened broadly in schools before turning to prisons. Such anecdotal evidence leads both the friends and foes of judicial intervention to suppose that one can predict a judge's propensity to intervene by knowing the political party of the president who appointed him or her and related background characteristics. In chapter 9, however, Robert Bradley suggests that, contrary to the fears of some or the hopes of others, more "Republican" judges on the federal bench does not spell the end of judicial activism in this area; such background characteristics of judges are powerful predictors neither of judicial intervention nor of the extent of that intervention. Bradley's timely and sophisticated analysis bolsters our basic premise, derived from more casual observations of judicial behavior in this area, that judges have become a permanent part of the nation's correctional policy "subgovernments."

Chapters 1 through 9 reflect mostly academic analyses of our topic by individuals who have studied much but participated little, if at all, in actual instances of judicial intervention in prisons and jails. Chapter 10 presents the thoughtful reflections of an insider. Clair A. Cripe draws on his experiences as general council to the Federal Bureau of Prisons, one of America's finest corrections agencies, to suggest that corrections officials rather than judges deserve credit for many or most of the improvements that have occurred. His account deepens our understanding of what may be required to enhance judicial capacity in this area.

In the concluding chapter I summarize the central findings and implications of the various contributors to this volume. Basically, our conclusion is hopeful: there probably are ways to enhance judicial capacity that presuppose neither a boundless supply of human and financial resources nor the happy accident of outstanding judges possessing extraordinary political skills, administrative savvy, and prudence. But we recognize that our exploratory volume leaves us—and our readers—a long way from possessing definitive knowledge on this topic. That is not an excuse but a promise and a goad to future research.

More broadly, it is hoped that our academic colleagues with no direct interest in the subject of corrections may learn something by reading this volume. Let me, therefore, conclude this introduction by enticing our peripheral readers to continue reading.

In recent years, political scientists have been wrestling with "public choice" theory. In essence, this theory suggests that viewing government officials as rational, self-interested actors out to maximize votes (legislators), budgets (bureaucrats), or personal well-being (voters) is the best way to understand political institutions and the policy process. Among other advantages, this theory lends itself to both formal (mathematical) modeling and quantitative analysis. An analysis of the general weaknesses and limitations of this theory is well beyond the scope of this volume. But we do suggest that this theory applies poorly, if at all, to judicial behavior and to the behavior of correctional administrators. The battles that have been waged over how to administer prisons and jails, and concomitant disputes over whether judges can and should be involved in the process, have normally been fought by public-spirited individuals motivated by competing visions of good government and what constitutes good correctional practice. And, as any reader of our "three faces of *Ruiz*" must testify, the behavior of many of those involved has been anything but rational, in the narrow sense the term is defined by public choice theorists.

In recent years political scientists have begun to debate "the return of the state" to their discipline, essentially meaning a return to studies in which the preferences of government officials, and not only the demands and pressures generated by societal groups, appear as the major determinants of which issues get on the public agenda, which policies are adopted, and how those policies are implemented. Contrary to conventional "pluralist" notions of the policy process, "statists" believe that government officials and organizations are largely autonomous and that they often make and administer policies at odds with both public opinion and the preferences of powerful, well-organized lobbies. The central question in this debate is not whether the pluralist or the statist model applies universally but what accounts for the variations in "state autonomy" across policy areas, organizational contexts, and time.

The rise of judicial intervention in prisons and jails furnishes one interesting but as yet largely unexplored test case for "the return of the state." In most popular and scholarly accounts, this development is attributed to the efforts of civil liberties groups, prisoners' rights lobbies, enhanced media scrutiny, and other societal pressures that ended the autocratic reign of iron-fisted wardens. But a plausible argument holds that this development represents a historic intrastate transfer of power from one set of government officials to another, namely, from state and local wardens to federal court judges.

Public management scholars may find herein grist for the mill of their interest in theories of executive leadership and organizational innovation. State corrections commissioners in the United States have an average tenure of three years. They direct public agencies with multiple, vague, and contradictory goals (e.g., punish, deter, rehabilitate, incapacitate), often without clear and sustained bureaucratic authority, technical ability, or political support. As our cases illustrate, some corrections executives who had assumed office before the eve of judicial intervention were reluctant to accept the judges' involvement. In responding to judicial orders, several dragged their feet, and at least one openly defied the bench for many years.

But for today's corrections executives, all of whom landed their first job as director after 1970, judicial intervention offers blessings as well as burdens. On the one hand, it is a way of gaining public attention and coercing legislators into supplying the funds needed to hire staff and house inmates under decent conditions; hence, some commissioners knowingly encourage lawsuits that may lead to intervention. On the other hand, in responding to the court's orders, which may involve fundamental changes in official administrative practices and organizational customs valued by the staff, commissioners must sometimes choose between being held in contempt of court and being held in contempt by their line workers.

Since the late 1920s, sociologists of the prison system have produced one of the largest, most interesting, and most widely read bodies of literature in their general discipline. In recent years, however, interest has dwindled. Little of substance has been written about the precise nature of the changes that occur either in "inmate society" or "guard culture" as a result of judicial intervention. Among other unresolved questions, it remains unclear whether judicial intervention has any unique effects on relations among and between inmates, line staff, and correctional managers, or whether other "external shocks" (e.g., the appointment of a maverick director from outside the agency, the establishment of correctional officer unions) work to change cellblock relations in much the same way and to much the same degree. The reigning conjecture among sociologists of the prison is that judicial intervention has been responsible for many or most of the social changes in the "Big House." Our volume hints that "opening the gates" to more complex conjectures might help to revive interest in the sociology of the prison.

Contemporary legal theorists are fortunate—or cursed—to be living through one of the most fertile and tumultuous periods in the intellectual history of the field. The days of "Professor Kingsfield" and "black-letter law" are nothing more than memories in the nation's leading law schools. "Critical legal theorists" draw on literary criticism, political theory, and Marxist economics. "Law and economics" theorists draw on policy analysis, political theory, and market economics. Among "constitutional law" theorists there are some who believe in "original intent" and others who have never read *The Federalist Papers* and rarely, if ever, cite the Constitution.

Our volume may have the dubious distinction of providing aid and comfort to each of these schools of legal theory. For example, as is evident in each of our cases, the "text" and meaning of court decrees, even in their narrowest and most mundane procedural provisions, are often different for different actors in the drama of judicial intervention. Judicial intervention, and the case law that sustains it, can be "read" either as a pretext for "expanding the net of social control" over the nation's "underclass" or as a genuinely humane and well-motivated effort to treat even heinous and remorseless criminals better than they have treated their victims. Meanwhile, almost any given interventionist decision can be understood as a hallowed imperative of constitutional law, a bald usurpation of constitutional prerogative, or an example of what happens when decision makers do not know and apply quantitative cost-benefit analysis.

While we hope that our colleagues in areas of study distant from, or bordering on, our topic will find something of interest in these pages, our main "constituency" is those whose primary concern, intellectually and practically, is how to enhance judicial capacity in this field. And so we dedicate this book to those readers for whom the ménage à trois of the courts, corrections, and the Constitution is a vital and ongoing concern.

1

The Impact of
Judicial Intervention
on Prisons and Jails:
A Framework for Analysis
and a Review of
the Literature

MALCOLM M. FEELEY and ROGER A. HANSON

During the past thirty years the federal courts have become one of the principal agents of change in the nation's prisons and jails. In the 1960s federal courts used the First Amendment's protections of free expression and the Fifth and Fourteenth amendments' due process clauses to protect prisoners' religious observances and access to communication and to impose orderly procedures on disciplinary hearings and classification systems. The courts then began to rely on the Eighth Amendment's prohibition against cruel and unusual punishment to place limits on crowding and to order changes in the delivery of medical and food services, recreational opportunities, and the like. Despite some cutbacks, courts have continued to set standards for prison administration, and by now virtually every facet of institutional life has been constitutionalized in ways that directly affect prisons and jails in all fifty states. The extent of this involvement is suggested by an ACLU survey which found that there were major court orders in prisons and jails in forty states.[1]

In these cases courts have ordered improvements in institutional services, required the expenditure of vast sums of money, ordered the early release of thousands of inmates, and appointed special masters to design and implement detailed administrative plans to effect these and other aspects of institutional life. The extent of this involvement by the federal judiciary in overseeing major changes in the nation's jails and prisons is perhaps second in breadth and detail only to the courts' earlier role in dismantling segregation in the nation's public schools. However, as many commentators have pointed out, this type of judicial activism extends well beyond these two issues and is part of the general pattern of an expanded judicial role.[2]

This shift has precipitated a lively debate over the appropriate role of the courts. One side is skeptical of these developments, arguing that such activism by the judiciary undercuts the popular branches of government and weakens the democratic process[3] and that such actions by the judiciary are often unproductive or counterproductive.[4] Others defend these developments, arguing that the courts are expanding public access for traditionally powerless groups and forcing public institutions to adhere to their constitutional obligations and facilitate the democratic process.[5]

Not surprisingly, how one assesses court orders in prison and jail conditions cases depends on which side of this debate he or she accepts. Contending normative orientations influence the choice of alternative strategies and shape the questions asked, the data collected, and the conclusions drawn.[6]

Our purpose in this chapter is to offer a framework for assessing the impact of court orders on prisons and jails in ways that advance the general debate about the capacity of the courts to make social policy. We begin by reviewing the debate about the role of the courts and then argue that although empirical research cannot resolve the debate, it can help clarify issues and thus advance the debate. In particular, we suggest that three sets of impacts should be examined: the impact of the courts on the *structure* of correctional institutions; the impact on *policies* promulgated in the wake of court action; and the impact of court orders on *delivery of services* within the institutions. These concerns move from the general to the specific.

The first issue raises the question as to whether judicial intervention has altered the organizational character of correctional institutions. Has it affected their sense of mission and the way correctional officers and inmates view each other? In the context of the current debate, has judicial intervention contributed to increased violence within institutions?

The second issue, concerning policy, raises the question of whether court orders have been generalized? Have they been institutionalized in legislation and administrative regulations? If so, will they endure once the court withdraws?

The third issue, concerning delivery of services, is prompted by the policy analyst's experience with implementation or, more properly, the widespread failure of implementation. Even though new policies have been enacted and formally embraced, have they been put into place? Are they working as expected? Do they make a difference? As obvious as these questions are, research on implementation has shown that public agencies often fail to implement even the most uncontroversial new policies. When policies are imposed by courts upon a highly resistant institution, problems of implementation are likely to be even greater.

The Debate Over the Role of the Courts

There are two schools of thought about the role of the courts in contemporary public law litigation. Drawing on Lon Fuller's classic analysis of the legal process in "The Forms and Limits of Adjudication,"[7] the "traditional" view holds that the distinctive competence of courts resides in their ability to resolve disputes according to an established regime of rules by affording those directly affected by a dispute the opportunity to present proofs and arguments in their own behalf. In the traditional view, courts overreach both their authority and capacity when they order far-reaching changes that affect social policy.

An alternative view of adjudication has been called "structural reform." According to this view a unique function of the courts, and especially the federal courts, is to give meaning and content to constitutional values as they affect public institutions. When institutions fail to appreciate these values, the task of the court is to impose therapeutic relief in order to alter their institutional personalities so that constitutional values are more fully appreciated. Hence Owen Fiss's use of the phrase "structural reform" to describe this type of litigation.[8]

This review attempts to speak to both those who understand courts as dispute resolvers and those who see them as structural reformers. This is a challenging task, since the different views emphasize different features of the same process and accept different types of evidence as indications of success and failure.

In discussing the impact of the courts on various aspects of institutional structure, policy, and service delivery, we recognize that no firm line divides these three areas and that each one is likely to point to a different set of activities, entail a different focus and methodology, and perhaps even address a different theory of adjudication. The first two address issues most directly raised by the structural reform orientation, and the last raises issues of concern in the dispute resolution model. We hope this review clarifies the nature of the debate and suggests ways to make the empirical components of each position—as it applies to prison and jail conditions litigation—more explicit.

Two other issues are central to, and inform, our analysis. Regardless of the level of analysis used to assess court-ordered changes in prison and jail cases, researchers must confront two distinctive features of correctional institutions. First, like other "street-level" bureaucracies,[9] prisons and jails have something of a pyramid of discretion: those with greatest discretion are at the bottom of the organizational structure.[10] Second, to a considerable degree, the norms governing the behavior of prisoners are a consequence of informal, symbiotic relationships among prisoners and between prisoners and staff members.[11] Although correctional institutions are command and control institutions whose effective operations are clearly influenced by the nature and quality of their leadership,[12] a great many of the operative rules governing the society of captives are formulated and enforced by the captives themselves.

These two features of prisons pose a challenge for those fostering planned change and assessing its impact: policies are likely to be aimed at hierarchical organizations but received by institutions in which power is dispersed among those not formally recognized as possessing it. Under these circumstances accountability and compliance are problematic.[13] The least controversial new policy can generate ripple effects throughout the organization in ways that are not easily anticipated. Even seemingly simple orders, such as those requiring greater access to legal services or medical care, can be radically altered in the process of implementation.

The Impact of Federal Court Orders

Notwithstanding these problems of implementation, there is no doubt that court orders have had a significant impact both within individual institutions and in entire correctional systems. They have altered the structure and process of authority, increased resources, and ordered new and different policies to be put into effect. However one assesses these changes, all agree that they have been significant and far reaching.

These cases have also spawned a lively debate. Critics, drawing on the dispute resolution model of adjudication, maintain that court orders have made prisons and jails more unruly and difficult to manage and fostered violence among inmates. Defenders counter with claims that court orders have reduced brutal treatment of inmates, reduced the worst crowding, and increased availability of much-needed health and legal services.

In general we believe that the critics of structural reform have put forward the more well-developed model of adjudication and have posed a set of serious problems that defenders of structural reform must address. They have raised a set of questions about the capacities of courts to effect far-reaching social change, meaningfully oversee implementation of complex administrative changes, and minimize the undesirable side effects of their actions. These concerns have been raised by as diverse a group as Horowitz, Glazer, Scheingold, Bumiller, Freeman, and Handler.[14] If we emphasize the concerns of these critics—and our discussion has been informed by them—it is because we believe that their positions are more clearly stated than those of the proponents of such judicial involvement. But we emphasize that both sides of the debate generally proceed by a selective use and interpretation of relevant data, and this chapter is a call for more systematic inquiry on a fuller range of issues than has generally been the case. Critics must do more than point to the worst instances of court orders run amok and defenders must address the very real problems of judicial oversight that critics have identified.

Structural Reform

Authority, Safety, and Violence

Opponents of institutional reform litigation frequently argue that court orders not only fail to achieve their goals but undermine existing institutional authority, thus exacerbating the very problems they seek to solve. Whereas no responsible critic opposes the Supreme Court's ruling in *Brown v. Board of Education* (1954), many do question the lengths to which the courts have gone when interpreting it. Sweeping school desegregation orders which disrupt neighborhoods and natural boundaries, some critics claim, contribute to white flight, the proliferation of private schools, and increased racial tensions and are often pursued at the expense of improvements in instruction and programs.

One of the most articulate of the critics is Nathan Glazer, who in a series of articles has argued that court orders aimed at restructuring public institutions undermine the authority of leaders and staff of those institutions and thus ironically contribute to their decline.[15] According to Glazer, court-imposed due process requirements prevent officials from acting decisively and undermine their authority in the eyes of their clientele. This in turn leads to a decline in staff morale, an increase in staff turnover, and an increase in the unruliness of clientele groups. Acceptance of such court orders by institutional leadership widens still further the gulf between them and their staffs and accelerates the downward spiral. Although Glazer developed his arguments with public schools and welfare agencies in mind, he could as easily have directed them at prison and jail conditions suits.

Several reports on the effects of prison conditions litigation echo Glazer's general concern. The most dramatic indicator of this has to do with the consequences of court orders on safety and security within institutions. Researchers who have focused on this issue—and it is probably the most frequently addressed issue in research in this area—report increases in inmate to inmate and inmate to staff violence in the immediate aftermath of court orders.[16]

The issue of the effects of court orders on violence has been developed most fully in an article by Engel and Rothman.[17] Drawing on a number of important studies of prison structure and life from the 1950s to the 1980s, they argue that the prisoners' rights movement and court orders expanding the rights of inmates have undercut the traditional authority of prison personnel in ways that have led to a significant increase in violence among inmates. This reform effort, they believe, has politicized prisons and in turn provoked a more militant inmate posture and still more litigation. "Because prison administrators are fearful of inmate suits," they assert, "they are sometimes reluctant to enforce punishment."[18] The result, they conclude, is predictable: As the courts mandate changes in institutional policies, staff and inmates lose respect for the authority of the prison personnel. This limits the administrators' ability to run the prison effectively. The loss of authority, coupled with fear of litigation and negative media coverage, has caused a shift in the control that was historically reserved for prison administrators and further threatens the lives of inmates and guards. Daily, guards face the fear of being taken hostage or being assaulted. They argue that "the consequences . . . can be seen as one of those classical 'unintended consequences of social change,' increased gang activity, increased violence, and no clear evidence that either the rehabilitative effort or the rights movement has yielded appreciable benefits to the inmates."[19]

Engel and Rothman's essay has been widely cited for the proposition that litigation and an increased rights orientation foster increased violence. They may be correct. But to be convincing they must develop their assertions more fully and present more systematic data. For instance, in their California "case study," they provide no evidence to show that there was an increase in violence during the period they consider. Although they provide officially reported data on certain types of violent incidents between 1970 and 1973 and state that the incidence of violence declined in the mid-1970s, they offer no longitudinal data of either rates of violence of frequency of litigation. Indeed, litigation in California increased significantly during the mid-1970s, a period in which they report a decline in violence.

In addition, they call for a better system of inmate classification and tighter management instead of more litigation and prisoners' rights, but they do not even attempt to show how these goals are incompatible with each other. Hence, the causal inference they draw between violence and court orders is questionable. The several other "case studies" appended to and discussed in their essay are equally flawed.

However, their study does reveal that rates of inmate violence fluctuate and appear to be related to the introduction of new programs and new regimes of all sorts. If anything, their essay suggests a more general conclusion: Any number of changes may disrupt the fragile equilibrium of prison life and produce aftershocks. For instance, one of the consequences of the civil rights revolution and the black power movement is that people of color are more assertive than they were in earlier eras. In light of the fact that inmates in custodial institutions are disproportionately brown and black while authorities are white, we can easily hypothesize that these social changes have contributed to new problems of social control within these institutions. But we need a much more fine-grained analysis before we can draw the type of casual connections Engel and Rothman make in their article.[20]

This need is suggested by other information that challenges Engel and Rothman's conclusions. Interviews with corrections officials in California indicate no widespread belief that there is a strong connection between court orders and inmate violence. James Rowland, commissioner of the California Department of Corrections (CDC) and no friend of prison conditions litigation, has frequently noted that despite the crowding and large numbers of lawsuits, during the mid-1980s, incidents among inmates and between in-mates and guards decreased. Similarly, Anthony Newland, former statewide coordinator of litigation for the CDC and now deputy superintendent in charge of the thirty-five hundred-person facility at Vacaville, believes that court orders have generated increased problems for prison managers but not necessarily increased vio-lence.

In Newland's view, the most significant impact of the litigation on prisons has been on management.

> [T]he problem [of staff resistance to court orders] is resistance to change and the lack of understanding and leadership by prison management. The system is manageable. The manager's authority is not limited, it is just different. Prisons now have to use 20th Century management techniques. . . . The changes in prison management parallel the changes in the free community during the 60's and the 70's. Prison must adapt, just like the welfare department did, to equity, due process, and humane conditions. The staff may feel a loss of control because the method of control must be changed from a decentralized, feudal system, to a centralized bureaucratic system. If staff are resistant and allow violence to occur, it is the fault of poor management, managers who refuse to change, untrained management, and legislative inertia—the refusal to provide the dollars which are necessary for change to occur in a system-wide manner.[21]

Thus, while he believes that court orders increased tensions and may have contributed to an increase in inmate violence in some facilities immediately following some of the orders, Newland also believes that such disturbances were short-lived and part of the readjustment to new management styles.

Still, Engel and Rothman have developed a theme echoed by others. Indeed, the concern about the violent side effects of court orders is one of the most frequently addressed issues in studies of the impact of court orders on institutions. Much of this work has focused on a single case, *Ruiz v. Estelle* (1980), in which the entire corrections system of the state of Texas was subjected to a compre-hensive court order requiring massive changes in virtually every facet of institutional life. All of those who have examined the impact of the court's order in this case agree that it was associated with a sharp increase in inmate-on-inmate and inmate-on-staff violence. But, as chapters 2 through 4 of this volume make clear, analysts disagree widely over whether, and to what extent, the court's actions were catalysts for this increase in violence.

Some researchers have argued that although court orders may be destabilizing for brief periods, eventually they lead to declines in staff violence against inmates as departments hire more and better trained guards, promulgate and enforce written procedures, and the like.[22] These changes, they argue, more than offset any temporary increases in inmate violence that may have been occasioned by court orders which had the effect of destabilizing the status quo.

One problem in all the studies to date which purport to assess the effects of court orders on institutional conditions is the time frame. Conditions suits take a number of years to come to fruition, so that those who explore the process of litigation are usually not in a good position to report on the impact of the court's orders. In selecting sites for research, scholars have also gravitated toward the more troublesome cases, and thus the impression that court orders foster increased violence may be a function of site selection. We note, for example, that the especially troublesome *Ruiz* case has been the subject of sustained attention by researchers, and that other less problematic cases have not been subject to such scrutiny. Thus, generalizations about the effects of court orders are likely to be drawn from a skewed sample that overemphasizes resistance to change.

Institutional Morale and Leadership

Nathan Glazer and others claim that court intervention affects in substantial ways the distribution of authority within large-scale institutions.[23] All things being equal, he holds, litigation puts people with theoretical knowledge and training into positions of power at the expense of those with practical experience and training. He argues that this involvement takes several forms, which in combination affect in significant ways the character of an institution. In turn, he continues, this can undermine staff morale and effectiveness.

A variation of this theme was put forward by James Jacobs in his 1980 review of the impacts of the prisoners' rights movement.[24] Jacobs and others have concluded that court orders have propelled better educated and more sophisticated people into positions of leadership in prisons, and because of this, "there is some basis to believe that today's correctional officers are more insecure vis-à-vis inmates than were their predecessors."[25] More recent work reinforces this assertion. For instance, Jacobs,[26] DiIulio,[27] and Chilton[28] report that court orders have made guards more receptive to unionization. Similarly, Samuel Brakel[29] has warned that new rights gained through litigation may simply enlarge the scope of mutual harassment between correctional officers and inmates and weaken the authority of the former:

> The general lesson is that an introduction of new procedures into the prisons tends to upset the balance of inmate–staff relations and is likely to lead to a situation in which the level of mutual psychological harassment and the inclination to engage in other petty tests of power—significant features of prison life under any circumstances—are raised to new heights. Such a deterioration in the prison "climate," it should be recognized, carries with it the potential for defeating whatever benefits are intended to be conferred by the new rules or regimen.[30]

Similarly, DiIulio has characterized the rules promulgated by the new administrators in response to court orders as "pseudo-scientific," "pseudo-bureaucratic" measures imposed at the expense of sound management practices and often harmful to staff morale.[31] In ongoing studies of litigation in California, Feeley and Little have found major changes flowing from litigation.[32] In Santa Clara County, the Board of Supervisors responded to protracted litigation against the county sheriff by creating a new department of corrections with its own director, a corrections professional. This in turn precipitated a crisis of morale among the jail staff.

More generally, Jacobs has concluded that court orders widen the gap between correctional leadership and prison staff by facilitating appointments of a new type of administrator whose values are more closely attuned to those of the court than traditional line staff and is more sophisticated in handling reporting requirements, queries from the press, and the like.[33]

The foregoing discussion rests upon extremely limited evidence and thus must be regarded as highly tentative. Indeed, the history of court-ordered changes is too brief to allow for anything more than tentative conclusions about short-term consequences. For this reason it may be useful to compare these concerns about the dysfunctional effects of litigation on prison violence and morale with the effects of earlier court orders in other areas where massive changes have also been mandated. Court rulings affecting the police provide one such basis for comparison. Beginning in the 1960s the U.S. Supreme Court handed down a series of major decisions restricting the authority of the police and broadening the rights of criminal suspects. Although the initial indications were that the landmark Supreme Court decisions of *Escebedo*, *Mapp*, and *Miranda* significantly limited police power to act decisively and negatively affected police morale, a generation later researchers are much more sanguine about the impact of these rulings.

Three recent studies have attempted to assess the longer term impact of these and related decisions. Studies by Skolnick and Simon[34] and Slocum[35] both conclude that however controversial they were at the time, the limits imposed on the police by *Miranda v. Arizona* (1966) and *Mapp v. Ohio* (1961) and related cases are now viewed by leading police officials as part of the landscape in which they operate. More important, they continue, these decisions had a major catalytic effect on improving the quality of law enforcement. They have fostered rulemaking within police departments, led to improvements in training, facilitated additional resources, and contributed to police professionalism in a host of other ways. In his survey of the long-term impact of these decisions on the police, Samuel Walker has observed:

> There is abundant evidence that the working environment of American policing improved significantly as a result of the rule-making initiatives of the Supreme Court. The level of educational attainment has risen significantly, pre-service training has improved both in terms of the number of hours and the range of subject covered, most states now mandate pre-service training of all sworn officers. . . . The policy and procedure manual has developed as the primary tool for closer supervision of officers. Some departments successfully curbed corruption through the combination of formal policies and more intensive supervision.

> In short, there is a broad consensus that the American police are far more professional today than they were twenty-five years ago and that the intervention of the courts played an important role in stimulating change.[36]

Walker goes on to describe this transformation as follows: Although at the time veteran officers "regarded the new rules as an intrusion or as a disruption of established practices," twenty-five years later, officers socialized into a new working environment take them for granted and have come to accept them as legitimate. In short, a broader perspective and time frame in assessing the impact of Supreme Court decisions affecting the police have led some researchers to conclude that the most enduring consequences of these rulings, which once were bitterly denounced by the police, has been to strengthen law enforcement agencies.

Still another perspective on prison conditions litigation derives from the contrast between responses to court-ordered changes in prisons and jails and responses to changes initiated by "reformers" within correctional systems. Those few studies which trace such internal changes report the same type of staff resistance, decline in morale, moves to unionize, and the like, that critics of court-ordered changes have identified.[37] Thus, it appears that change, whether initiated by judges or reform administrators, is inherently disruptive.

If so, the question is: How long does this disruption last? Is it temporary or permanent? And to what extent are these responses disruptive? We need to know much more about the *long-term* consequences of such change, yet such knowledge is difficult to obtain.

Writing while the issues were still being litigated, Samuel Brakel appeared to be pessimistic about the long-term benefits of the court's efforts, suggesting, as it were, that they simply enlarge the area of conlfict between guards and inmates.[38] In contrast, writing two or three years after introduction of the most controversial features of the court orders had been put into place in Texas, DiIulio[39] and Martin and Ekland-Olson[40] appear to agree that the intense frustration, turmoil, high staff turnover, and violence were subsiding and that a new order and stability were emerging. Similarly, Harris and Spiller,[41] Chilton,[42] and Storey (see chapter 6 of this volume), as well as others, suggest that even when it does occur disruption and violence may be short term only. For instance, in his study of court-ordered prison reform in Georgia, Bradley Chilton concluded that

[t]he inhuman practices and conditions at GSP [Georgia State Prison] . . . in 1979 no longer exist. [The] "reign of terror" against inmates has ended. Guards do not routinely beat, mace, and shoot inmates at GSP today. Inmates and guards no longer die from a lack of safety and protection. Guards can walk the cells without illegal knives and pickax handles to protect themselves. . . . The medical, mental, nutritional, education, and recreational needs of inmates are now provided for. . . . Inmates are humanely cared for and most have a practical opportunity to rehabilitate. These changes were the result, in large part if not solely, from the *Guthrie* litigation.[43]

Ongoing studies being conducted at the University of California at Berkeley on the impact of both jail and prison conditions orders report that interviews with defendant officials, attorneys, and guards reveal no widespread belief that court decrees have exacerbated continuing problems of inmate violence. Even those officials who are most critical of these orders at times concede that they may have reduced the potential for inmate-to-inmate violence, since they have reduced crowding and led to increases in the number and training of staff. Although the warden at San Quentin is highly critical of the ruling of the court-appointed special master in one suit, arguing that it undercuts his ability to isolate especially dangerous inmates, he and other officials at San Quentin acknowledge that the court orders have provided them with more resources and more opportunities and have substantially reduced the facility's population in ways that make supervision and control of inmates easier. In their continuing study of the Santa Clara County jail case, Little and Feeley have found no evidence that the court's orders have affected inmate unrest and violence.[44] Indeed, even those officials most critical of the settlement agreement and subsequent court orders acknowledge that these decisions resulted in a better classification system and a less crowded and safer jail.

Modernization of the Correctional Bureaucracy

Theorists of structural reform believe that the ultimate aspiration of institutional litigation is to transform institutions, to perform as it were a type of organizational therapy so that institutions will have a greater appreciation for constitutional values and a greater institutional capacity to pursue them. In this sense the impact of litigation is general and systemic. Indeed, in prison systems it may have its greatest impact on institutions which have not even been subject to court orders. There is considerable evidence that jail and prison conditions litigation has had this type of general effect.

Perhaps the single biggest change brought about by court orders has been the transformation of southern prisons. A number of suits in the 1970s challenged in fundamental ways the very premises upon which southern prisons had long operated and rejected the plantation model on which they were built. Although this model, and the assumptions of self-sufficiency, limited rights of the inmates, and the like, had long been under attack, intervention by the courts removed whatever vestiges of legal legitimacy has survived in this system. In effect the courts rejected the southern model and declared that prison administration federalism was a failure.[45]

More generally, the operations of prisons and jails throughout the country are now governed by a amalgam of statutes, regulations, and guidelines and are subject to greater accountability. Indeed, since the 1960s the principles of organizational rationality and legality have emerged to structure the governance of the entire operational life of correctional institutions and systems. One consequence is that the rule of law has not only penetrated these institutions; it has contributed to the professionalization of the administration of these institutions in much the same way that a decade earlier the expansion of due process requirements on the police fostered dramatic changes in police administration. These changes far exceed the sum of the particulars in any set of court orders.

State corrections departments are now better able to diagnose their problems and obtain resources to meet their needs. A number of states, largely as a consequence of court orders, have developed proactive capacities to review their compliance with constitutional conditions of confinement. The California Department of Corrections now employs a number of lawyers and compliance officers whose jobs are to develop and review correctional policies and practices in order to anticipate legal problems and avoid litigation. Indeed, there is an emerging new specialty in the corrections field, which, according to some proponents of the idea, trains and designates officials to perform "constitutional audits" of facilities and procedures in order to reduce legal liabilities. These officials are beginning to perform the same types of functions that affirmative action officers now routinely perform in a variety of public and private institutions.

Such developments cannot be attributed wholly to litigation and court orders. There has been a longstanding, independent effort to professionalize corrections, and many of the changes in recent years are a result of this movement. For the most part, courts have incorporated these emerging professional norms into their orders rather than inventing their own requirements.[46] But court orders have clearly served as an impetus for professionalization. The result is a growing acceptance of professional standards and a growing network of professional organizations which are having an impact on state and local correctional institutions. The American Medical Association, the American Bar Association, and the American Association of Architects all have promulgated correctional standards within their respective spheres and perform training and clearinghouse functions. Their various activities are also shaped in part by a concern with meeting court-imposed constitutional standards, and in turn more of their standards have been incorporated by courts into their orders.

Similarly, the American Correctional Association (ACA) has been aggressive in developing and implementing a system of accreditation of state prisons.[47] Initially launched by substantial grants from the Law Enforcement Assistance Administration (LEAA) in the 1970s, in the 1980s this program continued to receive support from the National Institute of Corrections (NIC) and the U.S. Department of Justice.

ACA's accreditation initiative, designed in part to try to ward off litigation, has also been responsive to it. Authors of the standards have been informed by and made an effort to incorporate and anticipate constitutional issues into their own standards. In California and elsewhere some of these standards are being incorporated into state administrative law; in the future, challenges to conditions of confinement are likely to be based on state administrative law in addition to constitutional law.

Local jails have distinctive difficulties institutionalizing responses to litigation. In most communities, jails are run by sheriffs with backgrounds in and continuing responsibilities for law enforcement. Even in larger communities, these organizations lack administrative depth and expertise, and counties lack the capacity to provide correctional law specialists other than in response to litigation. Still, there are indications that local jails are institutionalizing a response to constitutional issues. Training programs now routinely emphasize constitutional conditions of confinement in ways they did not earlier. Hospitals, architects, and food service agencies contracted by local jails now regularly consider constitutional issues. At another level, regional and national meetings of professional organizations, such as the American Jail Association, routinely devote time to correctional law issues. Indeed, in 1987 the American Jail Association officially established a Compliance Officer Network as a way of recognizing and enhancing the status and training of jail officials who have responsibility for monitoring conditions in jails. This new organization grew out of meetings of sheriffs' deputies from across the country who had been assigned to serve as liaisons with courts and court-appointed monitors, and its leaders are developing a clearinghouse of resource materials, promoting the notion of a continuous "self-audit" of conditions and services, and trying to develop a new and permanent position in the field. All this indicates that a number of prominent figures in the field see the continued litigation as an opportunity to expand their institutional capacities as well as their own careers.

As states are being drawn into the financing of local jails, they are also strengthening their oversight and regulatory functions, reviewing jail operating procedures, designs for new facilities, health, food, and safety standards, and the like, in light of constitutional requirements and state administrative procedures. As states assume a larger share of the costs for constructing and operating local jails, such state involvement is likely to expand.

Prison and Jail Policies

Despite the large number of court orders affecting prison and jail conditions, few clear-cut policies have emerged from these cases. Once the very worst practices were successfully attacked, court-based action in other areas was more problematic.[48] This is due in part to the fact that most federal courts have employed a "totality of circumstances" or "conditions" standard, which weighs one condition in light of other factors. Although lower courts have frequently found that conditions in prisons or prison systems violate Eighth Amendment standards, these rulings have not resulted in unambiguous *general* rules or policy guidelines because conditions vary from institution to institution. A factor that may trigger a finding of unconstitutionality in one place may not do so in another because of compensating factors. Furthermore, courts have interpreted "totality of circumstances" differently. Some have weighed the aggregate or cumulative effect of several conditions to determine whether the total conditions warrant a finding of unconstitutionality, whereas others have taken a narrower view and assessed the "spillover" effects of combinations of conditions, so that two or more conditions may be weighted against each other.[49] Thus, for instance, crowded cells are considered in light of the amount of time prisoners spend in their cells.

Typically a trial court opinion in a conditions case reads more like a consultant's report than a legal opinion. The opinion may trace the evolving scope of the Eighth Amendment's prohibition against cruel and unusual punishment, but this discussion is often perfunctory. The core of the opinion is a detailed description of conditions in the institution which emphasizes the gap between the magnitude of the functions to be performed and the failings in the effort to perform them—lack of funds, lack of staff, incompetence, and the like. The opinions often seize, in no systematic way, on a wide variety of standards against which to compare practices in the institutions: the institutions' own guidelines, state regulations and laws, minimum standards set forth by professional organizations, and the like. Often the court characterizes conditions and services in graphic detail and concludes that they are "brutal," "savage," "barbaric," or "horrifying" and then orders the institution to take immediate steps to rectify the situation, leaving a management plan to be worked out later, often by the parties themselves or under the auspices of a special master.

The point we wish to emphasize here is that the very approach of the courts is better understood in terms of managerial concerns than legal argument. Indeed, when courts invoke standards as criteria for making judgments, they are likely to be those promulgated by the Federal Bureau of Prisons, the ACA, and related professional groups rather than court-generated standards. For instance, when assessing the quality of an institution's medical staff, courts might turn to the relevant standards set by the American Medical Association. When assessing sleeping arrangements and per prisoner floor space, they may turn to the Bureau of Prisons practices or the ACA standards. In this sense the courts have not been developing an evolving set of rules or standards. Rather they have been expressing their disgust at conditions they find fall far short of professionally articulated standards and then ordering the institutions to do something to improve the situation. We stress this not to criticize the approaches taken by the courts but to emphasize just how thoroughly managerial judicial involvement has been. In these cases judges are managerial not only in their preferences for negotiations over adjudication, reliance on special masters, and protracted involvement in the remedial process, but in the very ways they define the issues. The result is a great deal of litigation but very few clear constitutional rulings. This, for instance, is suggested in a recent review of the literature by Smolla, who found it difficult to summarize the law in the area and instead had to resort to descriptions of what courts did and the conditions under which they acted.[50] This approach may be part of a more general trend in the bureaucratic state; if so, it has manifested itself clearly in prison cases.[51]

State Budgets and Federal Responses

One way policy analysts have tried to assess the impact of court orders on correctional policy has been to try to measure the effect of court orders on correctional budgets. In recent years, prison and jail budgets have jumped markedly. The question is, "What portion of this increase can be attributed to court orders or anticipation of such orders? In some states partial answers are fairly clear because courts have played such direct roles in securing increased funding. For instance, in *James v. Wallace*, Judge Frank Johnson ordered improvements which led to a dramatic increase in the state's correctional budget. The connection between his order and the expenditures was direct, and few would dispute the estimate that the court was responsible for increasing the state's correctional budget by as much as two-thirds.[52] Similarly, Harris and Spiller indicate that

Judge Henley's order in *Holt v. Sarver* resulted in a sixfold increase in the Arkansas correctional budget and that court orders in other cases could be credited with "breaking loose money for prison improvements."[53] In New York City former mayor Edward Koch used a federal court order to lobby successfully for an increase in funds for jail construction at a time when the city was still recovering from its near bankruptcy.[54] Similarly, DiIulio[55] and Martin and Ekland-Olson[56] agree that the court's orders in Texas required the state to increase significantly its correctional budget.

There have also been some studies assessing the general impact of court orders on state correctional budgets. Harriman and Straussman[57] compared state correctional budgets before and after litigation, and in states with and without major litigation, and concluded that the courts have forced states to increase significantly their correctional expenditures and that "on balance, the courts have forced states that have been defendants in prison conditions cases to spend closer to the level of states that have not experienced legal challenges to their corrections systems."

This finding has been challenged by William Taggart, who reported that per capita correctional budgets remained the same or even declined in states that have been subject to court orders.[58] However, Feeley noted that most of those states which experienced the largest increases in correctional expenditures in the wake of major court orders are in the South.[59] This reinforces the point that he and Rubin made elsewhere, that to date the most significant impact of prison conditions cases has been on correctional systems in the South.[60] By rejecting a long-standing tradition of correctional federalism, the courts put an end to the plantation model of prisons.

The national government has responded to prison conditions litigation with two major policies. Both are designed to improve conditions in prisons, enhance professional capabilities of correctional administrators, and reduce prison conditions litigation. We have already described the U.S. Department of Justice's sponsorship of the American Correctional Association's efforts to develop and implement a system of accreditation of correctional institutions. Another potentially far-reaching effort is the Civil Rights of Institutionalized Persons Act (CRIPA) of 1980, which permits the attorney general of the United States to sue state institutions that subject state inmates to "egregious or flagrant conditions which deprive such persons of any rights, privileges, or immunities secured or protected by the Constitution." Additionally, the law gives responsibility to the Department of Justice to develop and apply standards to state prison inmate grievance procedures. If the department finds that a state's procedure satisfies the criteria of timeliness, responsiveness, and fairness, these procedures can be certified and used to avert litigation (federal courts may require that inmates exhaust certified procedures before initiating litigation against prison officials). The Reagan Administration was not aggressive in using CRIPA to pursue prison reform, but the act has a vast potential for an aggressive Department of Justice.

Service Delivery

Ultimately the aim of court orders is to alter the nature and quality of service provided to inmates. Court orders are expected to alter the conditions of confinement, reduce crowding, expand access to recreation, provide better medical service, provide more nourishing and appetizing meals, and the like. Although institutional budgets have been increased and organizational structures have changed as a consequence of court orders, ironically there is a dearth of research that carefully charts specific changes flowing from specific court decisions. Despite the fact that this is an area where we are likely to think we know the most, in fact we may know the least. Too often we assume that court orders affect service delivery, simply because that is what is supposed to happen. We emphasize this not because we believe that when courts speak nothing happens—earlier discussion suggests that they have had a profound impact—but because there are few systematic studies reporting on the specific effects of specific decisions; and in those few studies that address the issue, the focus is often on the process of litigation, not on the nature of its impact on the inmates.

Thus, for instance, we know that prisons have established law libraries for inmates, budgeted more money for health professionals, and the like, but we lack knowledge about how these changes affect inmates, which is difficult or impossible to know. Still, it is possible and valuable to chart the impact on service delivery of most court-ordered changes. We emphasize this because if policy analysis of implementation has anything to teach us, it is that policies are not self-executing. Problems with implementation plague even the most enthusiastically embraced new policies and are even more serious when changes are imposed from outside upon a reluctant recipient.[61] "Street-level bureaucrats" have a myriad of ways to thwart even the most noncontroversial new policies.[62]

Service delivery can be categorized by the degree of *effectiveness* and *quality*. Although prior studies of prison conditions suits have not emphasized these categories, published and unpublished accounts of court interventions provide illustrative examples of each. Concerning the effectiveness of court orders and crowding, there are two issues: (1) the degree to which the objectives of the court are achieved, and (2) the problems of displacement. In a crowding case the number of prisoners may have been reduced, but does this translate into increased space for inmates? Do improvements in the ratios of prisoners to services (e.g., medical care, access to legal services, privacy, exercise) lead to actual increased opportunities to use these services? Similarly, do population reductions in one institution lead to net reductions in crowding, or are the problems transferred to other institutions? Additionally, when old institutions are remodeled or new institutions constructed, what is the change in crowding as measured by various indicators such as cell space, opportunity for exercise, and privacy?

The pursuit of answers to such questions is of course complicated by the steady increase in prison and jail populations. During the 1980s, the numbers of people in jails and prisons nearly doubled nationwide. As a consequence, conditions in prisons might have deteriorated despite the court orders, but the courts still might have been important in that conditions would be even worse in the absence of such intervention. The challenge for researchers is to factor out the effects of court orders from numerous other influences.

Court orders both aim to eliminate poor conditions and mandate new and improved services. Orders requiring new services, such as medical or legal services, may be easier to document, although as we have suggested even the most seemingly straight-forward issues can be elusive. Reports of failures to put newly adopted procedures into practice are common, and this is one reason that litigation in this area is so protracted.

Even with court-appointed monitors and masters, routinely translating orders into practice is problematic. Samuel Brakel has provided a detailed description of "the movement from the court's opinion detailing the prisoners' access rights, to the formulation of an implementation plan, its monitoring by the special master's office, the writing of a compliance report, and the final step . . . towards having the findings of the report adopted by the court and its recommendations translated into practical directive."[63] This lengthy process, he reports, was filled with pitfalls he did not anticipate:

> One point that can be made at this moment is that the very introduction of the access rules into the prison system generated—like any other new set of rights or rules would—considerable conflict and controversy. Inevitably, the availability of these new rights led to a spirited assertion of them by inmates and an explosion of charges that they were being violated by prison staff. The staff in turn reacted to these charges, often in a fashion that matched the unproductive and frivolous character of too many of the inmate complaints.[64]

It remains to be seen if and how these new access rules will take root in the long run.

Little and Feeley have found repeated instances where obstacles and resistance thwarted what the court thought was a simple, clear, and unambiguous order.[65] At one hearing to review the expanded housing capacity brought about as a result of court order, the court heard the good news that more beds had been put in place, only later to learn casually that they were not yet being used because new bedding had not been obtained. In this same case, in which the court's jurisdiction was set to end as soon as a new jail was opened, the sheriff, when questioned as to how he would cope once the new facility reached capacity, responded that it would not be difficult since he would not be operating under the court-imposed population caps and could squeeze more people into his facilities.

Courts face a particularly difficult challenge when trying to expand services available in men's facilities to women's facilities. Some studies and our own interviews with prison and jail officials reveal that court-ordered improvements often are not extended or extended as fully to women's facilities.[66] In addition, when the courts have addressed the distinct medical needs of women with respect to pregnancy and newborns, jail and prison officials have fiercely resisted, justifying some actions on grounds that women would not get "special treatment" and justifying other features of custodial organization, such as generally higher security classifications for women, on grounds of economies of scale.

We raise these types of issues not to conclude that nothing works but to warn against inferring actual practice from formal policy, and to suggest that it is important to trace court orders through their long paths from judgment to routine practice. It is understandable but nevertheless unfortunate that most studies of court orders focus on short-term effects. However, what is needed for a comprehensive assessment of court-ordered change are detailed examinations of the process of translating orders into responses and immediate responses into institutionalized practices.

Formulating and Implementing an Order

There is some truth to the observation that institutional litigation has forced courts to assume some of the characteristics of the very institutions they are trying to change.[67] Like the institutions they are trying to reshape, judges must improvise and expand their own capacities. They must improve their management capacities, acquire staffs, and negotiate budgets. At times they must become politicians to build public support for their objectives, either working through the media or working quietly to foster agency and legislative support for the massive changes and increased expenditures.

One common judicial response to these problems is the appointment of special masters knowledgeable about custodial institutions who can assist the court in formulating a solution to the mess the court found and can oversee implementation of a complicated management plan.[68] Known as "special masters," "monitors," "ombudsmen," "human rights committees," "compliance officers," and "experts," these agents of the court are appointed by federal courts under their inherent powers of equity and under Rule 53 of the Federal Rules of Civil Procedure, which specifically authorizes the appointment of special masters in "exceptional conditions."[69] State courts have similar powers under state law. This development has led one pair of sympathetic observers to characterize the remedial process in institutional conditions cases as the work of "judge and company."[70] Less sympathetic observers of the increased use of special masters argue that the routine appointment of special masters is transforming the courts into the very types of ineffective bureaucracies that they are trying to combat.[71] According to this view, the courts are abandoning their distinctive function of deciding legal issues and are in danger of becoming just one more public service agency.

Whatever their merits, the use of special masters has certainly increased in recent years. They now routinely perform a great variety of functions in both the predecretal and postdecretal stages of litigation. At the predecretal stage, they conduct evidentiary hearings and undertake specialized fact-finding functions, as in *Costello v. Wainwright*, a case in which a special master was used to aid in the evaluation of the quality of medical care in the prison system, and *Guthrie v. Evans*, a case in which a monitor conducted hearings to ascertain facts on a variety of issues.[72]

In prison and jail conditions cases, however, masters have been most active at the postdecretal stage where they have been used to formulate detailed plans for implementing a general court order. For instance, in *Palmigiano v. Garrahy*, a master was appointed to "advise and assist the defendant department to the fullest extent possible" to develop a plan for complying with the court order; and in *Jones v. Wittenberg* and *Taylor v. Perini*, the court appointed masters to "coordinate and approve all steps taken by defendants to effectuate compliance."[73] In *Ruiz v. Estelle*, the court appointed a master with extensive powers to aid the defendant Texas Department of Corrections in devising detailed plans for implementing the extensive relief the court had granted and in turn authorized the master to assemble a staff the size of a small law office to assist in the effort. In a Santa Clara County jail suit, a state court judge granted the court-appointed "compliance officer" extensive powers to assure that the county sheriff's department was moving toward compliance with its orders, and by all accounts the master ended up running the jail for extended periods.

Although there are a number of general discussions of the functions of special masters in prison and jail conditions cases,[74] there are few systematic studies of their multiple duties and conflicting roles. And there is nothing comparable to the literature on special masters in school desegregation cases.[75] Many of the discussions focus on their formal authority. Very few examine their actual behavior. We know of only one study by Susan Sturm, that has attempted a comparative assessment of the effectiveness of masters and monitors in prison conditions suits.[76] Sturm reviews the duties of masters in six different prison conditions suits and concludes that they perform a variety of different and incompatible functions. She notes, for example, that the orders of reference of appointment for masters are often vague and open ended, and that this generates confusion and unrealistic expectations among prisoners and prison officials as to what the authority of the special master is. She reports that masters are expected to be unbiased fact finders and advisers to the court, enforcement facilitators and arbitrators when working with defendants, and sources of information about problems of compliance for the plaintiffs. Some of these roles, she argues, are incompatible with each other. In addition, she emphasizes that masters must operate in a highly charged atmosphere in which defendants are alienated and resentful and plaintiffs' lawyers may be interested in publicizing the "symbolic victories." Thus the master's work is likely to take place under conditions that polarize the parties and in a process that may obscure and intensify conflict. Indeed, it is often the case that named plaintiffs are unrepresentative of the plaintiff class as a whole and that many of the most important concerns of the inmates have not been addressed by the court order.

The result, Sturm asserts, is a role conflict. For instance, if a master is active as an informal fact finder and arbitrator as a way of increasing his or her effectiveness as an administrator and enforcer, this may lead the master to assume the role of the judge in interpreting the order. Similarly, if a master helps to formulate a compliance plan, this may undercut his or her ability to act as an impartial hearing officer with respect to compliance with the plan. Finally, she notes, "the master's advisory, intermediary and enforcement roles are usually outside the court's visibility and control unless the parties formally challenge their legality." Sturm's recommendation in light of all this is greater specificity in judicial orders of appointment of special masters, a clear division of responsibility at the remedy formulation and remedy implementation stages, with different masters for each stage.

Although some tend to agree with this assessment of the role conflicts of masters, others would question the value of trying to seek such clarity in defining the master's roles and responsibilities. Harris and Spiller, for instance, emphasize that the master's functions evolve in ways that cannot be anticipated.[77] Little and Feeley have explored the emerging role of the special master in a jail case and found that his expanded powers, both formal and informal, were due to his discovery of a vacuum of effective knowledge and administrative skills in the sheriff's department and the judges' growing confidence in his abilities.[78] Kirp and Babcock have examined the work of special masters in several school desegregation cases and found that even when orders defining their functions were similar, their actual responsibilities varied widely.[79] Their major conclusion was that one cannot meaningfully talk about "the role" of a master because almost by definition masters are called upon to deal with extraordinarily complex situations, and judges who appoint them have little or no experience in working with them. Furthermore, they emphasize, the federal judiciary is so decentralized and judges so isolated from one another that each judge's appointment of a master is likely to be a new and ad hoc arrangement, the details of which must evolve as both judge and master get to know each other and the case continues to unfold.

Each of these studies found that formal fact finding and other "legalist approaches" formed only a small part of a master's work, and that all masters, however their roles were initially conceived, inevitably augmented their formally prescribed duties with a wide variety of informal information-gathering methods. More generally, despite specifications of the masters' formal duties, Kirp and Babcock found that the most important jobs of the special masters were not—and could not be—specified in advance of their appointments. Their jobs largely consisted of "selling" the court's orders to the defendants. In some instances masters acted like politicians, quietly working behind the scenes; in others they performed the role of expert and fact-finder; in still others they went public, hoping to build public support for their recommendations. When trying to account for variation in masters' styles and their effectiveness, Kirp and Babcock could find no relationship between provisions in the court's orders of reference or the similarities and differences in the problems addressed by the courts.[80] Rather, they found that variation was rooted in the personal characteristics of the judges and masters, and especially how judges perceived their roles in the cases (i.e., what they thought needed to be done, whether they thought a case had a "political dimension," and how they viewed change occurring in complex organizations).

Thus, we are presented with two views of special masters. Both identify the ambiguity and multiplicity of roles of the special master. Sturm regards this as a liability and recommends that the role conflicts be reduced in order to increase the effectiveness of the masters. In contrast, Kirp and Babcock and others regard the multiplicity of roles and responsibilities as a strength of great value to the special master. We see something of this controversy in a brief exchange in the American Civil Liberties Union's National Prison Project's *Journal.* Arguing for the need for greater specificity of roles, Susan Sturm observes: "The master must be able to define and maintain a position of neutrality in order to function effectively. In the past, masters have sometimes carried out their responsibilities in the absence of any clear guidelines as to how to proceed, what to achieve and what to avoid. The absence of a clear mandate can lead to unrealistic expectation and mixed signals among inmates and prison officials alike. . . ."[81] In response, Gordon Bonnymore, who has served as a special master, asserted that he had found the ambiguity in the order of reference for his appointment in Tennessee valuable.[82] In his opinion that open-ended specification of the master's duties was an effective way of communicating to the state that the master had the court's full confidence and that it should cooperate fully with him.

Our own view is that the factors most likely to explain variation among masters' styles or roles (assuming we can even identify them) are related to what judges want to accomplish, and how effectively the master exploits whatever "political" skills he or she possesses. So far as we can tell, the process of appointment of special masters in prison conditions cases and the factors that distinguish their style and effectiveness have to do with a host of contextual and personality factors that became apparent only after they are deeply involved in their work. To the extent this is true, no list of formal tasks set forth in the orders of reference of appointment will adequately capture their responsibilities. Hence, we suspect that more systematic research is likely to show that role conflicts are inherent in the job of mastering and monitoring, and that efforts to specify in the orders of reference the tasks of the masters will not meet with much success. This difficulty in defining and limiting the role of special masters is just one more indication of how thoroughly managerial judicial involvement in prison and jail conditions cases is. As we suggested at the outset of this chapter, judicial invention in prison and jail conditions transforms judges into administrators of large and unwieldy institutions. Nowhere is this more evident than in the activities of special masters, those agents of the court who have continuing responsibilities for overseeing the myriad of planned changes and unforseen consequences set in motion by a court order.

Conclusion

Generalizations concerning prison conditions litigation are shaped by what cases are examined and how they are examined. For prisons and jails, this has meant we know most about a small number of atypical cases, those that are large, dramatic, or especially controversial. There are few systematic studies of smaller cases. Still, it is possible to identify some general issues and themes.

First, there is common agreement among researchers that federal court intervention into prisons and jails has altered in significant ways the authority of institutional administrators and officers. In particular, the early cases directed against conditions in southern prisons resulted in the transformation of the organization of those institutions and a jump in state expenditures to maintain them. While this intervention by the courts has contributed to the enhancement of the administrative capacity of correctional agencies, in some instances it also appears to have affected administrators' abilities to maintain safe and secure institutions, at least in the short run. Court orders disrupt existing arrangements between officers and inmates; in some instances, this disruption has contributed to inmate violence, including attacks against both other inmates and officers. However, this pattern is neither permanent nor inevitable. Research in some settings reveals no increase in violence after the court orders, and even where it has occurred it often is relatively short-lived. This mixed picture will, of course, become clearer as more studies examine both the short- and long-term effects of litigation.

Second, although the ostensible purpose of litigation is to bring conditions up to constitutional standards, there are few studies that document how prisoners have benefited from these court-ordered services. Do, for instance, prisoners receive better medical services after a court has ordered them, budgets have been increased, and new staff appointed? Undoubtedly, there are many other factors, including rapidly growing populations, that affect the availability of such court-ordered improvements. Nevertheless, the acknowledged necessity of screening out external factors should not inhibit the development and refinement of indicators of the quality of prison life. Even more to the point, there is a need for more research on the *impact* of court orders on both policies and actual service delivery. Until those studies are conducted, it will be difficult to make any conclusive statements about the effects of judicial intervention.

Third, although there is always the fascination with process—how courts fashion complex remedies—this topic seems to defy meaningful patterns. At rock bottom, the relationship between the judge and the special master, and possibly monitors, hinges on the personalities of the participants and the exigencies of the situation. Differences in behavior appear to be a function of personality and style, not some more substantial structural dimension. As a result, it is unlikely that variation in the degree of the court's success in modifying prison structure, policies, or service delivery is likely to be accounted for in terms of formal procedural styles.

The implication of these themes for practitioners and researchers is that caution and modesty are called for. Judges, masters, attorneys, and correction officials lack well-documented models of successful federal court intervention. Although some situations have been less contentious than others, there is no clear path to ensure quick compliance nor any key to minimize negative side effects.

For researchers, the absence of a cumulative body of testable propositions should be sobering—and a stimulus to more careful research. Much of what we know rests on a limited number of cases, not necessarily representative of the world at large. Although past research has tackled a meaningful set of issues, improvement is necessary in the design of both longitudinal and comparative studies.

Notes

1. The National Prison Project, *Status Report: The Courts and Prisons* (Washington, D.C.: American Civil Liberties Union, December 1, 1988).
2. For example, see Donald L. Horowitz, *The Courts and Social Policy* (Washington, D.C.: Brookings Institution, 1977); and his "Decreeing Organizational Change: Judicial Supervision of Public Institutions," *Duke Law Journal* 1265 (1983).
3. Gerald Frugg, "The Judicial Power of the Purse," 126 *University of Virginia Law Review* 715 (1978); Robert F. Nagel, "Separation of Powers and the Scope of Federal Equitable Remedies," 30 *Stanford Law Review* 661 (1978); and his "Controlling the Structural Injunction," 7 *Harvard Journal of Law and Public Policy* 395 (1984); Paul Mishkin, "Federal Courts as State Reformers," 35 *Washington and Lee Law Review* 949 (1978).
4. Horowitz, *The Courts.*
5. Abram Chayes, "The Role of the Judge in Public Law Litigation," 89 *Harvard Law Review* 1281 (1976); Owen M. Fiss, "Foreword: The Forms of Justice," 93 *Harvard Law Review* 1 (1979); John Hart Ely, *Democracy and Distrust* (Cambridge: Harvard University Press, 1980).
6. Roger A. Hanson and Joy A. Chapper, *A Framework for Studying the Controversy Concerning the Federal Courts and Federalism* (Washington, D.C.: Information Report of the U.S. Advisory Commission on Intergovernmental Relations, 1986); and Hanson, "Contending Perspectives on Federal Court Efforts to Reform State Institutions," 59 *University of Colorado Law Review* 19 (1988).

7. Lon Fuller, "The Forms and Limits of Adjudication," 92 *Harvard Law Review* 353 (1978).
8. Fiss, "Foreword: The Forms of Justice," p. 1.
9. Michael Lipsky, *Street-Level Bureaucracy* (New York: Russell Sage Foundation, 1980).
10. This point was stressed in The President's Commission on Law Enforcement and Administration of Justice, *Task Force Report: Corrections* (Washington, D.C.: U.S. Government Printing Office, 1967). But as Clair A. Cripe indicates in chapter 10 of the present volume, the degree of discretion exercised by those at the bottom of the "pyramid" (both inmates and staff) may vary from system to system and among institutions within a given system.
11. The classic study is Gresham M. Sykes, *The Society of Captives* (Princeton, N.J.: Princeton University Press, 1958). Also see Sykes and Sheldon Messinger, "The Inmate Social System," in *Theoretical Studies in the Social Organization of the Prison* (New York: Social Science Research Council, 1960), 5–19; and James B. Jacobs, *Stateville: The Penitentiary in Mass Society* (Chicago: University of Chicago Press, 1977).
12. John J. DiIulio, Jr., *Governing Prisons: A Comparative Study of Correctional Management* (New York: The Free Press, 1987); see especially chapter 4.
13. Richard F. Elmore, "Organizational Models of Social Program Implementation," 26 *Public Policy* 185 (1978).
14. Horowitz, *The Courts*; Nathan Glazer, "Towards an Imperial Judiciary?" 41 *The Public Interest* 104 (1975); Glazer, "Should Judges Administer Social Services?" 50 *The Public Interest* 64 (1978); Glazer, "The Judiciary and Social Policy," in *The Judiciary in a Democratic Society*, ed. Leonard J. Theberge (Lexington, Mass.: Lexington Books, 1979, 34–57); Stuart Scheingold, *The Politics of Rights: Lawyers, Public Policy, and Political Change* (New Haven: Yale University Press, 1974).
15. Glazer, "Towards an Imperial Judiciary," "Should Judges Administer Social Services," and "The Judiciary and Social Policy."
16. DiIulio, *Governing Prisons*, pp. 212–226; Kathleen Engel and Stanley Rothman, "The Paradox of Prison Reform: Rehabilitation, Prisoners' Rights, and Violence," 7 *Harvard Journal of Law and Public Policy* 413 (1984); Kenneth C. Haas and Anthony Champagne, "The Impact of *Johnson v. Avery* on Prison Administration" 43 *Tennessee Law Review* 275 (1976); James W. Marquart and Ben M. Crouch, "Judicial Reform and Prisoner Control: The Impact of *Ruiz v. Estelle* on a

Texas Penitentiary" 19 *Law and Society Review* 557 (1985); M. Kay Harris and Dudley Spiller, *After Decision: Implementation of Judicial Decrees in Correctional Settings* (Washington, D.C.: National Institute of Law Enforcement and Criminal Justice, 1977); Bradley Chilton, "*Guthrie v. Evans*: Civil Rights, Prison Reform, and Institutional Reform Litigation" (doctoral diss., University of Georgia, 1988).

17. Engel and Rothman, "The Paradox of Prison Reform," p. 413.

18. Ibid., p. 431.

19. Ibid., p. 435.

20. Though DiIulio reaches conclusions similar to those of Engel and Rothman, he too questions the causal links in their argument; see DiIulio, *Governing Prisons*, pp. 21, 323.

21. Anthony Newland, Memorandum on "The Impact of Jail and Prison Conditions Litigation," (typescript, November 1988).

22. Harris and Spiller, *After Decision*, pp. 16–21; James B. Jacobs, "The Prisoners' Rights Movement and Its Impact, 1960–1980," 2 *Crime and Justice: An Annual Review of Research* 429 (1980); Chilton, "Guthrie v. Evans," pp. 179–183; Tinsley E. Yarbrough, *Judge Frank M. Johnson and Human Rights in Alabama* (University: University of Alabama Press, 1981).

23. Glazer, "The Judiciary," p. 34.

24. Jacobs, "The Prisoners' Rights Movement" pp. 460–463.

25. Ibid., p. 461.

26. Jacobs, *Stateville*, pp. 190 –198.

27. DiIulio, *Governing Persons*, pp. 220–27.

28. Chilton, "Guthrie v. Evans," pp. 168–170.

29. Samuel Jan Brakel, "Mastering the Legal Access Rights of Prisoners" 12 *New England Journal of Criminal and Civil Confinement* 1 (1986).

30. Ibid., p. 69.

31. DiIulio, *Governing Prisons*, pp. 223–25.

32. Deborah Little and Malcolm M. Feeley, "Courts, Jails and Organization Theory: A Case Study of *Branson v. Winter*," (paper prepared for delivery at the annual meeting of the American Society of Criminology, Reno, Nevada, November 9–11, 1989).

33. Jacobs, "The Prisoners' Rights Movement." pp. 458–59.

34. Jonathan S. Simon and Jerome Skolnick, "Federalism, the Exclusionary Rule and The Police," in Harry N. Scheiber and Malcolm M. Feeley (eds.), *Power Divided: Essays on the Theory and Practice of Federalism* (Berkeley: Institute of Governmental Studies, 1989), pp. 75–88.

35. Priscilla Slocum, "The Exclusionary Rule and Structural Reform of Police Organizations" (doctoral diss., University of California at Los Angeles, 1987).

36. Samuel Walker, "The Rule Revolution: Reflections on the Transformation of American Criminal Justice, 1950–1988" (University of Wisconsin, Institute for Legal Studies, December 1988).

37. Richard McCleery, "Communication Pattern as Bases of Systems of Authority and Power," in *Theoretical Studies in the Social Organization of the Prison* (New York: Social Science Research Council, 1960), pp. 49–77.

38. Brakel, "Mastering the Legal Access Rights," p. 69.

39. DiIulio, *Governing Prisons*, pp. 228–29.

40. Steve J. Martin and Sheldon Ekland-Olson, *Texas Prisons: The Walls Came Tumbling Down* (Austin: Texas Monthly Press, 1987).

41. Harris and Spiller, *After Decision*, pp. 14–20.

42. Chilton, "Guthrie v. Evans," pp. 180–85.

43. Ibid., p. 185.

44. Little and Feeley, "Courts, Jails and Organization Theory," pp. 42–49.

45. Malcolm M. Feeley and Edward Rubin, "Federal-State Relations and Prison Administrations," in Harry N. Scheiber and Malcolm M. Feeley (eds.), *Power Divided: Essays in the Theory and Practice of Federalism*, (Berkeley: Institute of Governmental Studies, 1989), pp. 63–74.

46. Ibid., pp. 65–69.

47. Dale K. Sechrest and Ernest G. Reimer, "Adopting National Standards for Correctional Reform" 18 *Federal Probation* 75 (1982).

48. Harris and Spiller, *After Decision*, pp. 18–42.

49. Rod Smolla, "Prison Overcrowding and the Courts: A Roadmap for the 1980s," *Illinois Law Review* 389 (1984).

50. Ibid., pp. 405–20.

51. Feeley and Rubin, "Federal-State Relations and Prison Administration," p. 63.

52. Harris and Spiller, *After Decision*, pp. 18–42.

53. Ibid., p. 25.

54. Ted Storey, "Courts and Corrections: The New York City Jail Litigation," (paper prepared for the annual meeting of the Law and Society Association, Vail, Colorado, June 1988).

55. DiIulio, *Governing Prisons*, pp. 230–34.

56. Martin and Ekland-Olson, *Texas Prisons*, pp. 238–39.

57. Linda Harriman and Jeffrey Straussman, "Do Judges Determine Budget Decisions?" 43 *Public Administration Review* 343 (1983).

58. William A. Taggart, "Redefining The Power of the Federal Judiciary: The Impact of Court-Ordered Prison Reforms on State Expenditures for Corrections," 23 *Law and Society Reviews* 241 (1989).

59. Malcolm M. Feeley, "The Significance of Prison Corrections Cases: Budgets and Regions," 23 *Law and Society Review* 273 (1989).

60. Feeley and Rubin, "Federal-State Relations and Prison Administration," p. 68.
61. Jeffrey Pressman and Aaron Wildavsky, *Implementation* (Berkeley: University of California Press, 1973) pp. 7–34; Lipsky, *Street-Level Bureaucracy*, pp. 16–23.
62. Lipsky, *Street-Level Bureaucracy*, pp. 23–26.
63. Brakel, "Mastering the Legal Access Rights," p. 68.
64. Ibid., p. 69.
65. Little and Feeley, "Courts, Jails and Organization Theory," pp. 46–49.
66. Judith Resnick and Nancy Shaw, "Prisoners of Their Sex: Health Problems of Incarcerated Women," in *Prisoners' Rights Sourcebook*, ed. Ira P. Robbins (New York: Clark Boardman, 1984); Kathleen Daly, Shelly Geballe, and Stanton Wheeler, "Litigation-Driven Research: A Case Study of Lawyer–Social Scientist Collaboration," 10 *Women's Rights Reporter* 87 (1988).
67. Horowitz, "Decreeing Organizational Change," p. 1266.
68. Vincent Nathan, "The Use of Masters in Institutional Reform Litigation" 10 *The University of Toledo Law Review* 419 (1979); Joanna Weinberg, "The Judicial Adjunct and Public Law Remedies," 1 *Yale Law and Policy Review* 357 (1983).
69. Irving Kaufman, "Masters in Federal Courts: Rule 53," 58 *Columbia Law Review* 452 (1958); Nathan, "The Use of Masters," p. 419.
70. David Kirp and Gary Babcock, "Judge and Company: Court-Appointed Masters, School Desegregation and Institutional Reform," 32 *Alabama Law Review* 313 (1981).
71. Horowitz, *The Courts* and "Decreeing Organizational Change."
72. Chilton, "Guthrie v. Evans," p. 81ff.
73. Nathan, "The Use of Masters," p. 442.
74. Ibid.; Allen Breed, "Special Masters Ease Prison Reform," 23 *Corrections Today* 262 (1979); Susan Sturm, "Special Masters Aid in Compliance Efforts" 6 *National Prison Project Journal* 9 (1985); Gordon Bonnymore, "Letter to the Editor," 7 *National Prison Project Journal* 5 (1988).
75. Kirp and Babcock, "Judge and Company," p. 313.
76. Susan Sturm "Special Masters Aid in Compliance," p. 9; idem. "Mastering Intervention in Prisons," 88 *Yale Law Journal* 1062 (1979).
77. Harris and Spiller, *After Decision*, pp. 26–28.
78. Little and Feeley, "Courts, Jails and Organization Theory," p. 40.
79. Kirp and Babcock, "Judge and Company," p. 315.
80. Ibid., p. 367.
81. Sturm, "Special Master Aid in Compliance," pp. 9–10.
82. Bonnymore, "Letter to the Editor," p. 5.

THE THREE FACES OF *RUIZ*

In 1972 David Ruiz, an inmate in the custody of the Texas Department of Corrections (TDC), sent a handwritten petition to Judge William Wayne Justice of the Eastern District Court. Ruiz challenged conditions of confinement in TDC under section 1983 of the U.S. Civil Rights Act. In 1974 Judge Justice combined Ruiz's petition with those of seven other TDC inmates. The then director of TDC was W. J. (Jim) Estelle, Jr. The case, a class action suit, was titled *Ruiz v. Estelle.*

The trial began in 1978 in Houston Federal Court. On December 12, 1980, Judge Justice issued a 248-page memorandum opinion.* He found that TDC prisons were overcrowded and understaffed, provided inadequate medical care and fire safety, subjected inmates to brutality by officers and by other inmates, unduly restricted inmates' access to attorneys and legal resources, and sanctioned intimidation and harassment of inmates who brought (or merely threatened to bring) suits against prison officials. He held that, in their totality, these conditions constituted cruel and unusual punishment under the Eighth Amendment of the United States Constitution. He further held that TDC deprived inmates of their due process rights under the Fifth and Fourteenth amendments.

Ruiz v. Estelle, 503 F. Supp. 1265 (S.D. Tex. 1980), aff'd, 679 F.2d 1115 (5th Cir. 1982), *cert. denied*, 460 U.S. 1042 (1983).

In his remedial decree, Judge Justice ordered fundamental changes in TDC and set deadlines for making these changes. Among other things, he ordered TDC to reduce its inmate population, expand its use of work furlough and community corrections programs, construct new prisons, enhance staff training programs, and develop a new inmate classification system. He also ordered TDC to abolish its "building tender" system. Building tenders were inmates used by TDC officials to control other inmates, often by sheer physical brutality.

Judge Justice appointed a special master to oversee the implementation of his detailed orders. The special master was empowered to hold hearings, make findings of fact, and advise the court about the state of TDC's compliance with the decree. In appointing the special master, Judge Justice cited Federal Rule of Civil Procedure 53 and the court's inherent equity powers. He also cited TDC's near-total lack of cooperation in working out solutions and its failures to comply fully with its own written policies and procedures.

In 1982 the Fifth Circuit Court of Appeals upheld Judge Justice's central finding about the unconstitutionality of conditions inside Texas prisons. While overturning several provisions of the decree, it upheld most of Judge Justice's orders, including the appointment of a special master with quasi-judicial powers. But the appeals court emphasized that the special master's discretion was limited to matters within the scope of the decree, vacating Judge Justice's order that all findings of the master were to be treated as correct unless "clearly erroneous." With Judge Justice's approval, court monitors were chosen by the special master to assist in overseeing the implementation of the district court's compliance plans.

In the June 1985 edition of *The Echo*, a Texas inmate newspaper, the headline read "Final Ruiz Settlement." By that time, most of the major issues in the case were settled, and implementation of the decree was well under way. As of this writing, however, TDC remains under Judge Justice's supervision.

During the nine-year legal struggle leading to Judge Justice's 1980 ruling, and in the five years between that ruling and the final settlement, *Ruiz* sparked a national controversy. Among corrections practitioners, activists, and analysts, opinions about the quality of TDC prison management, the propriety of the federal judge's involvement, and the causes and consequences of the court's intervention have varied widely.

The controversy continues. Chapters 2, 3, and 4 present three distinct interpretations of *Ruiz* and its aftermath. These "three faces of *Ruiz*" offer three different assessments of the impact of this important instance of judicial intervention on one of the nation's largest prison systems. We challenge the reader, however, not only to explore how these accounts differ but to probe what, if anything, they have in common as guides to enhancing judicial capacity. Our own ideas about what they have in common as guides to enhancing judicial capacity appear in the concluding chapter.

2

The Old Regime and the *Ruiz* Revolution: The Impact of Judicial Intervention on Texas Prisons

JOHN J. DiIULIO, JR.

As Malcolm M. Feeley and Roger A. Hanson suggested in chapter 1, there is no body of empirical research to tell us whether, on balance, judicial intervention has changed prisons for the better, altered correctional practices in a way designed merely to avoid unfavorable rulings, or led to undesirable or simply unanticipated results. As I see it, there are at least three schools of speculation and a prima facie case against each of them.[1]

One school argues that activist judges have emboldened the inmates, upset informal order-keeping arrangements among prisoners and between inmates and staff, and gutted basic custodial controls. Members of this school blame the courts for rising tides of prison violence. For example, Kathleen Engel and Stanley Rothman argued that court-imposed reforms have increased prison violence by undermining the "complex relationships among inmates" that had "contributed to the maintenance of order and inmate solidarity."[2] But the notion that such informal cellblock alliances were once a bedrock of prison order is a vivid but wholly unsubstantiated sociological myth; riots and disturbances have occurred most often precisely where prison administrators have relied on inmates to control other inmates and have failed to run things "by the book."[3]

A second school maintains that activist judges have done no more than force prison administrators to operate in ways that secure rather than deny prisoners' rights. Advocates of this view credit the courts with improving prison conditions. For example, the National Prison Project of the American Civil Liberties Union led the litigation efforts that expanded court intervention into penal affairs; indeed, the organization spearheaded the use of special masters and monitors. One of the ACLU's primary objectives in this area has been to decrease the number of people behind bars and to force a greater use of ostensibly less harsh and restrictive alternatives to incarceration; hence, whether the actual impact on cellblock conditions is good, bad, unknown, or nonexistent, the organization counts as "major victories" instances of judicial involvement where population limits have been imposed and negative media attention has been focused on the prison gates.[4]

Yet a third school believes that the courts have fostered a codification of prison policies and procedures resulting in the bureaucratization of the prison, which in turn has made prisons more orderly and humane.[5] This belief moves from a top-down conception of bureaucracy that focuses more on formal administrative trappings (bulky training manuals, elaborate central office policy directives, the existence of uniform institutional training programs, etc.) than on the real, day-to-day work of line employees. By definition, those in a bureaucracy who perform the agency's critical tasks have little discretion; successful job performance is not highly contingent on the integrity, personality, keen wit, or any other special talents of the workers.

Yet nothing can be more clear than that court-induced changes in how prisons operate have helped to increase the complexity of the corrections officers' work by vesting them with ever greater discretionary authority, personalizing their relationships with inmates, and obliterating the guards' once simple, paramilitary routine of numbering, couting, checking, locking, monitoring inmate movement, frisking convicts, searching cells, and so on. To the extent that prisons have undergone any sort of court-induced organizational metamorphosis, the barbed-wire bureaucracies have become less, not more bureaucratic, with effects on actual prison conditions that are hard to measure.

None of the leading theories fares well when considered in the light of actual cases. Perhaps the single most controversial, well-publicized, and revealing instance of judicial intervention into a major prison system is *Ruiz v. Estelle* in Texas. The case began in 1972, dragged on into 1985, and revolutionized the way that Texas ran its prisons. It provides much food for thought on the impact of judicial intervention on prisons.

The Case of Texas Prisons

In 1985 Dr. George Beto, for thirteen years a professor of criminal justice at an East Texas university, close to most of the prisons he had run from 1962 to 1972, sat in stunned silence as members of his graduate seminar who worked in Texas prisons lectured the class about their experiences. Beto's head drooped as they described in graphic detail how common it now was for Texas prisoners, especially new ones, to be raped or gang-raped; how every shakedown of cells turned up hundreds of weapons and other contraband; how certain inmate leaders ran prostitution and drug rings behind the walls; how prison gangs were putting out contracts on—that is, hiring inmates to kill—staff and other prisoners; how inmate classrooms and workplaces were, like the cellblocks, sites of inmate idleness punctuated by disorder; how demoralized officers, fearing inmate reprisals for disciplinary action and with little more than personal survival and a paycheck in view, were simply "keeping their backs to the wall" and ignoring most rule violations, major and minor.

During Beto's tenure and into the 1980s, the Texas prison system was hailed as one of the nation's best;[6] but in 1984 and 1985 a total of fifty-two inmates of Texas prisons were murdered, and over seven hundred were stabbed. More serious violence occurred in those two years than had occurred in the previous decade. As the disorder mounted, inmate participation in treatment and educational programs became erratic, the once-immaculate inmate living quarters ceased to sparkle, and recreational privileges were curtailed.

What happened to the Texas Department of Corrections (TDC) was the product of at least two sets of related factors: a major flaw in the model of penal administration fathered by Beto and bequeathed to his successor, W. J. Estelle, Jr.; and *Ruiz v. Estelle*, a landmark court case in which an activist federal district judge, William Wayne Justice, forced sudden, sweeping changes in TDC's philosophy, leadership, and day-to-day management practices while making the agency the bête noire of state policymakers and the press.

Beto instituted what came to be known in corrections circles as the "control model" of penal administration. Beto was a tall, lean Lutheran minister with a doctorate in education; his control model emphasized inmate obedience, work, and education, roughly in that order. Every TDC prison was run as a maximum security operation organized along strict paramilitary lines. Official rules and regulations were enforced rigorously. In the prison corridors, for example, clean-shaven, white-uniformed inmates were required to walk between lines painted on the floors rather than moving at random down the center. Talking too loudly was a punishable offense. Punishment for rule violations, major and minor, was swift and certain. Rewards for good behavior came in the form of better work assignments, sentence reductions, and trustyships. Each inmate spent his first six months doing backbreaking stoop labor, a cog in the machine of TDC's then enormously successful agribusiness complex. All inmates were required to attend school and learn how to read.

Beto earned the nickname "Walking George" for his practice of appearing unexpectedly at the prisons and roaming relentlessly to see that every phase of the operation met his exacting standards. He was a charismatic leader who made both his subordinates and the inmates feel that he knew or could trace their every move; in fact, he normally could. A man as comfortable in the aisles of the state legislature as he was in the cellblocks, Beto successfully courted governors, lawmakers, and others influential in state business and saw to it that TDC got the legal authority and the money it needed to run its custodial and treatment program in accordance with his correctional precepts.

The "Building Tender" System

Beto was perhaps the most well-read man ever to run a prison system; the influences on his thinking about how to govern prisons ranged from the Bible (which he read each morning in ancient Greek) and classic works of moral and political philosophy to writings in public administration and texts by leading sociologists of the prison. It was in deference to the last of these that Beto fashioned as part of his control model the "building tender" system in which inmates were used to control other inmates.

From his reading of the sociological literature on prisons, which included such powerful treatises as Gresham M. Sykes's *The Society of Captives*, Beto came to the helm of TDC believing that if prisons were to be safe, clean, programmatic, and cost-effective, then it was imperative that some way be found to minimize or, better still, to neutralize the influence of convict leaders. Beto saw himself as a prison reformer out to habituate society's criminally wayward to the norms and values of a decent, law-abiding, and socially useful way of life. He was convinced by what Sykes had counseled; namely, that any attempt to reform the prison that "ignores the social system of the prison" (the language, leaders, laws, rites, and rituals of the convict population) was bound to be "as futile as the labors of Sisyphus."[7]

Beto, however, was determined that the TDC's way of coopting inmate leaders would not involve lax rule enforcement, illicit privileges, and the corruption of formal authority that characterized "con boss" systems. Rather than allow the most aggressive and violent inmates to rule, Beto tried to select certain inmate leaders, give them special official status beyond a mere trustyship, and use them to preempt the influence of more hard-core and incorrigibly antiadministration convict chieftains. "Either you pick their leaders," he explained, "or they do."

Beto's building tenders were to be rewarded officially with better food, job assignments, and other amenities in return for watching the officers' backs, providing information, turning cell doors, "tending" to the physical upkeep of the institutions, and so on. In short, the building tender system was a calculated gamble aimed at turning the "natural" leaders of the society of captives into the official allies of the government of keepers.

Beto did everything imaginable to tilt the odds in the administration's favor. For one thing, he hand-picked his "supertrusties," choosing inmates who were tough but not predatory (or, in Beto's words, not the "kind who would rape a snake through a brick wall"). He permitted neither the building tenders nor the staff to "get too big for their britches." Walking George fired officers who violated their offical trust, usually on the spot. Any building tender who grasped or demanded illicit privileges in return for his services was sent back into the fields to do stoop labor flanked by "fish" (new inmates). As Beto recalled, the Texas control model "was, at heart, a system in which power was highly centralized. Power can be used well or ill, but unchecked it tends, as has been observed by better minds, to corrupt. It was therefore imperative that abuses, most especially abuses by staff members, be uncovered quickly and stopped."

When, in 1972, Beto resigned amid cries from all over the state that he remain as director of TDC, most parts of his control model were well institutionalized—the paramilitary procedures, the liberal awarding of good time (i.e., sentence reductions), the stress on inmate discipline, work, and education. The building tender system, however, was never a well-integrated part of the model. Beto and his top aides were aware that, without unremitting efforts to keep it honest, the building tender system could easily degenerate into the very system of inmate dominance and corrupt inmate–staff relations that it was meant to forestall. As one high-ranking veteran of the TDC noted perceptively, "The tenders were always like a sort of sore thumb of the control model. . . . I mean here you had the bosses [officers] and the 'Yes sirs' and the steady discipline, all of it done formal-like and run by the authorities. . . . But then there were the tenders, inmates who were "first among equals" so long as they did our bidding. . . . But you know Dr. Beto, he'd never let it get out of control!"

Beto's extraordinary degree of personal involvement in keeping the building tender system from degenerating into a species of inmate self-rule was a symptom of its essentially prebureaucratic nature. The fact that he had to exploit fully his blanketing and charismatic leadership merely to keep the system on an even keel was a sign of its weakness. Virtually every other part of his control model could be mastered and implemented by any competent and dedicated team of prison officials—but not the building tender system.

The Destruction of the Control Model

Whether they baptize their inmate allies building tenders, con bosses, or "inmate advisory council representatives," and whether the in-mate–staff alliance is tacit or formal, it is never good policy for prison administrators to rely on inmates to control other inmates. There are dozens of post–World War II sociological monographs on the prison asserting that such relationships are both inevitable and desirable as means of keeping order, rehabilitating inmates, and attuning the prison to "democratic values."[8] Yet the factual record of this same period shows that all species of "participative prison management" have turned higher custody cellblocks into versions of Hobbes's state of nature in which the inmates' most basic right—the right to safe incarceration—has been forfeited. Prison managers who have de-pended on convicts or their leaders to maintain institutional control have consistently lost it, giving rise to situations in which the inmates, not the officers, dictate what happens behind bars. This could have been learned from the wave of prison riots that occurred in the early 1950s. But in deference to sociological theory, and in contradiction to his belief in prison governance by duly constituted authorities, Beto enlisted the support of building tenders, sowing the seeds of the control model's destruction.

Under Beto's hand-picked heir, W. J. (Jim) Estelle, the number of TDC inmates increased by the thousands and the agency's prisons more than doubled to over two dozen institutions. Though in many respects a brilliant prisons man, Estelle was no Walking Jim. Under Beto, the building tender system was like an overly sharp knife wielded by a master chef in a calm kitchen. This knife was handed to Estelle, who, by comparison, was a good short-order cook behind a busy counter. Estelle was a younger man with a mostly office-bound style of executive leadership; word of abuses did not always trickle up to his headquarters in Huntsville, and there were no upward-flowing, independent channels of information, like the channels that had enabled Beto and his aides to check on the veracity of reports from the field and caused them to notice when no such reports were forthcoming.

Predictably, while most other parts of the control model survived and were strengthened under Estelle, the building tender system ran amok and became nothing more than a con boss system in which selected inmates were allowed to carry weapons and were given illicit privileges for "keeping things quiet." In some instances, this meant administering beatings to fellow inmates who had defied an officer or refused to work. At a few TDC institutions, the administration became a virtual hostage to the building tenders, relying on them to perform many or most custodial functions. In at least one prison, the weekend staff consisted of only a dozen officers who supervised some forty building tenders who made counts, searched cells, frisked other inmates, and administered harsh and arbitrary discipline.

The corruption of the building tenders was infectious. Inmates abused by staff, or by building tenders at the behest of staff, were often unable to get a fair hearing (or any hearing at all) within TDC. In a complete perversion of the esprit de corps and sense of mission that had characterized the agency, wrongdoers at some prisons were shielded by their co-workers and, in some cases, by their superiors.

In 1978 the state's first Republican administration in 105 years took the reins in Austin and wasted little time in shaking things up. With new appointees, the Texas Board of Corrections, a body once dominated by leading Texas businessmen who had never been anything but supportive of TDC, started to cast unprecedented split votes and to voice public criticism of the agency. Political pillars of TDC, such as Texas State House Appropriations Chairman Bill (The Duke of Paducah) Heatly and H. H. (Pete) Coffield, were passing from the scene. Meanwhile, the state's oil revenues were drying up, forcing Texas policymakers to scratch for ways to be even stingier than was customary with financial support for public agencies. Estelle lacked the political instincts that had made Beto so successful with the state's political establishment; TDC lost its "sacred cow" status and was targeted for budget cuts.

Ruiz v. Estelle

It was in this context that the case of *Ruiz v. Estelle* was litigated. The case began in 1972 shortly before Estelle's appointment. Inmate David Ruiz, a chronic offender who had been incarcerated many times, sent a handwritten petition to Judge William Wayne Justice of the Eastern District Court. While in prison, Ruiz stabbed several of his fellow inmates and was often placed in solitary confinement. In his petition, Ruiz charged that conditions in "the hole" were inhumane. He claimed that he slit his wrists so that prison officials would release him from isolation. Ruiz challenged conditions of confinement in TDC under Section 1983 of the U.S. Civil Rights Act. In 1974 Judge Justice combined Ruiz's petition with those of seven other TDC inmates, thereby framing a class action suit.

Unaffectionately called "Willie Wayne" by TDC officials, Judge Justice came to the *Ruiz* case with a record of strong judicial activism in education and other areas. He separated the damage claim at stake in the case from the injunctive issues, thereby making his control over the litigation absolute. In addition, he instituted a procedure whereby issues not raised by the inmate plaintiffs—crowding, recreational facilities, prison land use, and many others—came under his review. He appointed a few of the country's leading prison litigation attorneys to represent the inmates and brought in the United States Department of Justice as an adversary to the State of Texas.

The trail began in 1978. In the four years preceding the trail, Judge Justice imposed a number of orders on TDC. In 1975, for instance, he ordered that prison authorities be prohibited from censoring inmates' mail. In 1980 the judge issued a 248-page memorandum opinion requiring scores of changes in the way that Texas ran its prisons, among them the following: an end to the use of building tenders; a requirement that the agency double its officer force and retrain veteran officers; a revision in the procedures for handling inmate grievances; a complete overhaul of the prisoner classification system that would reduce the number of maximum security designations; a division of the prison population into management units of not more than five hundred each; a radical improvement in health delivery systems that would give inmates easy access to state-of-the-art medical treatment; and the provision of a single cell for each inmate. All of the major issues in the case were decided wholly in favor of the plaintiffs. The judge dismissed without formal comment TDC's contention that certain of his requirements were likely to spawn inmate violence; and he rejected summarily the agency's plea that the timetables he had established for implementing these changes were unrealistic.

During the nine-year legal battle leading up to Judge Justice's 1980 ruling, TDC's control model had received mixed reviews. Some experts credited Texas corrections officials with running the only safe, clean, cost-effective prison system in the country. Others denounced TDC as a repressive agency that treated its inmates like slaves. The judge readily agreed with the system's critics, holding that TDC imposed cruel and unusual punishment on inmates as a result of the "totality of conditions" inside its prisons.

In 1982, a decade after the litigation began, the U.S. Circuit Court of Appeals for the Fifth District upheld Justice's central finding about the unconstitutionality of conditions inside Texas prisons but overturned several provisions of the original order. "Taken as a whole," the three-judge panel wrote, "the district court's decree administers a massive dose when it is not yet demonstrable that a lesser therapeutic measure would not suffice." Among other things, the panel reversed Justice's one-man, one-cell holding, noted that the "Constitution does not require that inmates be given the kind of medical attention that judges wish to have for themselves," and vacated orders that TDC get Justice's approval for any construction plans and that the reports of the special master appointed by Justice be treated as findings of fact.

At the same time, however, the panel chided TDC officials for failing to run better prisons and warned that the "implementation of the district court's decree can become a ceaseless guerrilla war, with endless hearings, opinions and appeals, and incalculable costs." The panel also warned Judge Justice and his team of monitors to "respect the right of the state to administer its own affairs so long as it does not violate the Constitution."

Unfortunately, neither the judge and his monitors nor the TDC officials fully heeded the panel's warnings. The litigation continued to boil for three more years amid bitter charges and countercharges. Estelle was the proud director of a proud agency. He challenged TDC's critics on the bench and elsewhere to measure its performance in terms of safety, cleanliness, programs, and costs. Compared to prisons in California, Michigan, and many other major jurisdictions, TDC prisons had been quite good. For example, between 1973 and 1980 Texas had a total of 19 prison homicides while California had 139; rates of prison assaults in Texas prisons ran well below the national average while costs per inmate were the lowest in the country; and TDC boasted the only fully accredited prison educational system in the nation.[9]

Effective Prison Management

TDC's relative success was due mainly to its tight, formal system of managing prisoners. While other prison systems experimented wildly with "participative management" schemes designed to "demilitarize" the institutions, TDC's internal management remained security-driven and autocratic. While other corrections departments rushed to create loosely structured "treatment milieus" in the name of rehabilitation and inmate "self-development," TDC required inmates to work, go to school, speak respectfully to authorities, dress neatly, wash regularly, and obey the rules. While maximum security prisons in other states became places where predatory felons were free to walk, talk, and behave pretty much as they did on the streets, TDC subjected inmates to a rigorous daily routine of numbering, searching, locking, and frisking. Whereas other prison agencies gave inmates good time automatically, TDC employed a "point-incentive system" under which well-behaved inmates received two days off for every productive, infraction-free day they served (the country's most generous good time program) while poorly behaved inmates did "flat time" and lost visiting and other privileges. Finally, whereas in most other prison systems directors changed every few years, wardens played musical chairs, and line employees were unionized, TDC enjoyed remarkable administrative stability at all levels, developed a clear sense of organizational mission, and had serene labor–management relations.

These and other elements of TDC's management regime were worth preserving. In 1982, with Estelle still in the director's chair and with a good possibility of measured, effective organizational changes that could provide most of the remedies mandated by the court, a blue-ribbon panel noted that TDC had been described as "the best example of slavery remaining in the country" and "probably the best prison system in the world"; as the panel's report concluded, the reality "lay somewhere in between."

The judge, however, painted an image of TDC that was unrelievedly bleak, while his staff acted in ways that were almost calculated to breed ill will, confusion, and low morale among the very persons—from the director to the junior officials in the cellblocks—who would ultimately have to translate the court's decree into administrative action. No matter how Estelle and his staff moved to bring the agency into compliance with the court's sweeping orders, public criticism and a barrage of new orders followed. Echoing the complaints of cellblock workers, a central office administrator observed:

> Compliance of staff to our orders or of inmates of staff orders was never really a major problem here. . . . But now, with the court action and the rest, every day has become a goal line defense. . . . Officers must look at the bulletin board each day to see if the essence of the job they had the other day has changed. . . . How would you like to be given a new syllabus every day to teach from? One day you emphasize one theme, the next day another. Pretty soon everyone is confused; people get disgusted, some quit, and things just break down.

Estelle's defense of the agency, like the judge's attack, was undiscriminating, even desperate. He fought fiercely to protect Beto's control model and to shore up staff morale. By 1983, however, Beto himself recognized that the building tender system was a cancer ripe for the cutting, a rotten administrative crutch that TDC could and should throw away at the judge's invitation in order to preserve and strengthen the rest of the system. This, however, was not Beto's fight. At Estelle's insistence, TDC maintained in its legal defense that the building tender system—documented in agency pamphlets, experienced by thousands of inmates and staff, and known even outside of Texas as one feature of Beto's control model—did not exist. Under fire from the Board of Corrections, and having had the agency's budgetary requests rebuffed by a state legislature that was about to launch critical investigations into TDC's financial management, Estelle resigned in late 1983. Later he explained:

> I was determined, as all of us were, to fight for our ideas about how to run prisons. We had self-proclaimed prison reformers telling us how horrible we were at doing our jobs. Of course, what these people knew about prisons you could fit into a tiny thimble with room to spare. They wanted to effect changes and baptize every change a reform. Well, every change in a prison setting is not a reform and correctional institutions are ill-equipped to handle sudden administrative changes. . . . We were wrong on some things, short as hell in some areas of the operation. We were willing to usher in reasonable changes and remedies. But we had been doing most things very well and would not be part of simple-minded so-called reforms that, as sure as I'm sitting here, were bound to kill inmates, injure staff, and destroy our programs.

The principled intransigence of the fallen director was mirrored, albeit crudely, by his staff. The thrust of the court's decree was caricatured by many of the uniformed officers. In a typical remark, one veteran officer stated: "The judge says an inmate can spit in your face. I won't have it. That's no good for the inmate! What does that teach him but to misbehave the way he's always done?" A warden asserted: "We don't need people coming in here—judges, monitors, politicians, professors—telling us what to do. We have our lives invested in these prisons. Our inmates are kept well. They're not getting raped right and left. . . . But I guess that's what the judge and them others want."

Cleaning Up the Mess?

Following a brief stint by an acting director, in mid-1984 Estelle was replaced by Raymond Procunier. Known in corrections circles as "The Pro," Procunier had directed several prison systems, including California's. A salty mouthed man with a brash style who approached inmates and staff on the prison yard like an old-time ward politician seeking votes, Procunier announced that he would "clean up the mess" in Texas within two years and fully implement the court's orders.

Initially, Procunier had a honeymoon with state policymakers and the press and won the trust and support of TDC's "old guard." But rather than focusing on the serious business of running decent prisons with a demoralized and beleaguered staff, Procunier sponsored empty but progressive-looking measures (e.g., a complete redrafting of the agency's prisoner classification system) and rushed TDC into the latter stages of compliance with Judge Justice's decree. He fired employees who did not jump to cooperate, subjected the officers to lie detector tests, and took other actions that undercut his popularity within the department. Meanwhile, political support for his administration crumbled as murders multiplied, inmate-on-officer assaults skyrocketed, programs were disrupted, costs escalated, prison gangs organized along racial and ethnic lines blossomed, and outside contractors were brought in to do the agricultural and other work once solely the province of TDC inmates.

In the wake of the political and judicial tumult, Texas officers relaxed the unyielding attention to basic security procedures that had once been a hallmark of TDC management. Out of a mix of spite, wounded pride, and simple confusion about the state of their authority, officers in some prisons started letting inmates congregate freely out in the yards and inside the cellblocks. The formal chain of command and standard operating procedures governing cell searches, contraband interception, and the like, were weakened and in some places abandoned. In a typical remark, one veteran TDC officer confided sadly: "Nobody felt like keeping it up. All you heard was that we beat the inmates, we didn't care for the inmates, that we let them rip up each other. . . . Then the outsiders are giving us orders. . . . So we let go, let everything go."

As more TDC inmates were being buried, rates of staff turnover reached all-time highs, and officers took the unprecedented step of unionizing, Judge Justice, who had not once set foot inside a TDC prison since the *Ruiz* case began, continued to pressure the agency. The court's actions—repeated stabs against the officers' sense of mission—encouraged TDC workers at all levels to abdicate responsibility for the inmates, enervating any desire they might have had to go above and beyond the call of duty at a time when enormous demands were being made on them. Judge Justice and his staff made it clear they were out to revolutionize TDC, not reform it. As one of the court's aides later confided, they acted on the assumption that TDC was "rotten from top to bottom, that everything had to change"; they denied that TDC's paramilitary system of formal governance, as opposed to its use of building tenders and later con bosses, was mainly responsible for the historical lack of disorder inside Texas prisons.

The court joined the agency's new director in explaining the rampaging institutional violence not as the result of a breakdown in the formal aspects of the control model but as the product of a "power vacuum" created by the abolition of the building tender system and filled by a new, more vicious, less controllable cadre of inmate chieftains who headed TDC's budding, California-style prison gangs. In a twist of historic irony, both the critics of the agency and its supporters (including, to the surprise of many, the generally liberal *Texas Monthly* magazine) joined in repeating Beto's initial mistake of assuming that prison administrators cannot govern without somehow harnessing the support of the "society of captives" and its leaders. The violence, it was claimed, occurred because proadministration building tenders were "inevitably" replaced by antiadministration prison gang leaders.

In California and other places where prison gangs had become dominant, prison officials had entered into quasi-formal power-sharing arrangements with the inmates, brokering truces among the prisoners and between inmates and staff via "men's advisory councils." Even with former California director Procunier in charge, however, TDC's tradition of control by duly constituted authorities remained too strong to permit that folly from being reenacted in Texas. Instead, after hiring a couple of sociologists to analyze the situation, Judge Justice and his aides concluded that more officers should be hired, and quickly.

Assuming that hiring more officers will necessarily improve the administration of a prison is like assuming that hiring more violinists is bound to improve the sound of an orchestra. The new TDC "violinists" were hurried into the cellblocks, many without even the most basic preservice training. Their in-service training amounted to a socialization in the false but self-fulfilling prophecy that, minus the building tenders, nothing could be done to gain (or regain) control. There was a rapidly shrinking minority of veteran TDC officers and higher ranking officials who knew better, but by 1985 only a very few of them cared to fight for and demonstrate the efficacy of the rest of the control model. Instead, in the face of the court's order, and under new and less popular leadership, those TDC administrators who had allowed the building tenders to run wild surrendered their inmate allies and gave up their formal means of control as well. In a comment typical of TDC veterans who lived through the turmoil, one ranking agency official observed: "We throwed the baby out with the dirty bathwater. We had a good program that didn't have nothing to do with the building tenders. Hell, I worked places in this system where we always made it run by the book, like a military operation. That's the way it was under Dr. Beto and mostly under Mr. Estelle."

In opposing minor parts of this interpretation, Ekland-Olson and Martin (see chapter 3) trumpet the judge's embrace of a court-sponsored staffing "study" by two TDC officials and two paid National Institute of Corrections (NIC) consultants with "a combined total of almost a hundred years of prison administration experience." They lambast me for slighting this ostensible evidence of judicial prudence, and for characterizing the credentials of other court confidants in the way that they were presented at the time in the press and by TDC leaders. They doth protest too loudly.

The "TDC/NIC study" was viewed as a joke by top TDC officials with a combined total of a few thousand years of experience. Likewise, outside experts with views contrary to the court's were not consulted; some were enjoined from entering testimony for TDC because the court had made their agency a party to the dispute on the side of the inmate plantiffs. Several of the court's advisers had themselves presided over prisons where staff-to-inmate ratios were lower than in many of the TDC prisons they "studied"; and the final report contained neither statistical evidence on the relationship between staffing patterns and institutional problems, nor a systematic survey of TDC line staff.

As in too many other facets of the intervention, here the court kept its own counsel, heard what it wanted to hear, baptised supporting opinion as fact, and banished competing opinion as legally contemptible. I would not, however, characterize Ekland-Olson and Martin's apologetic interpretation of the court's behavior as they do my more unsparing one: "marked distortion," "misrepresentation," born of confusion about the "facts." But I would suggest that by treating the court-sanctioned official record as definitive in all respects and virtually the sole locus of analysis, their interpretation naturally unfolds like an insider's history of the dispute written from the viewpoint of only one of the contending parties; concomitant dangers of relying so exclusively on court records are highlighted by Clair A. Cripe in chapter 10. Where the complex human drama of sweeping judicial intervention is concerned, the "facts" do not speak for themselves; reasonable minds with varying degrees of disinterest in the case and sources of information and perspective can disagree, both in broad outline and on specific points, about what the record shows.

The Activist Judge: Savior or Villain?

In 1985 Procunier resigned and was replaced by O. L. (Lane) McCotter, a former commandant at the military barracks at Fort Leavenworth, Kansas. Beto had influenced then-Governor Mark White to appoint McCotter as head of TDC. Prodded gently by Beto, McCotter effected what one TDC veteran praised as "a return to a few of the basics" minus the building tenders. Within months, the homicide rate shriveled to nearly zero, assaults became rare, education and industry programs started to hum again, and the quality of food and recreational services ascended to their pre-Procunier levels.

Nevertheless, in 1987 Judge Justice was threatening to hold TDC in contempt and fine it tens of thousands of dollars if its inmate population rose above the arbitrary quota that he had set. As had been true of his behavior in the early days of the *Ruiz* litigation, "Willie Wayne" ignored reasonable arguments concerning the validity of his assumptions about the causes and consequences of prison crowding and remained deaf to other assaults on his expertise as TDC's de facto director of corrections. Meanwhile, since 1972 Texas taxpayers had spent over a billion dollars to implement the judge's muddled vision of how to govern prisons, millions of it having gone to inmates' attorneys and the court's special masters and monitors.

A few years earlier, however, while the dead inmate bodies were piling up in TDC prisons, Judge Justice spoke before a large audience consisting mainly of corrections practitioners. Ironically, he was introduced to the group by none other than Dr. George Beto, who, in a courteous and conciliatory spirit, praised the judge's concern for corrections. Justice returned the personal compliments, noted that "the courtroom is a less than ideal setting for the development of correctional policy," and mentioned a "growing awareness of the centrality of the role of corrections administrators in the process of maintaining prisons that are safe, lawful, and humane."

In Texas, the activist judge was neither a savior nor a villain. Instead, he was a force for sweeping changes, some of them good, lots of them bad, many of them wholly unanticipated, and others yet to unfold. Technically, there was absolutely nothing about the court's ruling, least of all in Judge Justice's order to abolish the corruptive building tender system, that made good prison government in Texas impossible; the worthwhile parts of the control model, including the paramilitary system of formal prison governance, were not ruled completely out of existence. While parts of the court's order (e.g., the provision of numerous amenities for inmates in solitary confinement) wrested important carrots and sticks from the hands of Texas keepers, nothing in the letter of the court's decree gutted TDC's basic custodial controls or made tight, security-conscious institutional management illegal.

It was not so much the letter as the spirit of the judge's attack on the agency that courted the tragedy of 1984 and 1985. Though by no means perfect, compared to many other agencies TDC had a remarkably good record, because it had stable executive leadership, conscientious managers, and dedicated workers who assumed strict responsibility for the care and custody of adjudicated felons and organized themselves accordingly. Infusing the members of any large, complex organization with a genuine sense of mission and identification with their agency is no easy task. Corrections is a dangerous, dirty, difficult, and thankless profession, but through two decades of careful nourishing, first by Beto and then by Estelle, TDC staff at all levels had come to share a deep belief in the worth and rightness of their work. Unlike most state corrections departments, TDC's prison workers were proud of their agency and attached to a disciplined, no-nonsense way of getting the job done.

What Beto and Estelle had taken twenty years to build, Judge Justice, aided and abetted by Estelle's successor and by grandstanding state policymakers eager to make fresh political hay and headlines out of the system's legal troubles, helped to put asunder, by making the task of formal prison governance inside Texas prisons much harder and much less personally rewarding. TDC employees were sensitive to how the agency's detractors on the bench and elsewhere had portrayed them as nothing but a "bunch of redneck guards and contraband carriers." As one veteran TDC employee recalled: "The judge and the politicians and the newspapers was all over us like stink on a skunk. No sooner did we fix one thing, broken or not, than we was told to fix another, and another. . . . We didn't think so much was wrong to begin with, so it just got crazier and crazier. . . . I worked here the better part of my adult life, and honest to you, I never seen nor heard the half of what they was accusing. . . . If I'd a believed TDC was all they said, I'd a been after it too."

To this day, there are those who insist that Judge Justice imposed a "straitjacket" on TDC and blame him for the horrors of 1984 and 1985; but it is nearer to the truth to say that he forced the agency to wear an ill-fitting garment that eventually, and predictably, burst at the seams. In 1984 and 1985 TDC personnel could have kept a close watch on tools in the industrial plant, frisked inmates regularly, segregated inmate predators, identified and brought special charges against prison gang organizers, limited the flow of inmates in and out of the cellblocks and around the dining halls, rewarded inmates for good behavior, and taken the scores of other basic and once reflexive measures that would have prevented or reduced the level of individual and group misconduct behind bars. Instead, the judge fostered a situation in which formal controls were relaxed, infractions were ignored, and the inmates were increasingly left to their own murderous devices. As it complied with his decree, TDC stopped governing prisons, doing less than it had at any time since before the Beto era to protect and guide those in its custody.

The court's intervention resulted in the imposition of hitherto unknown legal, political, and budgetary constraints on the agency. If the judge had been more judicious, his understanding of prisons sounder, his appreciation for what TDC had achieved in the past less miserly, and his preoccupation with its failings less total, or if he and his aides had troubled themselves to consider the possible unintended effects of their actions on both inmates and staff, there can be litle doubt that things would not have degenerated as they did. The special master in *Ruiz*, Vincent Nathan, has argued forcefully that it is wrong to assign even this degree of blame to the court and its aides.[10] He is joined in this view by many others who were intimately involved in overseeing TDC's compliance with Judge Justice's orders, including William G. Babcock, who served as a court monitor.[11] And in chapter 3 of this volume, Steve J. Martin, who once worked as a TDC corrections officer and represented the system in court, has joined with Texas-based sociologist and criminal justice expert Sheldon Ekland-Olson in waging a powerful defense of the court and condemnation of the defendants.

The fact that many such defenders of the court have a personal stake in challenging critical assessments of its role does not in any way invalidate their arguments. But some "insiders" have been more self-critical. For example, former *Ruiz* monitor Samuel Brakel has criticized the court's "implementation strategy," recounting how Judge Justice simply ordered changes "and hired a special master to ensure the change occurred, without giving careful consideration to the functions served by each [existing TDC] policy or practice. . . ."[12] According to Brakel, the court's failure to order and enforce changes in a more discriminating manner had several harmful consequences, including an increase in inmate-on-officer verbal and physical abuse, inmate disregard for the rules, and inmate disturbances and riots.[13] Brakel concluded:

> [T]here is every indication that the federal judge was fully aware that the [Texas Department of Corrections] had a strongly established set of

policies and management practices, not to mention a clear stratification of management, staff and inmates. . . . It was, in fact, many of those policies and practices which served as the focal point for the decision. Therefore, it would seem self-evident that the implementation of change in such a system should be informed by organizational theory. However, this seldom has occurred in the history of institutional legal reform, and it certainly did not occur in *Ruiz*.[14]

Similarly, Roy H. Reynolds, who worked as an assistant to Brakel, has reviewed the mastership of *Ruiz*. Reynolds has faulted the court's intervention: "The reforms which have been mandated in the name of the Constitution go beyond enforcement of the constitutionally required minimal standards and constitute the imposition of an inchoate view of prison administration that can result in harsh, unintended consequences for the inmates the courts intended to protect."[15]

Conclusion

Commenting on the pre-*Ruiz* regime in TDC, an inmate who had served time in two other state prison systems stated: "You know what to expect. You don't have to worry about getting stabbed or raped by other inmates, or what's going to happen from one day to the next, because it's the administration that's totally in control. After a short time here, you realize that if you go to your cell, go to mess, wash up, go to work quietly, all will go well."[16] Commenting on the post-*Ruiz* regime in TDC, an official who had spent most of his adult life working behind bars stated: "TDC was never perfect, Lord knows. But we kept inmates safe, gave them real chances to better themselves, insisted on civilized behavior. . . . The judge gave us no credit. . . . Now the inmates can rape, stab, and kill each other at will."

Before the judge issued his orders, TDC's ancien régime was rotting from within as building tenders became con bosses. Instead of helping to preserve those elements of the existing administration that were worth preserving, the court excused itself as TDC went from a mostly benevolent paternalistic despotism run by prison officials to a malevolent anarchy of competing prison gangs and their leaders. By gradually returning to something like the control model without building tenders, and given the judge's prudence and forbearance, TDC may yet substantially improve the quality of life inside its prisons.

Notes

1. This chapter is a slightly modified and updated version of my "Prison Discipline and Prison Reform," *The Public Interest* 89 (Fall 1987), 71–90.
2. Kathleen Engel and Stanley Rothman, "Prison Violence and the Paradox of Reform," *The Public Interest* 73 (Fall 1983), 97.
3. John J. DiIulio, Jr., *Governing Prisons: A Comparative Study of Correctional Management* (New York: The Free Press, 1987).
4. American Civil Liberties Union, ". . . nor cruel and unusual punishments inflicted," promotional pamphlet, 1988.
5. For example, see James B. Jacobs, *Statesville: The Penitentiary in Mass Society* (Chicago: University of Chicago Press, 1977).
6. For an overview, see R. Craig Copeland, "The Evolution of TDC" (master's thesis, Institute of Contemporary Corrections and the Behavioral Sciences, Sam Houston State University, 1980).
7. Gresham M. Sykes, *The Society of Captives* (Princeton, N.J.: Princeton University Press, 1958), p. 134.
8. For example, see Charles Stastny and Gabrielle Trynauer, *Who Rules the Joint? The Changing Political Culture of Maximum-Security Prisons in America* (Lexington, Mass. Lexington Books, 1982).
9. DiIulio, *Governing Prisons*, chapter 2.
10. Vincent Nathan, "Reflection on Two Decades of Court-Ordered Prison Reform," Fortunoff Colloquium, speech delivered in New York City in April 1988.
11. William G. Babcock, private correspondence with the author, 1988.
12. Samuel Jan Brakel, "Prison Reform by Judicial Decree: The Unintended Consequences of *Ruiz v. Estelle*," *Justice System Journal* 9 (1984), 302.
13. Ibid.
14. Ibid., p. 301.
15. Roy H. Reynolds, "The Role of Special Masters in Federal Judicial Supervision of State Prisons: The Need for Limitations," *American Criminal Law Review* 26 (Fall 1988), 511.
16. Cited in Reynolds, "The Role of Special Masters," p. 503.

3

Ruiz: A Struggle over Legitimacy

SHELDON EKLAND-OLSON
and STEVE J. MARTIN

We have discussed our view of litigated prison reform in Texas in a number of places.[1] In this chapter our primary objective is to present what we see as the more general conclusions to be drawn from prison conditions litigation in Texas. Although we see our accounts as largely consistent with other "faces" of *Ruiz* presented in chapters 2 and 4 of this volume, we will discuss some important exceptions.

Defining Legitimate Authority

Above all else, *Ruiz v. Estelle* was a hard-fought struggle to define legitimate authority. It is this struggle that makes the *Ruiz* case so important. Much has been written about whether courts should intervene in administrative matters of institutional management. That administrative boundaries are permeable is a settled issue.

Courts have the legitimate right to intervene. But how much, and with what success? A court's capacity for effective intervention depends in large measure on its ability to translate broad constitutional principles into specific normative mandates, viewed as legitimate in the distinct day-to-day context of prison life. Perceptions of legitimacy by cellblock officers and prison administrators will greatly influence whether these principles become patterns of action. Perceptions of legitimacy and the "bureaucratic will" to change are closely intertwined. This is true of implementation problems in *Ruiz* as well as in other prison conditions cases. It is equally true of cases involving educational and mental health institutions.

However, even a cursory examination of institutional reform cases, some of which are discussed in later chapters of this book and elsewhere,[2] reveals wide variation in the struggle to redefine or affirm legitimate authority. In many ways what makes the litigation surrounding *Ruiz* unique is the intensity with which the battle was fought. The tenacity of the writ-writing prisoners and their lawyers, the intensity of administrative resistance to the litigation process and eventual court-ordered reforms, the symbolic importance of battles won and lost, and the disruptive impact of many of the court's rulings can be viewed in this light.

Whether it is to uncover common features of litigation or to understand important patterns of variation, *any framework for studying litigated institutional reform should focus on how legitimacy comes to be affirmed or redefined and implemented.* We offer this as the central issue for future comparative studies of litigated institutional reform.

From this starting point, we address two aspects of the experience of prison reform in Texas: What factors were related to the intensity of the struggle? How was the litigation process related to an upsurge of violence in some prison units?

The Intensity of the Struggle
to Define Legitimate Authority

The TDC of the late 1960s through the beginning of the *Ruiz* trial was a separate moral community, conceived and nourished by geographical isolation, labor recruitment patterns, and the influence of politically astute and efficient leadership. As the national civil rights movement gained momentum, the moral distance widened between TDC and the emerging more inclusive definition of the human community. The intensity of the struggle between TDC's administration and challenging inmates, their lawyers, and Judge Justice was initially kindled by this moral gap. As the *Ruiz* case progressed, the struggle was fueled further by an ongoing sense of mutual distrust. These two factors, structural and moral isolation along with mutual mistrust, form the foundation of our analysis.

As litigated reform efforts got under way, TDC was operating in large measure as a law unto itself. As such, it was in a position to question the authority of any intruder, including lawyers and the federal courts. The "law" of TDC was embodied in a system of control in which a strong sense of routine and one's "place" in the hierarchy dominated. Routine was organized around the idea that the prison system should be self-sufficient and that therefore inmates were expected to work. Inmates were firmly entrenched in their place as slaves of the state, civilly dead, and therefore without legitimate standing to assert their rights. Undergirding these expectations and sense of place was a system of intimidation and corporal punishment.

The rigid sense of place and the importance of intimidation were the contested points of legitimacy in *Ruiz*. Any assessment of Judge Justice's ruling should keep this firmly in mind. In chapter 2, DiIulio suggested that the "rotten crutch" of the Texas control model was the ill-advised use of the much discussed building tender system during the administration of W. J. Estelle. In fact, however, what crippled the legitimacy of TDC was deeper and more pervasive than DiIulio suggests.

The model of control in TDC evolved from the cultural traditions of East Texas. More than other regions of the state, East Texas had been settled by migrants from the Deep South. Slavery, plantation life, and sharecropping were part of its heritage. Lynchings during the late nineteenth and early twentieth century were concentrated in this region of the state. In particular, there was a disproportionate number of lynchings in Brazos, Grimes, and Waller counties,[3] the counties wherein the TDC of the 1960s had its roots and from which it drew its contemporary labor pool. As one observer wrote of the years when litigated prison reform was beginning: "[East Texas] is a region where rural ways still shape urban life, a society which is only gradually opening itself to a wider world, only gradually yielding to external pressures. . . . Now much weakened in power and influence and much less typical in cultural patterns this oldest province is, nonetheless, no less distinctive a part of the Texas empire than it was a century ago."[4]

This distinct sense of community was magnified within the Texas Department of Corrections when writ-writing inmates and their lawyers began to exert pressures for reform in the latter years of the 1960s. The Texas prison system of this time was a graphic illustration of the general tendency of closed communities to develop a unique moral order and a feeling of "we" and "them." In this context, the *Ruiz* case was not just a challenge to clarify legal ambiguities; it was a challenge to a way of life, to a sense of place, belonging, and control.

There is a deep moral significance in the idea of one's "place." Mountains of data suggest that the treatment we receive or impose as well as our beliefs about our own identity are shaped by perceptions about location in the human community. Clearly, this is true of war and genocide, of abortion and euthanasia, as well as of suicide and capital punishment. Various forms of sanctions are viewed as more or less legitimate depending on the status of those on whom they are imposed. Slaves could be beaten in that they "belonged" to their owners as property, closer to stock animals than to independent members of the civil society.

This link between place and the legitimacy of sanctions was well established in TDC. In the 1930s Lee Simmons, then director of the Texas prison system, testified before a state legislative committee concerning the use of the "bat," a twenty-four-inch leather strap with a wooden handle: "I told my friends on the legislative committee: 'Gentlemen, it's just like using spurs. You get on an old cow horse without spurs—and you can't head even a milking-pen cow; but when you've got your spurs on, the old horse will do the job.' And you don't have to use the spurs, because all he needs to know is that the spurs are there. It's the same with us and the 'bat.' The record shows we seldom have to use it. But the boys all know it is there."[5]

In 1973 testimony was taken before another state legislative committee from a TDC lieutenant who had been involved in forcing ten inmates to work in the fields.[6]

Q: If the inmate continued to refuse to go to work, what force would you use to cause him to go to work?
A: That force that was necessary to effect that change.
Q: In other words, if you were to go into a cell to give an order to move—to go to work—and he continued to refuse to go to work?
A: Yes.
Q: Would you continue to hit that inmate if the inmate continued to refuse to go to work?
A: Yes.
Q: At what time would you stop hitting the inmate?
A: When he went to work.

Further testimony in *Ruiz* repeatedly underscored the importance of physical intimidation in the Texas model of control. In September 1977 an inmate who had been "treed" after trying to escape while working in the fields was forced to come out of the tree and fight the pursuing dogs.[7] According to the physician who later attended the inmate, this resulted in "a tremendous number of puncture wounds where something had bitten him" as well as bleeding welts across his back, consistent with the use of a whip. It was, the doctor summarized, the worst example of brutality he had seen. This, of course, implied the doctor had been witness to other occasions of physical intimidation. When asked by the lawyer if this were the case, the doctor replied that he had been witness to "hundreds" of cases where "it happened to be obvious that another human being or more than one had inflicted the injuries."

Such testimony was supplemented by numerous examples in the *Ruiz* trial, instances Judge Justice found credible, where inmates were beaten with fists and clubs, kicked and maced by officers. Confronted with this evidence, Judge Justice found that "brutality against inmates [was] nothing short of routine in Texas prisons."

This conclusion is not only supported by trial testimony. It is entirely consistent with the findings of Crouch and Marquart.[8] Staff brutality was routine in TDC, although not in the sense that it happened every day, in every dispute between staff and inmates.

Rather it was routine in that it was deeply embedded in the subculture of prison life as a legitimate alternative. Guards were socialized to its use. Acceptance and promotion depended in part on "skilled" intimidation.

It is the longstanding, deeply rooted role of physical intimidation in keeping inmates in their place in the Texas prison system which, in our opinion, all but escaped DiIulio's notice. DiIulio chose to note how, under the Texas control model, staff were to forget the crime "only insofar as that meant refraining from any imposition of extralegal pains on the inmate. Inmates were to be kept wholly secure from any abuses by other inmates or staff."[9] For George Beto and his staff, DiIulio concluded, "governing prisons was a form of soulcraft in which orderly conditions were to provide the foundation for the inmates' enforced habituation to a civilized round of daily life."[10]

The point is, of course, what constitutes legitimate punishment from one perspective may constitute extralegal abuse from another. The "soulcraft" of Texas prison administrators that DiIulio noted could be interpreted by the court as intimidating brutality. This became the major point of contention in *Ruiz*. Neither the "soulcraft" nor the routine brutality view of the TDC control model is complete by itself. Life in TDC prisons was characterized by both. What is important, for present purposes, is to note what the court found illegitimate. Clearly it was not kindly soulcraft and habituation to a civilized routine of daily life. It was routinized physical brutality directed at some to control many. Where the court saw brutality, administrators saw order, safety, and cleanliness. It is in this unbalanced view of the same reality that the seeds of mutual distrust were sewn.

Trust is multifaceted. On one level, it is a practical matter. We trust those we see as competent. We trust those we believe are reliable. We mistrust those we perceive to be deceptive. Trust is also normative. We trust those we see as fair. We mistrust those we see as biased. Finally, trust generates emotion. We respond positively to those we trust and with some antagonism to those we do not. On all counts, the intensity of resistance in any contested dispute over legitimacy is likely to rise and fall with the level of mutual trust.

It is important to recognize that the level of trust is not constant. It changes with ongoing assessments over the course of a relationship and across social contexts. It can be built. It can be destroyed. Persons may be seen as quite competent, and therefore worthy of trust, in one arena of expertise, less so in others. Bias may be accentuated or absent, depending on the issue. The intensity of the contest over definitions of legitimacy will vary accordingly. Such was the case throughout the history of *Ruiz v. Estelle*. It is our opinion that the dynamics of trust building and destruction is an area ripe for study in any comparative analysis of litigated reform efforts.

It is in the realm of mutual trust or mistrust that much of the impact of interpersonal interaction plays out in litigated reform. As actors enter and leave the stage of litigation and negotiation they bring with them differing levels of credibility, charisma, and rhetorical skills. These attributes often translate into mutual respect and trust—or just the opposite. An important result is that the perceived legitimacy of reforms is determined as much by the personalities of those involved as it is by an objective balancing of the documented facts. Litigated reform thereby becomes more a matter of symbolic politics than rational assessment.

While exacting scales are missing, it is safe to conclude that the level of mutual mistrust was high throughout most of the years when *Ruiz* was wending its way through the federal courts. Judge Justice was seen as unfairly orchestrating the outcome of the trial from the time he consolidated the original petitions into a class action suit in 1974. Reflecting this distrust, in their petition to the Fifth Circuit Court of Appeals following the consolidation, attorneys for the state charged that Judge Justice was unfairly allowing the United States Department of Justice to "rampage through the Texas prison system in the hope of finding unconstitutional activities."

When the trial began in October 1978, inmate work stoppages, a phenomenon all but unheard of in the tightly controlled years before trial, prompted a news blackout by prison administrators. Once the demonstrations were quieted, prison officials were quick to note that their mistrust of the intrusive and, in their opinion, ill-informed and biased federal judge was well founded. The director of the prison system was quoted in the news media as lamenting: "I find little charity and less solace in bringing issues before a court that has no knowledge, direct or indirect, of what the real issues are

and could care less that their personal social philosophy, finding its
way into so-called law, jeopardizes not only our inmates' safety, but
the safety of prison staff as well." Given the belief that "so-called
law" was being shaped by an unfair, incompetent, and insensitive
judge, it is not surprising that prison officials were ready to energet-
ically resist what they saw as illegitimate intervention by other
government entities not knowledgeable to question, let alone reform.

This same mistrust of Judge Justice was evident throughout the
Ruiz trial proceedings. Misgivings were illustrated most dramatically when the state's attorneys attempted to present uncontested
facts in open court regarding the prison system's educational programs. Since the facts were uncontested, Judge Justice did not want
to take up court time. For their part, the state's attorneys felt it
important to represent a positive image of TDC in a public forum
to balance what they saw as misleading "horror" stories the court
had been hearing during the early phases of the trial. It was not fair
that these previous stories had received so much press coverage
while the positive civilizing efforts of prison officials were relegated
to private depositions. Feelings ran high as the lead attorney
charged Judge Justice with changing the rules of the trial and asked
that the record reflect his belief that the judge was committing
reversible error. Whereupon the following exchange took place:

JUDGE: I don't think any rule requires the court to sit and listen to
testimony that is uncontested that's not going to be denied.
ATTORNEY: That may be so, Your Honor, but I think we are entitled to put
on our case, and I think we are entitled to have the court
observe the demeanor of the witness.
JUDGE: If it's uncontested, what is there—what credibility choice is to
be made if it is uncontested?
ATTORNEY: Sir, there's still—the court still has to assess—I have gathered
the impression from the beginning of the trial, quite frankly,
Your Honor, that we have been adjudged guilty—.
JUDGE: Counsel, I'm going to hold you in contempt of court if you
keep up in this vein, and I advise you to apologize to the court
immediately.

In the end, an apology was extended, the witness was allowed to
testify, and a contempt citation was avoided. The climate of distrust
remained. Some two and one-half years after the trial had drawn to

a close, TDC Director W. J. Estelle, in a public speech, stated, "Going into Justice's courtroom is like playing poker in a strange town without a clean deck." It is our position that this and similar pronouncements by the prison system's leadership, questioning the fairness and competence and therefore the legitimacy of the court, set a moral tone which encouraged continued resistance to court-ordered reforms. Given such seeming support from the agency's leadership, lower level personnel could and did justify violations of court rulings. Such violations only accentuated feelings of mistrust that ran both ways.

Where the mistrust of Judge Justice by prison administrators and staff was grounded in perceptions of fairness and bias, the foundation of the judge's mistrust of prison officials was documented deception and defiance. The result in the case of prison administrators and staff was indignant pronouncements and continued resistance. The result of the judge's mistrust was intrusive oversight. Taken together they constituted the struggle for legitimate control.

There is ample evidence that Judge Justice did not believe all of what prison officials reported in court, nor did he always trust that his orders would be carried out. On one occasion he all but accused a witness from TDC of lying. On another, he expressed extreme indignation when informed that a previous protective order had been violated. When the attorney for TDC attempted to justify the violation, Judge Justice was vehement. "Well, I'm very interested that that's your opinion about the thing. That is the most outrageous opinion that I have ever heard of . . . . Let's get off on something else. I find the position of the Texas Department of Corrections in that proceeding arbitrary, tyrannical and any other word that you want to apply to it."[11]

Such vehement indignation came after earlier experiences with similar violations. By July 1976 officials at one TDC unit had been subjected to three hearings on violations of court orders. The violations ranged from rather petty harassments to more severe charges of brutality. On appeal in 1977, the state's attorneys did not question the factual findings regarding these violations and the Fifth Circuit found that the plaintiffs had been subjected to "intimidation, coercion, punishment and discrimination."

At yet another hearing, shortly thereafter, prison officials were once again charged with violating court orders. Part of the resulting agreement was that the officers involved would be reprimanded. The only disciplinary action taken was a written reprimand from Director Estelle to the assistant warden of the unit stating, in part, "I am pleased that you have already made the correction. You and I both had a shared responsibility in this matter and, while I realize there was no more intent on your part than mine to violate any of the court's Order, I know we will renew efforts to see that such violation does not occur again. Consider us both reprimanded by this document." The assistant warden was promoted to warden shortly thereafter. The warden of this same unit was promoted to assistant director and named warden of the year. This anemic reaction to violations of court orders continued well into 1983.

As part of the hearings on Order violations, Judge Justice heard testimony from prisoners and prison officials. For the first time in a *Ruiz* hearing TDC called prisoners to testify on their behalf. Of the five prisoners called, four were building tenders, though they were reluctant to acknowledge that fact when cross-examined. What they did testify to were the rather routine activities they claimed constituted the duties of building tenders.

This testimony was taken before the *Ruiz* trial actually began. As the trial progressed, Judge Justice became increasingly convinced that the routine activities of building tenders extended far beyond the rather mundane responsibilities of tending the buildings. If there was some question in Judge Justice's mind prior to the *Ruiz* trial about the activities of building tenders and the veracity of official testimony, by the end of the proceedings it was most certainly clarified. Inmates were used on numerous prison units in positions with supervisory authority to supplement the guard force. Abuses were present, often with the knowledge and complicity of the prison staff. Still, prison officials maintained their denials and failed to take remedial action. The fact that these denials were effective until some ten years after the passage of the state statute prohibiting such use of inmates is ample testimony to the idea that the Texas Department of Corrections remained very much a law unto itself until the early 1980s.

The "rotten crutch" of the Texas prison system again went deeper than the abusive use of the building tender system under the directorship of W. J. Estelle. The legitimacy of prison officials was undermined not only by abuses associated with the building tender system but also by the accompanying deception. It was deception that fed Judge Justice's mistrust in the prison system's administration and thereby invited involvement in internal administrative matters by the federal court, the court-appointed special master, and eventually other state officials.

Court Intervention, Legitimate Authority, and Prison Violence

By now there are numerous discussions about the link between court intervention, shifting structures of authority and control, and prison violence. Much has been discussed by the authors of this volume. Other sources include Jacobs, Glazer, and Engel and Rothman.[12] From this research several questions emerge.

Some have asked, "Is there something inherent in court intervention per se that destabilized the authority of organizational administrators and staff?" When federal courts first emerged from the self-imposed shell of the hands-off doctrine, the answer was a clear "yes." Today, as the legitimacy of court intervention has matured into a well-established fact of life, the same question yields a more qualified answer.

The structure of authority frequently is determined by who has the last say in any given dispute. In the years before active court intervention, prison administrators were for all intents and purposes the court of last resort. When the federal courts began to intervene and rule on the legitimacy of prison conditions, the balance of authority shifted. Court intrusion meant there was another ear to listen and other voices to be heard. By definition, this disrupted the existing equilibrium of legitimate authority. The new structure of authority, while uncertain at first, is now better established. Given the new equilibrium, comparative analysis of court intervention into the affairs of institutions in the late 1980s and beyond should reveal progressively less dramatic struggles for power.

Court intervention in the early years of institutional reform may have disrupted the structure of legitimate authority, but did it inevitably lead to violence? We have argued elsewhere that the answer is "no." It is not reform or intervention per se, but the way in which people react to the process of change that accounts for the noted upsurge in violent activity in some cases. The primary responsibility for this upsurge must be placed on the doorstep of opportunistic and predatory inmates and intergang rivalries. There was nothing in Judge Justice's ruling, or the ruling of any other court, that directly increased stabbings in the cellblocks. Although this hardly needs to be stated, we sometimes lose sight of this basic fact in our attempts to understand the role that court intervention plays. If anything, court intervention seems to affect the structure of opportunities and constraints. The question then becomes "How does this rearrangement of constraints and opportunities occur?"

General propositions that might explain why violence was more evident in one case than in another await further comparative analysis. Useem and Kimball have provided a formula for this work, and they too note the central importance of perceived legitimacy.[13] What we can accomplish in the present discussion is a summary of the events in the *Ruiz* case that may have weakened the constraints and increased the opportunities for inmate-on-inmate violence. Shifting perceptions of effective legitimate control, mutual mistrust, and antagonism between the court and prison administrators and staff, as well as the denial of legitimacy of the imposed reforms, were all major factors.

The importance of perceptions among inmates that there had been a shift in effective legitimate control was first evidenced in the inmate disturbances that accompanied the opening of the *Ruiz* trial in 1978. Inmate work stoppages in the past had been rare. Two of the six such disturbances in the years preceding the trial had occurred 1972, when the activities of Fred Cruz, Frances Jalet, and David Ruiz were beginning to have an effect. We have detailed these events elsewhere.

For those in powerless positions, increased freedom from constraints flows from the perception that others might be listening. For example, when asked what triggered the disturbances at the beginning of the trial, an inmate spokesman responded, "The *Ruiz* case. . . . Now is our chance to get some recognition." In another subsequent disturbance, this time following Judge Justice's decision, a notice was circulated among inmates stating, in part, "As of November 1, 1981, there were to be no inmates sleeping on the runs,

No Building Tenders, No Turnkeys. As we know, all three (3) still exist and will continue to exist until we show our support for Judge Justice and his rulings. . . . To make this work, WE ALL must stand firm together against the TDC's idle threats."

It is in perceptions of an expanded audience that court intervention had its most immediate effect on reduced constraints among inmates. It is hard to imagine, in the years before court intervention, that inmates would be referring to possible staff reprisals as "idle threats." Given Judge Justice's emotion-laden conclusion to his opinion, it became more plausible. Judge Justice wrote:

> It is impossible for a written opinion to convey the pernicious conditions and the pain and degradation which ordinary inmates suffer within TDC prison walls—the gruesome experiences of youthful first offenders forcibly raped; the cruel and justifiable fears of inmates, wondering when they will be called upon to defend the next violent assault; the sheer misery, the discomfort, the wholesale loss of privacy for prisoners housed with one, two or three others in a forty-five foot cell or suffocatingly packed together in a crowded dormitory; the physical suffering and wretched physiological stress which must be endured by those sick or injured who cannot obtain adequate medical care; the sense of abject helplessness felt by inmates arbitrarily sent to solitary confinement or administrative segregation without proper opportunity to defend themselves or to argue their causes; the bitter frustration of inmates prevented from petitioning the courts and other governmental authorities for relief from perceived injustices. For those who are incarcerated within the parameters of TDC, these conditions and experiences form the content and essence of daily existence. It is to these conditions that each inmate must wake every morning; it is with the painful knowledge of their existence that each inmate must try to sleep at night. (Ruiz v. Esrelle, 503 F Supp. 1265 [S. D. Texas 1980])

While it is impossible to state with certainty, this closing assessment was very likely in W. J. Estelle's mind when he replied over the ensuing months that Judge Justice had "vilified one of the finest prison staffs in the U.S." in an opinion that read "like a cheap dime store novel" reflecting a "crass, gross, almost incredible lack of literary skill."

Statements such as the foregoing from the court, along with the newly established oversight of the special master and his monitors, signaled to the inmates that they now had a sympathetic ear. When the court heard the message and evaluated existing practices as illegitimate, the moral bond to the authority of prison officials was all but destroyed. When conditions did not change in accordance with the new definitions of legitimacy, inmates were less constrained in expressing a sense of injustice and outrage. This newfound freedom to express indignation and a sense of power eventually translated into a rise in inmate assaults on staff during the *Ruiz* trial and in the year immediately following.

The question which no one, including us, has answered with any finality, is how Judge Justice's assessment of the TDC and the rancor between the court and prison administrators contributed to the wave of inmate-on-inmate violence which began to build in 1979 and came crashing ashore with fifty-two homicides in the years 1984 and 1985. In chapter 2, DiIulio seems to attribute much of the "blame" to ignorance, biased insensitivity, and an ill-timed, forced implementation schedule:

> To this day, there are those who insist that Judge Justice imposed a "straitjacket" on the TDC and blame him for the horrors of 1984 and 1985; but it is nearer to the truth to say that he forced the agency to wear an ill-fitting garment that eventually, and predictably, burst at the seams. . . . If the judge had been more judicious, his understanding of prisons sounder, his appreciation for what the TDC had achieved in the past less miserly, and his preoccupation with its failings less total, or if he and his aides had troubled themselves to consider the possible unintended effects of their actions on both inmates and staff, there can be little doubt that things would not have degenerated as they did.

The portion of this summary which we find least convincing is the idea that Judge Justice and "his aides" (the special master and his monitors) did not trouble themselves to consider the possible unintended consequences of their sweeping actions. This statement simply does not correspond with the record.

When disturbances broke out in the beginning of the trial, there was concern that the situation might turn into "another Attica." Judge Justice troubled himself enough to hold hearings on the possible consequences of the trial and issued the following statement, directed largely at the demonstrating inmates: "The court is greatly concerned for the safety of both inmates and guards and what is described as a volatile situation in two of the units. At this time, the court is seeking to determine the issues in this litigation in a deliberate and impartial manner. Now, orderly progress of the trial could be impeded if violence and disruption continue. It is my hope that they cease."

This statement was widely publicized and had the desired effect in that shortly after it was released the demonstrations subsided. The last unit to return to normal was Ellis. Here, inmates charged, in a letter to Judge Justice, that officials were "not allowing us to return to work, and with the constant inhuman treatment, they realize it's only a matter of time before somebody's temper explodes, which would cause a chain reaction."

Further evidence that Judge Justice was troubled a great deal by the possible unintended consequence of his actions comes from a November 1982 hearing approving a negotiated settlement on a use-of-force issue. In what turned out to be a prophetic assessment, Judge Justice noted:

> The elimination of these policies, procedures, and practices, without more, will create nothing more than a vacuum with respect to the control of TDC's institutions and prisoners. Such a vacuum, if it is allowed to occur, will remain unfilled only briefly. Aggressive and predatory prisoners, disorganized or otherwise, will seize the opportunity to achieve control. As the experiences of other states have demonstrated such illegal power structures, once they arise, take root quickly and defy the most vigorous efforts aimed at their elimination.

It is hardly the case that this statement reflects a mind untroubled by the possibility of heightened violence. Nor does the record support a lack of concrete efforts to implement reforms in a orderly fashion. In our opinion, the imagery that DiIulio presents of an agency rushed into taking on an ill-fitting system of control simply does not reflect the facts of the case.

Most obviously, the building tender system, as an exercise of inmate authority and control over other inmates, had been illegal since 1973. While the Texas legislature might be faulted for lack of funding to provide more acceptable inmate-to-guard ratios and thereby a lessened need for supplements to the guard force, it is hardly the case that Judge Justice and his aides were rushing the process. Less obviously, though no less important, is the fact that prison administrators could have been held in contempt of court for not meeting deadlines or for violating court orders on a number of occasions. They were not. Instead there was a constant emphasis on negotiated settlement between the parties. These settlements were informed by numerous lengthy monitor reports on such topics as augmentation of the security staff, crowding, classification, medical and psychiatric care, access to courts, treatment of mentally retarded and physically handicapped prisoners, occupational safety and health, the building tender system, and conditions of death row. In each case a compliance plan was negotiated with prison and state officials.

Our disagreement with DiIulio's assessment of *Ruiz*, detailed in the immediately preceding paragraphs, centers on statements made in *Governing Prisons*. In chapter 2 of the current volume DiIulio extends what, in our opinion, is a basically flawed analysis.

The time period referred to is 1984 and 1985. The focus is on strengthening of the guard force in the cellblocks. The image presented is again one of a hurried, thoughtless, incompetent Judge Justice. According to DiIulio, Judge Justice and his aides, "after hiring a couple of sociologists to analyze the situation," concluded that "more officers should be hired, and quickly." The analysis goes on to note, "Assuming that hiring more officers will necessarily improve the administration of a prison is like assuming that hiring more violinists is bound to improve the sound of an orchestra. The new TDC 'violinists' were hurried into the cellblocks, many without even the most basic preservice training."

The record supports the following. The analysis of staffing needs began some two years before the time noted by DiIulio. On June 1, 1982, Judge Justice approved the Stipulated Modification of sections II.A and II.D of the Amended Decree. This agreement came to be known as the "Building Tender Agreement," as section II.D of the judge's remedial order required the "elimination of building tenders." Section II.A required increased staffing.

In negotiating the building tender agreement, the parties recognized from the outset that eliminating building tenders would require significant staffing increases. Accordingly, section XII of the Building Tender Agreement, entitled "Staffing Increases," established a process for determining the minimum number of officers required to staff TDC. This process involved a study jointly undertaken by the National Institute of Corrections (NIC) and TDC, each utilizing two experts to perform a security staffing needs analysis of TDC during the summer of 1982. The NIC team was comprised of James D. Henderson, former regional director, Federal Bureau of Prisons, and Allen Ault, former director of two different state prison systems. The TDC team was comprised of Loyd Hunt, warden of the Retrieve Unit and a twenty-five year TDC veteran, and Bobby Maggard, director of staff development and personnel, with over twenty years of experience in TDC. These four career corrections practitioners represented a combined total of almost a hundred years of prison administration experience. It is more than a minor misrepresentation to characterize the effort as "hiring a couple of sociologists to analyze the situation."

It may be that DiIulio is confusing his facts. The two "sociologists" he refers to may be Ned Benton and Don Stoughton, two consultants retained pursuant to the use of force agreement to assist in the development of a use of force plan. Benton is a former director of the Oklahoma prison system; Stoughton was a career criminal justice practitioner prior to working as a consultant. These two issued a report in February 1984 entitled "Remedial Actions to Reduce Unnecessary Force in TDC." One section of this report addressed deployment of staff to assure that additional staff already provided for by the NIC/TDC staffing study were properly deployed and supervised.

The reason Benton and Stoughton found it necessary to address this issue was TDC's inability or refusal to properly deploy officers pursuant to the NIC/TDC staffing study. The NIC/TDC staffing study was completed in September 1982. One of the specific recommendations and requirements was placing correctional officers inside the cellblocks and dormitories. Pursuant to the terms of the building tender agreement, the staffing increases called for in the study (over twenty-five hundred officers) were to be phased in by January 1985 as the building tenders were phased out. The prison units that relied most heavily on building tenders (Ramsey, Ellis, and Eastham) received the first increases in January 1983. Coffield, Ramsey II, Retrieve, and Darrington received their additional staff January 1984. All of these increases occurred prior to Benton and Stoughton's report.

This phased-in approach was adopted to avoid the situation DiIulio describes as TDC "violinists" being hurried into the cellblocks. Rather than hurrying correctional officers into the cell-blocks, TDC simply refused to deploy officers in compliance with the staffing study. This issue was addressed in the December 1986 contempt proceedings, wherein it was found that "no officers were actually assigned to any housing areas at 10 of TDC's 27 units as of January 1985."[14]

There were most certainly undesirable consequences accompanying the implementation phase of *Ruiz*. However, the facile out-of-tune orchestra imagery, allegedly conducted by Judge Justice and his aides, is not very helpful in uncovering the primary reasons for the discordant results. While there are some aspects of DiIulio's analysis with which we agree, in this instance we find marked distortion. State policymakers and prison officials had the opportunity to make substantial contributions to the specific mechanism of reform as well as to the schedule on which these reforms would be implemented. Given the time and resources expended on interim negotiations and reports, it is difficult to support the claim that Judge Justice and his aides were not judicious or troubled about the potential consequences of their actions.

If not a hurried, ill-informed, untroubled judiciary, then what? If we stay with the actions of Judge Justice and the *Ruiz* proceedings for clues to possible contributions to heightened violence, there is an argument to be made concerning the "symbolic politics" of litigated reform. Clearly, messages coming from the court, such as those cited previously, were not accepted readily by prison staff and administrators. These messages, for these officials, were insulting and uncalled for. They appeared, as DiIulio notes, as an unkind preoccupation with the failings of TDC. As such they further symbolized the illegitimacy of the court's findings. This denial of legitimacy and perception of insult had very real consequences for the constraints on and opportunities for violence within the cell-blocks.

The effects of the court's ruling, however, went beyond symbols and resistance. There was eventually broad-based staff turnover from top to bottom. There was a rapid influx of new guards from backgrounds different than the traditional TDC community. There were new rules to be followed. Authority became more centralized. Discretion for the line staff was more limited. An active internal affairs office was established. There was a change in routine. Life became less predictable. Stress rose. Morale dropped. In the process, a system of control emerged, in which inmates relied on their own violent resources.

Confronted with a newly forming system of staff control, which for a time was ineffective because of lack of motivation, lack of experience, and faulty information about what was going on in the cellblocks, some inmates took advantage of the expanded opportunities to enhance their status and power in the socioeconomic system of prison life. Coalitions consolidated largely along racial and ethnic lines. Violence became a primary mechanism for dispute resolution.

Still questions remain: Why was violence rather than negotiated compromise chosen by the inmates? How could the disorganization of the emergent legitimate control mechanisms have been minimized?

A careful analysis of why inmates chose lethal violence is beyond the scope of this chapter. However, this much seems clear. There was an ordered quality to the outbreak of stabbings and homicides in the years following *Ruiz*. It is very important to recognize that the level of homicides in the TDC began escalating almost immediately after the main trial proceedings in *Ruiz* in 1980 and 1981, as opposed to an instant jump during 1984 and 1985 as is sometimes implied. Although leadership clearly makes a difference, each successive director during the post-*Ruiz* years was confronted with the history of the immediate past. A substantial majority of the homicides contained a strong element of reprisal for some perceived wrong. These homicides reflected a feudlike sense of justice. Gangs became armed, warring factions; duty to the gang "family" was invoked. Once again, we find a close link between "place"—a we–them mentality—and violence, much like that which justified staff violence against inmates. In this sense, there are parallels to be drawn between the coercion of the pre-*Ruiz* guard subculture and the emergent coerced order among inmate gangs.

Why violence, as opposed to negotiated compromise, was chosen as the primary mechanism for settling disputes and consolidating power is not clear. However, it is evident that intergang animosities were greatly influenced by racial tensions, personal feuds, and drug trafficking in the outside world. In this sense, the upsurge in lethal violence transcended the prison walls. The increase was not so much motivated by reform-related changes as it was facilitated by the reduction in contraints and the increase in opportunities which followed in the wake of a disorganized system of staff control.

How could the disorganization of the newly defined system of legitimate control have been minimized? Here we are in agreement with DiIulio. Leadership matters. The task, to be sure, was impressive. Few administrators, in prison or elsewhere, could have made an absolutely smooth transition in accommodating the massive influx of line staff that occurred in the TDC in the post-*Ruiz* years. Nor was it always easy to reeducate long-time veterans to the new definitions of legitimate action.

These tasks aside, we are convinced that denial of legitimacy to the court's rulings by the prison system's leadership set a moral climate in which staff could justify violation of court rulings. Such violations only prolonged the disorganized phase of the transition. The vehemence of the defiance was rooted in the noted levels of mutual mistrust and the lingering loyalties to a long-established way of life.

Notes

1. Sheldon Ekland-Olson, "Crowding, Social Control, and Prison Violence: Evidence from the Post-*Ruiz* Years in Texas," 20 *Law and Society Review* 389 (1986); Steve J. Martin and Sheldon Ekland-Olson, *Texas Prisons: The Walls Came Tumbling Down* (Austin: Texas Monthly Press, 1987); Sheldon Ekland-Olson and Steve J. Martin, "Organizational Compliance with Court-Ordered Reform," 22 *Law and Society Review* 359 (1988); Steve J. Martin, "Prisoners' Rights," 20 *Texas Tech Law Review* 573 (1989).
2. M. Kay Harris and D. P. Spiller, Jr., *After Decisions: Implementation of Judicial Decrees in Correctional Settings* (Washington, D.C.: U.S. Department of Justice, Law Enforcement Assistance Association, 1977); L. Ralph Jones and Richard R. Parlour, eds., *Wyatt v. Stickney: Retrospect and Prospect* (New York: Grune & Stratton, 1981); David J. Rothman and Shiela M. Rothman, *The Willowbrook Wars* (New York: Harper & Row, 1984); Ben M. Crouch and James W. Marquart, *An Appeal to Justice: Litigated Reform of Texas Prisons* (Austin: University of Texas Press, 1989).
3. Sheldon Ekland-Olson, "From Lynchings to Lethal Injections" (unpublished manuscript, 1988).

4. D. W. Meinig, *Imperial Texas: An Interpretive Essay in Cultural Geography* (Austin: University of Texas Press, 1969), p. 95.
5. Lee Simmons, *Assignment Huntsville: Memoirs of a Texas Official* (Austin: University of Texas Press, 1957), p. 64.
6. Martin and Ekland-Olson, *Texas Prisons*, pp. 66–69.
7. Ibid., pp. 145–47.
8. Crouch and Marquart, *An Appeal to Justice.*
9. John DiIulio, *Governing Prisons: A Comparative Study of Correctional Management* (New York: The Free Press, 1987), p. 176.
10. Ibid., p. 184.
11. Martin and Ekland-Olson, *Texas Prisons*, p. 147.
12. James Jacobs, "The Prisoners' Rights Movement," in *Crime and Justice: An Annual Review of Research, Vol. 2*, ed. N. Morris and M. Tonry (Chicago: University of Chicago Press, 1980), pp. 429–70; Kathleen Engel and Stanley Rothman "Prison Violence and the Paradox of Reform," 73 *The Public Interest* 91 (1983).
13. Bert Useem and Peter Kimball, *States of Siege: U.S. Prison Riots 1971–1986* (New York: Oxford University Press, 1989).
14. Memorandum Opinion, December 31, 1986, pp. 34–35.

4

Ruiz: Intervention and Emergent Order in Texas Prisons

BEN M. CROUCH and JAMES W. MARQUART

In 1972 a prisoner named David Ruiz filed a petition arguing that the Texas Department of Corrections (TDC) and its director, W. J. Estelle, Jr., unconstitutionally exposed prisoners to physically deteriorated, dangerous, and overcrowded conditions. The resulting suit, *Ruiz v. Estelle*, became the most comprehensive civil action in correctional law history. After years of legal conflict and a lengthy trial, Federal District Judge William W. Justice ruled in favor of the prisoner plaintiffs.

The *Ruiz* intervention in TDC is remarkable for the range of issues addressed and for the fact that ultimate reforms altered almost every aspect of prison operation. It is remarkable further for the extent to which the judicial reform orders were resisted by prison officials and, at least in the beginning, by state officials. That resistance cost the state millions in legal fees, undermined TDC's credibility with the legislature, and indirectly contributed to hundreds of injuries and dozens of deaths among prisoners. With the authors of the two preceding chapters, we believe that the consequences of the court orders for TDC raise important questions about judicial capacity to reform prison institutions. In this chapter we use data on these consequences developed over years of research to sketch the course of prison reform in Texas.[1] Specifically, we are concerned with the question of whether, despite the organizational change, conflict, and violence of the decree implementation process, it is possible to conclude that intervention can promote prison reform.

Our analysis yielded a conceptual model of TDC's reform experience. The model, presented in table 4.1, consists of three social orders which Texas prisons, their staffs, and prisoners experienced prior to and through the litigated reform process.[2] Specifically, TDC has moved from a *repressive order* (the prelitigation period), through a *legalistic order* (period of initial decree and compliance pressure), into a *bureaucratic order* (the emergent "new order"). These social orders vary considerably in terms of prison structures and relations. As court intervention prompted compliance through legal pressure and a new administration, prison organization became more formalized and rule-driven. These changes doomed the traditional TDC practices that had supported and defined the repressive order. The subsequent legalistic order enhanced compliance but produced social disorganization and violence. Specifically, a more formal organizational structure demoralized the staff because it, by design, limited their actions. At the same time, the new structure seemed to free prisoners to flout efforts to control them. Today, as we will show, much of this disorganization has been resolved with the emergence of a bureaucratic order.

Repressive Order and the Primacy of Control

Although table 4.1 describes the entire period prior to 1982 as reflective of repressive order, the period between 1947 and 1981 is most representative of our conception of this prison social order. While Texas prisons before 1947 contained many of the elements of

TABLE 4.1. Model of Litigated Reform in TDC and Variations in Major Structural Dimensions

Dimensions	Repressive Order (before 1982)	Legalistic Order (1982–85)	Bureaucratic Order (after 1985)
Primary objective of prison administration	Control; discipline	Constitutional legality	Control within judicially approved parameters
Legitimacy of prison actions	Tradition; management personality	Procedural fairness	Procedural fairness
Nature of rules	Many, but weakly binding on officials	Elaborate; strict accountability	Elaborate; tempered accountability
Official discretion and decision making	Pervasive discretion; ad hoc decision making	Very limited discretion; highly centralized decision making; narrow delegation of authority	Some increase in discretion and delegation of authority; much centralization remains
Prisoner control structure			
Rewards	Informal rewards extensive; important to control	Informal rewards essentially eliminated	Informal rewards very limited

Punishment	Informal, diverse; frequent force and coercion sanctioned officially	Formalized; force strictly limited; staff uncertainty	Formalized controls skillfully used by staff; "legalistic repression"
Prisoner–prisoner relations	Dominance of mass by officially coopted elites; fear of elites; minorities doubly subordinate	Elite cooptation eliminated; new groups/gangs; rise in racial tensions; fear of inmate aggression	Aggressive prisoners locked down; less fear of aggression
Official–official relations	Pervasive guard subculture; personalized interaction, promotion; line–administration values overlap greatly	Guard subculture dissolved; interaction and promotions highly formalized; line–administration values do not overlap	Guard work guided by bureaucratic rules and values; line–administration values overlap somewhat
Institutional relations of court and prison	Little court intervention; little conflict in relations; law subordinate to order in prison	Extensive court intervention; much conflict in relations; order subordinate to law	Limited court intervention; little conflict in relations due to compliance; order achieved within "letter of the law"

repressive order, those earlier prisons had limited organization, suffered massive neglect, and regularly lacked stability. Beyond a legislative desire that Texas prisons cost as little as possible, there was no strong principle or person to impose a definable order on them. The prisons were essentially anarchies in which state officials and even inmate managers largely abdicated responsibility.

From 1947 through the next three decades, however, Texas prisons operated under three powerful directors: O. B. Ellis, George J. Beto, and W. J. Estelle, Jr. These men and their staffs, over a thirty-year period, developed and maintained an authoritarian management style that epitomized repressive order. This style produced a level of prison control, stability, and productivity widely known and even envied by other state correctional agencies. It also carried considerable human costs for prisoners.

In 1947 the Prison Board hired O. B. Ellis, the man who began the refinement of TDC's repressive order. His success over the next dozen years produced a very favorable national as well as state reputation for the agency. During his tenure, an officer subculture, which controlled key staff behavior, began to emerge. That subculture stressed the work ethic, personal loyalty to supervisors, and paternalism and toughness toward prisoners, and it maintained solidarity in the security force, especially the middle and upper ranks. In the organization and to individual officers, control and order were paramount. Ellis underscored these values by systematizing disciplinary procedures (punishments) on the one hand and increasing inmate programs (rewards) on the other. These changes helped limit violence while agricultural reforms produced greater economic efficiency. Throughout this period, Ellis's skills in dealing with the legislature and the media muted criticism and largely precluded outside interference.

George J. Beto continued and extended the Ellis program. Like Ellis, he tightly controlled prison policy and unit-level operations. His penchant for showing up on a unit at any hour to check on staff and talk to prisoners earned him both a nickname (Walking George) and broad respect. Beto stressed educational and industrial programs for prisoners. Such progressive programs plus his considerable political skills helped ensure that the prison system enjoyed autonomy in many areas. In dealing with the legislature, the media, or citizens, he could point to a prison system with relatively little violence, one widely known as "the prison system that worked."

When W. J. Estelle, Jr., became TDC director in 1972, he maintained the traditional prison operations that were so widely approved. Like his predecessors, Estelle projected a powerful, charismatic persona. Known as the employee's director, he gave considerable freedom of operation to his many unit wardens and fiercely supported his staff. Estelle was also a master of public and legislative relations. Although during his administration a number of forces (several lawsuits, overcrowding, charges of brutality, and incipient pressure from reform groups and legislators) began to undermine TDC's traditional authority, Estelle's administration was relatively successful at keeping inmates submissive, violence low, and TDC's reputation intact through the 1970s.

In each of these regimes, staff attitudes and behaviors toward each other and toward prisoners were consistent with a repressive order. Legitimacy was based on tradition and the personal authority of strong directors and key unit personnel; the management objectives of prison officials—order and control—were clear and uniform. There were certainly written rules to guide official behavior, but they were not especially binding on officials so long as those officials could maintain productivity and control. Consequently, individual officers had much discretion in the treatment and control of prisoners. Even after the improvements wrought by Ellis and his successors, official actions were often idiosyncratic. Coercion, both psychological and physical, was routine and central to repressive order. The use of force by officers did more than foster prisoner obedience; it was also an indication of a "good officer," one who could be relied on and promoted. This valuation of personal toughness among officers was a key feature of the officer subculture that existed on each unit into the early 1980s in TDC.

Also central to TDC's repressive order, especially on the large units for "problem" or violence-prone prisoners, was the building tender system. This institutionalized use by officials of dominant prisoners as "building tenders" (BTs) to supervise and control other prisoners had existed throughout most of the twentieth century. Although there were always abuses of authority by these inmate elites, there appear to have been variations in the level of that abuse related to officer–inmate ratios. In the 1940s, when the prison system grew rapidly yet added few officers, reliance on BTs grew; greater official reliance on building tenders led to greater abuse of other prisoners by BTs simply because official supervision was thin to nonexistent. Significantly, the same scenario occurred in the 1970s when the inmate population grew tremendously and the security staff increased only slightly. In this period line officers again became excessively dependent on poorly supervised BTs. The result in both periods was greater abuse by these inmate guards. Interestingly, between these periods, during the more stable Beto era (1962–72), BTs appear to have been somewhat better controlled, relatively less free to abuse prisoners.

This recurrent problem with the BTs illustrates a fundamental point about the style of control and organizational structure in Texas prisons prior to court intervention. The prison operated on the basis of a highly personalized infrastructure. Individual reputations, personal intuition of guards ("convict sense"), control skill, and connections were paramount in all relations among officials and between officials and prisoners. Under stable organizational conditions and limited growth (e.g., the Beto period), this personalized infrastructure could more or less effectively guide the control of men (officers and prisoners) and the routine fiscal and political accounting required of a state agency. But pressures during the Estelle administration, especially population growth, began to stretch that personalized infrastructure to its limits. Evidence that the system was badly overextended (e.g., overreliance on BTs, "loose" accounting practices) made the system even more vulnerable to outside criticisms and especially to the court's tests of constitutionality.

Those tests were not forcefully applied until the *Ruiz* case went to trial in 1978. Through three previous decades, characteristic of repressive order, the courts either would not hear prisoner cases or focused on delimited legal issues (e.g., health care, mail privileges, integration). Consistent with a traditional "hands-off" doctrine, this judicial posture gave tacit approval to Texas prison practices and implied that law was subordinate to prison order. This situation changed drastically, however, as Judge Justice moved TDC from repressive order toward legalistic order.

Legalistic Order and the Rule of Law

The *Ruiz v. Estelle* trial and the reform mandates laid down by Judge Justice in 1981 did not immediately bring about fundamental change in TDC operations, despite the appointment of a special master to oversee compliance. For unit officers through 1981 and into 1982, the status quo remained largely intact. Though many old control and operating procedures had been ruled unlawful, new procedures remained ill-defined or irrelevant on the units while prison, state, and court officials negotiated or contested them.

Even when consent decrees on some issues were signed by state officials, unit staff and even central office administrators in TDC continued to operate in the old ways. After all, Estelle was still the director, and the new procedures seemed to many officers to be important only to the court. This official resistance, so central to understanding the Texas prison reform experience, derived from a deep commitment by TDC officials to a management and control system that over at least three decades had become not only legitimized but in some respects romanticized; it was solidified on the units through the socialization of staff to subcultural values. This commitment was such that traditional TDC modes of operation were, in the minds of officials at all levels, essentially unassailable; those officials simply could not find acceptable any other way of handling prisoners or running a prison, particularly if that other way was being imposed by an outside agent.

It is important to note, however, that not all points of Judge Justice's decree were equally resisted. On such issues as poor medical care, crowding, and sanitation problems, for example, there was relatively little resistance to change. Prison and state officials generally agreed that these areas needed improvement. The resistance came instead on those points in the decree that directly questioned the dominance of officers and their discretion to maintain control in ways they deemed effective. Traditional dominance and discretion were considered critical to the maintenance of order.

Although inmates during this time sensed and seized some new freedoms, they were regularly reminded that the old ways still held sway in the halls and cellblocks. Traditional means of control were still being used, although somewhat less openly. Consequently, in 1981 and 1982 the prison system drifted between a suddenly unconstitutional past and an uncertain future defined only by distant, negotiated settlements articulated by lawyers. Emergent policies growing out of those settlements lacked legitimacy for most unit-level officers, who felt little obligation to carry them out.

The legalistic order emerged full-blown when state and then prison officials finally decided to comply with the decrees and then imposed structural changes to that end. The Board of Corrections took the first step in this regard. In late 1983 the board accepted Estelle's resignation and declared that the prison staff would henceforth strictly abide by court proscriptions, especially those involving the use of force.

The major move in the erection of a legalistic order, however, was the appointment in mid-1984 of Raymond Procunier to the director's post. Procunier's board-imposed agenda was to bring TDC into compliance, to create as rapidly as possible a constitutional prison. A non-Texan with no concern for or commitment to TDC traditions, Procunier declared that the basis for future operations would be constitutional legality as defined by the court. To ensure compliance, Procunier centralized decision making. This move meant a rapid and immediate expansion of TDC's bureaucracy. Rules and the paperwork to explain and report on rule applications proliferated. The purpose of this formalization by headquarters was both to homogenize operations and to maximize compliance by holding staff strictly accountable for their actions.[3]

Formalizing procedures severely limited official discretion in rewarding and punishing prisoners. New rules specifically prohibited most traditional control devices, particularly official use of force and reliance on building tenders to control prisoners. Emerging policies so contrary to traditional practices and scrutiny from the central administration via internal affairs promoted great uncertainty and frustration among officers. In the face of polygraph checks and in-depth investigation for any alleged security staff misdeed, traditionally high officer morale plunged. Many officers expressed their disaffection by simply quitting; others expressed it by interacting with prisoners as little as possible in an eight-hour shift.

The centralization and accountability demanded by the new prison administration did more than reduce the power of unit staff from wardens to the lowest cellblock officer. These changes also altered the informal power relations within the inmate population. Aware of court-defined limits on official control, of officer uncertainty, and of the elimination of the building tenders, many prisoners began to exploit opportunities to extend their dominance over other prisoners. The result was an expansion of protection rackets, drug trafficking, prostitution, and prisoner-on-prisoner aggression generally. Such acts were frequently interracial, as racial animosities, former squelched under a repressive order, now more readily rose to the surface. Growing fear and racial tension among prisoners in turn became both causes and effects of the rapid growth of prison gangs in TDC prisons.

This general disorganization in the prisoner social system along with a lack of confidence in official protection, especially through 1984 and 1985, greatly heightened fear and actual violence among prisoners. The sense of impending danger from a riot, gang attack, or individual assault prompted a tremendous increase in the number of prisoners making or securing some type of weapon, primarily for self-protection. Many of these weapons were used, however, creating an unprecedented wave of violence in TDC prisons. Over six hundred nonfatal stabbings and fifty-two inmate-on-inmate homicides occurred during 1984 and 1985.

The rise of a legalistic order, where control seemed to many officers to be much less important than the promulgation of new, constitutional procedures, also dramatically altered relations between and among staff and prisoners. To improve the officer-inmate ratio administrations hired literally thousands of new security officers, many of whom were female. These new hires, along with the proliferation of rules and policies, undermined the highly personal infrastructure that had sustained the officer subculture and control system in the past. Personal ability to judge and deal with prisoners was no longer valuable in a system driven by paperwork, computer files, specialists, and a burgeoning clerical staff.

Generally, new standards for work and rewards on the job had a leveling effect among officers by significantly altering the bases for staff promotions and co-worker esteem. Exemplars of the traditional officer subculture were fired or disciplined while new officers, who were more comfortable with paperwork, got promoted.

Old loyalties to supervisors, other officers, and to the agency itself were deeply eroded, especially among veteran staff.

A leveling effect also became apparent among prisoners. As the building tenders lost their elite status, other prisoners rose to positions of dominance. At the same time, many regular prisoners, who had in the past benefited from official discretion to reward good behavior, found the limited official discretion no longer permitted the special considerations from guards they had enjoyed in the past. They learned that the new universalism demanded by the court and new administration meant they were being treated no differently than the problem prisoners.

Bureaucratic Order and Legalistic Repression

During the mid-1980s, despite low morale, uncertainty, and an apparent inability to restore order, TDC officials at all levels were nonetheless adapting, if not always willingly, to the new, court-approved operational policies. This adaptation to and eventual skillful use of constitutional means to achieve official ends (especially control) is the essence of a bureaucratic prison order. By the mid-1980s TDC officials began to adopt these new means to achieve traditional ends. In so doing, Texas prison officials were able to bring about a reemergence of stability.[4]

Although prisoner control seemed to recede in importance under the legalistic order, it certainly never disappeared as a significant objective. By late 1985 the turmoil and violence, together with much political pressure for prison officials to "do something," forced a reassertion of that control agenda, but this time within the parameters set by the court. Specifically, the TDC director ordered a massive lockdown of actually and potentially assaultive prisoners. This move helped both to raise staff morale and to reduce fear among prisoners. Both groups welcomed the lockdown since the prison environment had become extremely stressful for all. The lockdown announced that the administration was now interested in something besides compliance alone. More importantly, it communicated that the administration had at its disposal, and would use, legal means of punishing and controlling prisoners. This new approach to dealing with prisoners gradually filtered down to the unit level, and a new control structure began to emerge.

Of course, an important element in that new control structure was simply a much larger guard force. By 1987 TDC had been able to meet prescribed staffing levels in almost every area. Recruiting diligence by TDC, aided by a downturn in the Texas economy, which made state employment more attractive, produced through 1986 and 1987 enough people to meet unit needs despite continued turnover. Simply having officers "everywhere" helped thwart prisoner aggression and restore official control.

But a larger force alone was not enough to effect the greatly increased stability and safety that characterized Texas prisons after 1985; supervisors and officers had learned how to use the new policies to their advantage. With time, the once unfamiliar rules and procedures became routine, and supervisors, like their staff, learned what would work in the new bureaucratic environment. As newly promoted supervisors gained confidence, they became more able (and perhaps willing) to guide their subordinates in the ways of the new order. And most remaining veterans adapted to the new work demands, albeit in many cases grudgingly. At the same time, new officers, with little sense of the "old days," had less to overcome and adapted easily.

Specifically, the security staff learned how to use the sanctions legally available to them for inmate control, especially the "write up," or report of rule violation. Prisoners in TDC prisons today believe that the chance of getting written up for a minor violation is much greater than it was in the early 1980s, and most report a keen awareness that these "tickets" can affect their good time and eventual release. By varying the degree to which they apply the rules, by threatening, frustrating, and harassing prisoners with the multiplicity of rules, officers can intimidate and control most prisoners. The result can be as effective as the old "tune-up" or "ass whipping." Supporting the formal write-up procedures is administrative segregation, a readily available sanction for any troublesome prisoner. Today, through perfectly constitutional means, TDC officials have placed in "ad seg" thousands of prisoners whom officials have designated violence prone, gang affiliated, or unwilling to

follow prison routines. Prisoners can remain in segregation indefi-
nitely, and at this writing, some have been locked away for over five
years.

Though officers acknowledge that physical coercion is outlawed
except under the strictest circumstances, they have discovered that
applying the "letter of the rule" to control prisoners works. In this
way officials maintain control over inmates while not infringing on
their rights under law. By operating formally and universalistically,
even when rules are contradictory or when minor injustices are
obvious, officers can be punitive on solid legal grounds. This tactic
is a kind of *legalistic repression*. Of course, many officers do at
times bend rules either to punish a prisoner or to help him. But the
overriding impression is that the staff has become more confident
and proactive with respect to the rules, even those rules designed to
benefit or protect prisoners.

As the bureaucratic order has solidified in TDC, prison officials
have regained at least some degree of discretion and autonomy.
Under legalistic order, official discretion was highly constrained;
only court-defined and supervised operations were acceptable. As
TDC has approached compliance, however, especially on control issues, the court has accorded greater autonomy to TDC's
central office. Although monitoring continued in 1988, court
officials became much less aggressive in their oversight of TDC
operations.

In like manner, top TDC administrators, who in the early 1980s
centralized policy decisions because unit managers were simply not
trusted, have today returned considerable discretion to those (in
most cases new) unit managers. Indeed, the current director, Jim
Lynaugh, an accountant appointed to the post in 1987, has stated
that his concern will be with fiscal matters and that he will let unit
wardens handle security. This posture reflects Lynaugh's confidence
(and by implication the court's) that compliance is now sufficiently
institutionalized and that greater unit discretion will probably not
put inmate rights in jeopardy.

Clearly, the emergent bureaucratic order that has so altered
prison relations and structures in TDC is the result of court intervention. But has intervention actually benefited prisoners and improved the conditions of confinement as it was intended to do?

Inmate Life Under Bureaucratic Order

An important question in any reform litigation is whether the process has been in any sense a "success." But defining and measuring success is a difficult business for a number of reasons, for example, imprecise judicial decrees, conflicting views about reforms among prison interest groups, and, perhaps more important, the problem of weighing positive outcomes (less severe punishment) against negative outcomes (more inmate violence).[5] Because of these and other complexities, there is no established methodology, no "litmus test," for judging the success of intervention.

But there is one approach to assessing the ameliorative impact of court-mandated prison reform that is both reasonably straightforward and defensible, namely, to ask the supposed beneficiaries of litigated reform, the prisoners themselves. We did this by questioning nearly five hundred randomly selected prisoners on nine key TDC units in early 1987.[6]

How do TDC prisoners perceive the results of years of litigated reform (1981–87)? First, most prisoners believe that TDC has not changed all that much.[7] In one sense, this is not surprising. The place is still a prison with its routines, physical barriers, official surveillance, and deprivations. Yet most prisoners also believe that Justice's reform decrees and TDC's ultimate general compliance with them have made the prison a better place for the average inmate.[8] One example of that improvement is in the treatment of minorities by officials. Prisoners feel that there is somewhat less racial and ethnic discrimination in 1987 than there was before 1983.

A more fundamental example of improvement, however, is the prisoners' perception that under a bureaucratic order TDC is a safer place. Not only do institutional data reveal less violence, but inmates in 1987 perceived TDC to be a much less dangerous place compared to the late 1970s and early 1980s. Through 1985 approximately 60 percent of TDC prisoners felt that the prison was a dangerous place; by 1987 only 28 percent described the prison as dangerous. Other prisoner-reported improvements tied to the reforms include less inmate–inmate aggression and theft. These prisoner perceptions suggest that while intervention may initially promote disorganization and violence, these negative consequences do not necessarily become a permanent feature of the prisoners' world. That is, the "paradox of reform"[9] is paradoxical for a relatively short period only.

Court intervention produced improvements in other areas of prison life as well. These include much better medical services, the advent of grievance and appeal procedures, full-time "free-world" inmate advocates on each prison unit, correctional counselors, and explicit standards to guide official discipline. These changes, as we noted earlier, have generally become integral, accepted parts of the prison bureaucracy. Thus, from the prisoners' point of view, judicial intervention has made the incarceration experience in Texas relatively better.

Court and Prison Relations Under Bureaucratic Order

Through the protracted litigation process relations between the court and the prison have also changed. Under repressive order, the court was a distant presence at best and conflict between these institutions over prison operations was consequentially minimal. An opposite relationship obtained under legalistic order, however. The TDC's traditional control agenda and the court's constitutional agenda directly clashed. With the advent of a bureaucratic order, prison–court relations have again become less adversarial.

The course of prison–court relations in Texas parallels a national trend. That is, having moved from a hands-off philosophy to activism through the 1960s and 1970s, courts again appear less inclined to intervene in prisons. To a number of commentators, this is a welcome trend.[10] Brakel, for example, believes that the "litigation revolution" has been excessive and that courts should be limiting their involvement in prison operations. He writes:

> That before the court-ordered revolution many of this country's prisons were in deplorable shape does not justify, in my view, wholesale and continuous intervention that disregards the undesirable side effects of the reform mandate, and the alteration in normal lines of government authority and responsibility that accompanies the process. Rather than unequivocally endorse the revolution and its unabated continuation, I would conclude that the courts have gone far enough fast enough.[11]

A reduction in court activism has been noted, and frequently lamented, by many scholars. They sense the court is returning to a hands-off doctrine[12] in which courts either fail to intervene on behalf of prisoners or, when they do, rule in favor of prison officials. For example, a federal judge ruled against prisoners in *Bruscino v. Carlson*,[13] upholding the use as a prime control device the long-term, near-total lockdown of prisoners at the federal prison at Marion, Illinois.[14] A federal appeals court upheld this decision.[15]

There are several reasons for this generally less intrusive posture of the courts today. First, there appears to be an increasingly conservative political philosophy of the 1980s which has dampened judicial interest in questioning prison authorities.[16] Reduced court activism may also reflect the fact that today there are fewer young lawyers interested in prisoners' rights and there is less money to support their efforts.[17]

A third, and perhaps most important, reason for diminished court activism is that prisons have simply gotten better at operating constitutionally. Prison administrators have seen the intervention handwriting on the wall and have increasingly accepted judicially defined guidelines on caring for and controlling prisoners. Even those administrators of prisons not subjected to far-reaching decrees have learned vicariously from the experience in other states.[18] In this connection, Allen Breed, who has served in both state and federal correctional posts and as special master in prison reform lawsuits, suggests that the *Ruiz* case has been particularly instructive in this regard.

> Most [prison administrators] have moved away from the macho position of having to defend themselves in court and want to be a part of the solution. We are consistently seeing more consent decrees than remedial orders. Texas is the last large system for a remedial order. If the courts could win in Texas, as big and powerful and independent as it was, they [administrators] said "we'd better think about that in terms of future intervention."[19]

After years of intense litigation in *Ruiz*, Judge William Wayne Justice seems to be following this national trend of withdrawal in Texas, largely because of TDC compliance on almost all aspects of the decree. Compliance in TDC has progressed to the point that court officers today are more likely to view prison administrators as cooperative professionals than as obstructionists. In turn, the court has become less inclined to scrutinize every official action and policy.[20] In fact, in April 1987 Judge Justice went so far as to commend in writing the legislature, the governor, and TDC's administration on the progress made in compliance. Monitor reports and the judge's own observations on a tour of three TDC units in early 1987 documented that progress. As he does not have the reputation of compromising his principles, the judge's positive assessment of TDC's record is due to real improvements rather than a lowering of judicial expectations.

The only major decree in *Ruiz* which continues to call for court scrutiny concerns overcrowding. And even here the court has taken a somewhat less combative posture toward TDC and the state. For example, in the spring of 1987 Judge Justice threatened to fine the state twenty-four million dollars per month if progress was not made on the crowding problem. Subsequent efforts by the state to remedy the problem, however, led the judge to suspend the fine, citing the state's "good-faith" efforts.[21]

Conclusion

After a long and painful litigation process, a bureaucratic social order prevails in Texas prisons today. Though the court's intervention initially produced tremendous disorder, stability has re-emerged. Both the keepers and the kept have made an uneasy peace, with each other and with the new order. Guards are no longer a relatively elite force manifesting subcultural solidarity and capriciously dominating prisoners; they have become bureaucrats.[22] Because their rights are more readily recognized today and because current control mechanisms are not as intrusive or capricious as they were before intervention, prisoners in Texas generally do time with less pain and fear. But they also know that the staff has learned to use lawful sanctions very effectively. In short, organizational expectations have become clearer for all parties, and Texas prisons have become more lawful and predictable.

The transformation of Texas prison has placed TDC in the mainstream of American institutional corrections. No longer does TDC reflect the image of the Texas cowboy—independent, sure of traditional values, wary of outside intervention. This shift in organizational persona is symbolized, for example, by the waning popularity of Western boots and Stetsons and in the official TDC decision in 1987 to cancel the famous Texas Prison Rodeo for the first time since its inception thirty-five years earlier. The managerial image today is more that of the corporation man or woman, an image consistent with a bureaucratic order. Administrators in TDC are particularly sensitive to judicial, media, and political interests, managing themselves and their agency accordingly. They are more universalistic and at least open to professionalism and training.[23]

The rise of bureaucratic order in Texas prisons has prompted a return of prison control to prison officials. As the court approves of constitutional progress, an emerging stability has discouraged media and legislative attention to the prison system. Prison officials are thus freer to make their own decisions about how prisoners will be handled, so long as those decisions meet constitutional and legislative standards.

Certainly, regaining some autonomy does not mean that officials in TDC or other "reformed" prisons will move back toward the management and control systems that existed in earlier decades. Indeed, there are at least two reasons to expect that a retreat to repressive order is unlikely. First, constitutional standards, once formalized into bureaucratic rules, tend to become legitimate in their own right, accepted by staff as appropriate guides for behavior. Self-perpetuating and conservative prison bureaucracies will outlast personnel who come and go. The second reason is that the current large body of case law concerning prison conditions and prisoner treatment both educates and threatens administrators who would employ policies widely recognized as unconstitutional. We may assume then that prison officials will operate in terms of current judicial expectations.

On balance, the Texas experience suggests that court intervention can bring about very significant improvements in prison conditions, even when actively resisted by prison officials. Yet those improvements fall short of some ideal notion of "justice." In *Ruiz*, prisoner plaintiffs and prison officials both appealed to justice, arguing for their own version of this illusory ideal. Prisoners argued that as a class they were denied rights and fair treatment, while officials claimed that TDC's particularistic approach afforded individual prisoners the justice each deserved. There is no question as to who won the case itself; clearly the prisoners did. The result of over a decade of litigation is a fairer environment in which prisoners feel much safer, enjoy (at least technically) the major elements of due process, and receive care defined by external or "free-world" standards. But the letter rather than the spirit of "justice" tends to prevail. Abuse, indifference, and injury still occur,[24] tempering the results of litigated prison reform.

Notes

1. This chapter draws on our extensive study of the Texas prison experience in *An Appeal to Justice: Litigated Reform of Texas Prisons* (Austin: University of Texas Press, 1989).
2. Some of the elements in our model are analogous to concepts developed by Philippe Nonet and Philip Selznick in their analysis of the evolution of law in society. See *Law and Society in Transition: Toward Responsive Law* (New York: Harper Torchbooks, 1978).
3. J. Vagg, R. Morgan, and M. Maguire stress that prisons cannot be held accountable by outside agencies, such as courts, unless there is in place a system of *internal* accountability. See their "Introduction: Accountability and Prisons" in *Accountability and Prisons: Opening Up a Closed World*, ed. M. Maguire, J. Vagg, and R. Morgan (London: Tavistock, 1986), p. 4.
4. In his account of the transition of Stateville Prison in Illinois, Jacobs notes that after much turmoil and violence, the prison eventually reached a period of stability. A somewhat similar stage was reached in TDC in the years after 1985. Indeed, according to Jacobs, there is a close parallel between the stages through which Stateville prison passed and the stages we observed in TDC. Specifically, our repressive order includes his "anarchy" and "charismatic leadership" stages; our legalistic order includes his "drift" and "crisis" stages; and our bureaucratic order includes his "stability" stage. This parallel underscores the patterned nature of organizational change in prisons. See J. B. Jacobs, *Stateville: The Penitentiary in Mass Society* (Chicago: University of Chicago Press, 1977).

5. For a discussion of some of the difficulties in defining and measuring the success of litigation in prison, see J. B. Jacobs, "The Prisoners' Rights Movement and Its Impact, 1960–1980," in *Crime and Justice: An Annual Review of Research*, Vol. 2, ed. N. Morris and M. Tonry (Chicago: University of Chicago Press, 1980) 429–470; see also M. Feely and R. Hanson, "What We Know, Think We Know and Would Like to Know About the Impact of Court Orders on Prison Conditions and Jail Crowding," paper prepared for the meeting of the Working Group on Jail and Prison Crowding, Committee on Research on Law Enforcement and the Administration of Justice, National Academy of Sciences, Chicago, October 15–16, 1986.

6. For details of this survey, see Crouch and Marquart, *An Appeal to Justice*.

7. In the survey of prisoners, fifty-seven percent agreed with such a statement.

8. This sentiment was reported by approximately two-thirds of the survey prisoners.

9. See K. Engel and S. Rothman, "Prison Violence and the Paradox of Reform," *The Public Interest* 73 (Fall 1983), 91–105.

10. D. Horowitz, *The Courts and Social Policy* (Washington, D.C.: Brookings Institution, 1977); R. Gaskins, "Second Thoughts on 'Law as an Instrument of Social Change,'" *Law and Human Behavior* 6 (1982), 153–68.

11. S. J. Brakel, "Prison Reform Litigation: Has the Revolution Gone Too Far?" *Judicature* 70 (June–July 1986), 7.

12. See E. Alexander, "The New Prison Administrator and the Court: New Directions in Prison Law," *Texas Law Review* 56 (1978), 963–1008; B. Falkof, "Prisoner Representative Organizations, Prison Reform, and *Jones v. North Carolina Prisoner's Labor Union*: An Argument for Increased Intervention in Prison Administration," *Journal of Criminal Law and Criminology* 70 (1979), 42–56; I. Robbins, "The Cry of *Wolfish* in the Federal Courts: The Future of Federal Judicial Intervention in Prison Administration," *Journal of Criminal Law and Criminology* 71 (1979), 898–930; M. Ware, "Federal Intervention in State Prisons: The Modern Prison Conditions Case," *Houston Law Review* 19 (1982), 931–50.

13. *Bruscino v. Carlson* (Civil Action No. 84-4320, D.C. S.D. Ill. 1987).

14. Significantly for recent control practices in Texas, this federal lockdown strategy appears to closely parallel TDC's extensive use of administrative segregation for troublesome prisoners.

15. On July 22, 1988, the U.S. Court of Appeals for the Seventh Circuit affirmed *Bruscino*.

16. J. Thomas, "Law and Social Praxis: Prisoner Civil Rights Litigation and Structural Mediations," in *Research in Law, Deviance and Social Control*, ed. S. Spitzer and A. Scull (Greenwich, CT.: JAI Press, 1984), chapter 6; D. A. Timmer and D. S. Eitzen, "Controlling Crime in the 1980's: A Critique of Conservative Federal Policy," *Humanity and Society* 92 (1985), 67–80.
17. Jacobs, "The Prisoners' Rights Movement," p. 439.
18. P. Baker et al., "Judicial Intervention in Corrections: The California Experience, An Empirical Study," *UCLA Law Review* 20 (1975), 452–580. Indeed, W. Turner points out that some prisons become more constitutional even after prison officials have *won* a rights suit filed against them. "When Prisoners Sue: A Study of Prisoner Section 1983 Suits in Federal Courts," *Harvard Law Review* 92 (1979), 610–63.
19. Quoted in F. Klimko, "The Price of Arrogance: Texas Legal Fees," *Corrections Compendium* 11 (July 1987), 8. In this connection, Jim Estelle, Jr., recalled that shortly after he took the Texas post (1972), a friend, during a corrections conference in another state, suggested he visit with two attorneys active in prison litigation. In that visit, those attorneys, according to Estelle, laid out plans to reform American corrections through the courts. Because of its size and reputation, Texas was to be the key to the plan; if it "fell," all the other prisons could be reformed without a fight.
20. Interview with Scott McGowan, Enforcement Division of Texas Attorney General's Office, October 1987.
21. C. Robison, "Judge Suspends Fines over TDC, Cites 'Good Faith,'" Houston *Chronicle*, March 17, 1987.
22. This observation is also made by L. Lombardo, *Guards Imprisoned* (New York: Elsevier, 1981).
23. For a recent analysis of the problems and prospects of managing contemporary prisons, see J. J. DiIulio, Jr., *Governing Prisons: A Comparative Analysis of Correctional Management* (New York: The Free Press, 1987).
24. There are indications that TDC staff still at times employ illicit force and that the administration is less than diligent in trying to eliminate these occurrences. In March 1988 the special master reported to the court that TDC was being too lenient on guards who used excessive force on prisoners. See K. Fair, "Report Finds Continued TDC Brutality, Blames Inadequate Guard Punishment," Houston *Chronicle*, March 3, 1988.

5

Politics and Constitutional Interpretation in Prison Reform Litigation: The Case of *Guthrie v. Evans*

BRADLEY S. CHILTON
and SUSETTE M. TALARICO

Courts give meaning to values in law and equity through adjudication by converting whatever is submitted to them for decisions into claims of right or accusations of fault.[1] This process is particularly important in institutional reform litigation where subsequent meanings can shape years of litigation and policy. Contemporary American jurisprudence includes at least three theories related to this kind of constitutional interpretation: (1) adjudication of pre-existing principle; (2) adjudication by legislating policy; and (3) adjudication as a practice of rights.

Although criticized by legal realists and judicial behavioralists, the conception of the judge as a neutral, objective, and rational adjudicator of preexisting *principles* is part of the accepted ideology of courts.[2] Ronald Dworkin, as contemporary spokesperson, emphasizes the unique role of courts in adjudicating principles and posits an idealized Judge "Hercules," who can find "one right answer" in every case, even with competing principles.[3] Once the appropriate preexisting principles are discovered and applied to a case, the parties are rationally obliged to comply with the court's judgment as they would to any contract.[4] In judicially managed institutional reform, Judge Hercules seeks out and applies preexisting constitutional principles that impose a burden of adequate custodial care on the state.[5]

With its idealized Judge Hercules, Dworkin's rights thesis fails to convince many that judges merely discover and apply preexisting principles. For example, David A. J. Richards argues that judges simply make *policy* decisions in constitutional interpretation. As proof, he demonstrates (1) that decisions are granted to individuals who cannot claim a right to the result (e.g., Ernesto Miranda in *Miranda v. Arizona* [1966]); (2) that decisions apply prospectively and affect individuals whose rights were not presented or even anticipated in court; and (3) that the courts develop policy even in the "natural province of adjudication."[6] Dworkin faults this idealized Judge "Herbert" in a collection named after Judge Frank Johnson's personal papers ("A Matter of Principle"), although the argument seems to parallel his 1978 thesis with little elaboration: "This administrative business of courts, which Chayes thinks provides a new style of adjudication, raises a great many problems for jurisprudence and political theory . . . much more needs to be said about the energetic administrative role courts now seem to have assumed, and the impact of that practice on the rights thesis."[7]

Other scholars object to a rights thesis that idealizes adjudication by either a Hercules or a Herbert. From phenomenology, pragmatism, and linguistic analysis, Richard E. Flathman presents a theory of adjudication as a social *practice* of rights. As a framework for analysis, it accommodates both the individual and social dimensions of rights in a theory based on things that people do, not idealizations. Flatham introduces *The Practice of Rights* accordingly:

> Rights arise out of and are accorded within a rule-governed social practice. But they are accorded to and exercised by individuals whose actions

cannot be analyzed without significant remainder in terms of properties of the practice or the society more generally. Its aim is . . . to identify and give a systematic account and assessment of the assumptions, beliefs, ideas, values, expectations, and modes of action that are prominent in the practice as its participants understand it and engage in it.[8]

Do any of these three approaches to constitutional interpretation help to illuminate the analysis of a particular instance of institutional reform litigation? We offer the following analysis of the prison reform litigation encompassed under the rubric of *Guthrie v. Evans* (Civil Action No. 73-3068, S.D. Ga. 1973) in the hope that it will stimulate additional discussion of both rights theory and the nature of institutional reform litigation. In the process we ask two central questions: How did the *Guthrie* litigation address a very real and pressing problem? What are the ramifications of the resulting solution?

History of the Guthrie Litigation

On September 29, 1972, Arthur S. Guthrie, Joseph Coggins II, and fifty other black inmates of the Georgia State Prison (GSP) at Reidsville signed a four-page in forma pauperis complaint with the federal courts in Georgia that has led to one of the most detailed and comprehensive remedial decrees ever imposed on prison facilities.[9] Judge Anthony A. Alaimo of the U.S. District Court for the Southern District of Georgia, Savannah Division, presided over the suit, which has been entitled *Guthrie v. MacDougall, Guthrie v. Caldwell, Guthrie v. Ault,* and, finally, *Guthrie v. Evans.* In the litigation, Judge Alaimo condemned as cruel and unusual punishment the segregation, overcrowding, poor medical care, miserable conditions, and unfair treatment of black and white inmates at Reidsville and set in motion extensive changes in nearly every aspect of prison operations. These covered everything from racial discrimination to the right to retain up to six issues of monthly magazines for up to three months.

Judge Alaimo officially sanctioned the lawsuit by certifying a class action on July 23, 1973. The class was composed of "all black inmates" at GSP except those who expressly waived their involvement (more than five hundred did so). In 1983 the class was expanded to include all GSP inmates, white and black.

With the consent of the parties, Judge Alaimo first ordered mediation of the *Guthrie* case under Robert F. Greenwald of the United States Department of Justice. Representative parties and their attorneys met unsuccessfully from October 1973 to December 1974, after which Greenwald finally recommended its end. During this time, the U.S. Civil Rights Commission held hearings (November 16–17, 1973) concerning prison conditions and civil rights in all Georgia prisons, including GSP. Testimony noted the chronic underfunding of GSP and other Georgia prisons.

After mediation ended in December 1974, Judge Alaimo appointed Marvin L. Pipkin, an attorney from New Brunswick, Georgia, as a special master to help the parties prepare for trial. Pipkin handled pretrial motions and discovery, held fact-finding hearings, and frequently visited GSP. From December 1974 to July 1977, discovery by litigants included dozens of lengthy interrogatories, depositions of inmates and experts, and inspections of GSP files. Although some items were protected for reasons of prison security and order, most were discoverable.

Fact-finding hearings under special master Pipkin were very lengthy and extensive, involving over two hundred witnesses and one hundred exhibits over three phases from June 1976 to July 1977. The initial hearings from June 1976 through July 1976 included limited testimony by inmates, guards, and staff at GSP on the improper use of force and intimidation of inmates by staff. Judge Alaimo issued an order (November 26, 1976) for the protection of inmates as violence increased at GSP.

All fact findings, reports, and recommendations by special master Pipkin were filed by October 7, 1979, finding the defendants' liable. Judge Alaimo endorsed these reports in their entirety. No formal trial on these issues was held by Judge Alaimo.

Important nonprocedural orders and consent decrees from 1974 to 1978 were relatively few, designed only to push GSP in a direction until a finding of facts was completed. These included (1) an order on April 4, 1974, to complete racial integration; (2) an order on November 26, 1974, to protect inmates; (3) a consent decree on July 19, 1978, to set up a law library and to provide legal assistance for inmates; (4) consent decrees on August 4, 1978, and December

12, 1978, covering a wide range of prison conditions, practices, and policies in the GSP regulations; and (5) an order on December 12, 1978, mandating racial integration of all housing.

Important nonprocedural orders and consent decrees from 1978 to 1985 are too numerous to itemize. Sixty-one orders and consent decrees were handed down to resolve GSP problems in three major areas: (1) physical health and safety of GSP inmates; (2) due process of law and the equal protection of the laws in the fair treatment of GSP inmates in the employment practices of GSP; and (3) various programmatic improvements in medical services, vocational and educational programs, and a rehabilitative incentive plan for GSP inmates.

As remedy formulation developed, Judge Alaimo appointed Vincent M. Nathan as special monitor from June 1, 1979, to December 31, 1983, with the consent of the parties. Nathan was given broad powers beyond mere oversight of decree implementation and acted as fact-finder, mediator, manager, and planner. His expenses and time were reimbursed by court orders assessed against the defendants. Legislators objected to Nathan's fees when they exceeded the full-time salary of the governor.[10]

Special monitor Nathan, with the help of assistants, drafted a series of reports on the defendants' state of compliance. Negotiated decrees were issued throughout this period. In the process the monitor interpreted these decrees and refined their scope by setting the criteria for measuring compliance. The criteria changed over the years, even for the measurement of prison conditions and practices not subject to later consent decrees.

In his first report dated November 20, 1979, Nathan took a hard stand, reporting significant noncompliance by the defendants in all areas. Nathan expanded the scope of the remedial decrees in the second report (October 26, 1980) by bringing a nearby facility called "Building 2" under his scrutiny. In the third (December 31, 1980) and fourth (November 2, 1981) reports, Nathan indicated that "genuine and continuing cooperation" with the state correctional authorities was possible, yet GSP was still in substantial noncompliance.

However, by the fifth report (December 1, 1982) Nathan found substantial noncompliance and seemed less optimistic for reform. Defendants and their attorneys were argumentative and alleged that Nathan's change in standards and scope of remedies gave the appearance of noncompliance at GSP when conditions had actually improved. Nathan again found substantial noncompliance in the sixth report (December 1, 1983) and left GSP as special monitor with the recommendations that Judge Alaimo impose punitive coercive measures on the defendants.

Earlier in an order on July 14, 1982, Judge Alaimo promised a final injunctive order if substantial compliance was found in the special monitor's fifth report. He threatened "punitive coercive measures" (e.g., receivership or expansion of plaintiffs' counsel) if there was no substantial compliance. Although the monitor's fifth report was unfavorable, the judge imposed no punitive coercive measures.

Independent monitor Charles Bell was appointed by Judge Alaimo from February 1984 to June 1985, to follow the case to complete implementation. Bell served as an administrative hearing officer in equal employment opportunity cases in the Department of Corrections before working on *Guthrie* as a monitor. While plaintiffs' counsel expressed doubt about Bell's objectivity as a correctional employee, they consented to his appointment and later agreed that his report was "fair."

This perception of Bell's services as special monitor stemmed largely from the fact that Bell's approach differed markedly from Nathan's. Nathan would surprise the defendants and wait to notify them of potential problems with consent decree compliance. Specifically, he informed both the judge and the defendants in the official reports he was ordered to file with the federal court. In contrast, Bell would tell the defendants of any concerns or problems he observed and not wait until he issued his report to Judge Alaimo. Consequently, when Bell filed his report on June 1, 1985, there was no surprise with his finding of minimum compliance at the newly constructed Rogers Facility adjoining GSP.

With the receipt of Bell's report, Judge Alaimo made a surprise visit to Reidsville to view the conditions personally. He was impressed with the changes he observed and commented nostalgically about the improvements. Formally approving the report of monitor Bell, Judge Alaimo told the parties to prepare for the final permanent injunction. In a hurriedly called session in the GSP facilities on June 26, 1985, Judge Alaimo issued the final injunctive order in

Guthrie v. Evans. Alaimo enjoined the defendants from failing or
refusing to comply with all consent decrees and orders, specifying
the compendium of orders previously collected by Nathan as well as
other remedial decrees. He threatened that any failure would result
in court sanctions (e.g., contempt, fines) and kept plaintiffs' counsel
on for an additional year to monitor compliance with the permanent injunction. At the same time, Alaimo ordered the defendants
to pay the legal fees of the plaintiffs, subject to documentation and
the defendants' right to challenge, as well as the plaintiffs' fees for
the additional year of monitoring. Governor Harris commented,
"We are free now to operate George State Prison without federal
court intervention, although we are bound forever to the requirements agreed upon under *Guthrie.*"

During the year following the final injunction, plaintiffs' counsel
monitored compliance and pointed to a potential violation of *Guthrie*
orders in the death of an inmate, Ray Sharp. Sharp was trying to
escape from GSP when he was shot and killed by a guard. Judge
Alaimo, however, did not construe this as a violation of *Guthrie.*
During the same period, plaintiffs' counsel estimated that attorneys'
fees from 1978 through 1986 totaled in excess of three million dollars,
with slightly over one million dollars incurred prior to 1982. The
State of Georgia released official cost estimates of fifty-five million to
well over one hundred million dollars for the structural changes alone
that were completed pursuant to the Guthrie litigation.

The State Prison at Reidsville, however, looked and functioned
quite differently in 1986 from that featured in an earlier film, *The
Longest Yard.* In fact, the old prison, although still structurally
intact, was functionally replaced by new wings built from and
around the original ediface. Inmates were now single-celled and the
general population considerably reduced. Hundreds of staff were
fired and hired during the time period, and substantial improvements in the prison's sanitary, medical, legal, and recreational facilities were made. Regardless of one's perspectives on the role of the
federal court in the litigation, there was no question as to the
changes in Reidsville. By the end of 1986 it was indeed a new prison,
one that would be fully accredited by the American Correctional
Association in 1987.

What did the *Guthrie* litigation accomplish? Over its protracted
course, the *Guthrie* litigation appeared to have accomplished sev-

eral things. The class action suit prompted a wholesale rebuilding of the prison facility with the result that virtually all state authorities now proudly refer to Reidsville as a "constitutional prison." In fact, nearly all key decision makers in interviews stressed that this was the primary objective of the case. Included under the rubric of constitutional prison were single-cell living arrangements, up-to-date medical, sanitary, and custodial conditions, and nondiscriminatory procedures for prison disciplinary processes.

A less dramatic but equally important feature of a constitutional prison was the rational restructuring of correctional authority and operations. Under the scrutiny of the *Guthrie* litigation, the historical deference accorded to the warden gave way to a bureaucratic restructuring that put the prison squarely under the state's correctional authority. To be sure, Reidsville came under that central authority prior to *Guthrie*, but the litigation brought the traditional independence of the warden to an end. In the process, the conditions for staff changed dramatically too. Many guards and staff were fired for refusing to comply with the *Guthrie*-initiated changes, in a spirit of professionalization that seemed to be in keeping with Warden Newsome's preference and style. In fact, the professionalization of staff and the centralization of authority in the Department of Corrections seemed to be key to successful compliance with the *Guthrie* consent decrees and stipulations.

In summary, then, the protracted *Guthrie* litigation, although never proceeding to trial, resulted in sweeping changes in the maximum security Georgia State Prison at Reidsville. The pre-*Guthrie* prison with its overcrowded dormitory wings, segregated facilities, discriminatory proceedings, limited medical treatment, and poor sanitation systems gave way to a prison accredited by the American Correctional Association and held out as a model for the rest of the state. Of course, it is possible that the changes would have been forthcoming without federal court intervention. Given the state's historical reluctance to spend much money to improve prison facilities, however, it is, at the very least, doubtful. Equally obvious, perhaps, is the limited quality of such "what if" conjecture. The fact remains that the federal district court did intervene in the administration of the state's prison and that considerable change followed in the wake of that involvement.

Role of the Judge

Most of our knowledge of institutional reform litigation has depended on the opinions published by judges in institutional reform cases. The secondary literature surrounding these cases typically concentrates, then, on the personality of the judge.[11] Although some studies include details on judicial relations with public officials,[12] the existing literature focuses nearly all of its attention on judicial capacity, legtimacy, or managerial abilities. These sources provide an introduction and overview to institutional reform litigation but tend to narrow our focus on the judge as *the* key decision maker.

From this study of *Guthrie*, it is evident that there are many key decision makers in institutional reform litigation. They hold different positions, and not all of them are legally trained. To understand such litigation, then, it is necessary to look beyond the judge to the administrators, attorneys for both parties, and a variety of court-appointed personnel. It is true that at certain points in the *Guthrie* litigation Judge Alaimo did play a pivotal role in leading the case toward resolution, but these occasions were rare. More typically, he deferred resolution of the issues to the parties' attorneys in negotiated settlements or to court-appointed officials. In fact, the day-to-day control of the court-ordered mediation, hearings, and monitorship were placed almost entirely in the hands of court-appointed personnel, retrieved by Judge Alaimo only after he insisted on ending the litigation and after these other key decision makers acquiesced. To be sure, Judge Alaimo maintained a symbolic role throughout the litigation as a sort of catalyst[13] for change when mediation or negotiation failed as well as a scapegoat for criticism of the case by the media and public. But the litigation was actually driven by a larger set of key decision makers.

There were at least thirty-six key decision makers identified in *Guthrie* from archival and interview analysis. Of these, none were drawn from the large group of plaintiff inmates. Even the eponym of the lawsuit, Arthur S. Guthrie, quickly disappeared in the archives and the memory of those involved. Some key decision makers had no knowledge of Mr. Guthrie, although others remarked that they had heard Guthrie was "back in" the Georgia correctional system after a parole release from GSP. The lack of even one key decision-making plaintiff inmate directly affected by the changes from *Guthrie* dramatically illustrates how the polycentric institutional reform case differs from ordinary civil litigation. In ordinary civil litigation, cases depend on the decisions of the parties, especially the plaintiff.[14] Yet the plaintiff inmates in *Guthrie* were sometimes so invisible to the key decision makers that they complained for three years that they were not even informed of the progress on their own case.[15] In fact, the plaintiff inmates questioned whether plaintiffs' counsel was working for them or for the court, with the more aggressive inmates urging all others to ignore the lawsuit and make their own changes. "All the so-called do-gooders and the professionals are mere novices compared to the average convict, so if things are to change, we the inmates and convicts had better get in a position to insure that the changes will be for our benefit . . . not for the benefit of . . . some high-paid 'professional' criminologist."[16]

Included in the key decision makers in *Guthrie* were, then, the court, defendants' counsel, and plaintiffs' counsel. Court decision makers included Judge Alaimo as well as the mediator, a representative of the U.S. Department of Justice amicus curiae, one special master, the special monitor, and the independent monitor. Key defendants included the corrections commissioners, one assistant commissioner, two planners in the Governor's Office of Planning and Budget, six wardens at GSP, one executive assistant to the GSP wardens, and defendants' counsel.

During the fourteen years of the *Guthrie* litigation, various subgroups constituted different "triads" that included members of the court, plaintiffs' counsel, defendants, and their counsel. This gave the case a "generational effect," where parties implemented and monitored remedial decrees designed by earlier litigants in the case. Different generations of litigation teams would often have little knowledge of what earlier participants had done or even who had designed the remedial decree under review. Fourteen years of litigation, combined with this generational effect, appeared to cause Judge Alaimo and the few others who were with *Guthrie* in its entirety to completely forget earlier activities as well. For example, no key decision maker could recall Joseph Coggins II or remember that he had written the original complaint. And memories of the years at mediation were wistful at best ("[s]hould have let the mediation go on longer").

Additionally, over the course of the litigation, key decision makers in the same "part" played their roles differently. For example, while early defendants' counsel played the role of mediator, changes in the Georgia Attorney General's Office and a different assistant attorney general resulted in a more aggressive defense that threatened to go "all the way to the Supreme Court." The litigation strategies of mediation, pretrial discovery, hearings, negotiations, and implementation were marked by corresponding changes in plaintiffs' and defendants' counsel, defendants (wardens, commissioners, etc.), and court-appointed personnel. Although some scholars have noted the polycentric nature of institutional reform litigation,[17] they have focused on the large numbers of individuals affected at the conclusion of the litigation. This case study reveals that *Guthrie* was actually a set of separately staged lawsuits linked abstractly by a common concern with the conditions and practices at GSP. This generational effect may be unique to institutional reform litigation and may contribute to the protracted, complex, and highly stressful nature of this type of lawsuit.

The fast turnover of personnel seemed clearly due to "burnout" in most instances. Some personnel simply moved on from *Guthrie* to other, more attractive employment, but all key decision makers were affected by the intense pressure associated with the case. Litigation was extremely complex, growing from seven issues to over twenty-five hundred; it involved the coordination of many lives; and there was no relief in sight for most of its fourteen years. Relatedly, the "judicialization"[18] of procedures and practices at GSP prompted the aforementioned high turnover of officials and staff at the prison, many of whom found the remedial decrees too voluminous to assimilate even after they were condensed and published for all employees. Even the level of violence among inmates and between inmates and staff at GSP may have been associated with the lawsuit, according to several key decision makers. These respondents argued that the *Guthrie*-initiated change instituted a period of instability that resulted in even greater tension among inmates and between inmates and staff. Interestingly, some key decision makers believed there would have been less pressure and violence had the case simply gone to trial. Others speculated that these pressures may have played an important part in obtaining a permanent injunction from those tired of the fourteen-year lawsuit.

Budgetary Changes

Great interest has developed concerning the impact of federal court intervention in state prisons on state budgets. Early reviews of the law[19] claimed that there were strict constraints on federal judicial authority to direct the expenditure of state funds (i.e., for prison construction). However, more recent empirical assessments suggest that federal court orders may have an effect on state spending for prisons far beyond these limits.[20] Further, a survey of agency administrators in eight states indicates that this court intervention is changing the nature of state budgeting decisions.[21] In contrast, others argue that courts are merely the catalyst and handy scapegoats for long-overdue legislative expenditures on capital improvements in corrections.[22]

What did *Guthrie* cost? Of course, there is no simple answer to this query. At the time of Judge Alaimo's final permanent injunction, the newspapers estimated that over "$100 million worth of changes [were] made" during the fourteen-year litigation.[23] However, these figures included only the costs of structural changes made at GSP and not attorneys' fees, the fees of court-appointed personnel, and the time of and expense to the plaintiffs and defendants. Nor did these figures include the related costs of alternative correctional institutions built to house the inmates diverted by court order from the overcrowded GSP.

Some estimates of costs were available, however, from archival and focused interview data. Table 5.1 summarizes GSP budgets from FY1976 through FY1986. The dollar figures include both capital and non–capital expenditures at GSP during *Guthrie* (e.g., $410,000 for a new prison cannery in FY1978); most capital and non–capital expenditure—nearly all expenses at GSP—related in some way to the litigation. The aggregate cost, then, to the defen-

TABLE 5.1. Costs in *Guthrie*, FY1976–FY1986

Fiscal Year	Staff	Personal Services	Operating Expenses	Medical Costs	Subtotal	Cannery Operation	Capital Outlay	Legal and Court Costs	Total
FY1976	455	$ 4,710,681	$3,251,746	$ 194,689	$ 8,157,116	0	$ 375,000	$ 85,475	$ 8,617,591
FY1977	504	5,083,974	2,803,842	639,640	8,527,456	0	1,082,000	92,000	9,701,456
FY1978	524	5,911,645	3,793,872	1,274,719	10,980,236	0	583,925	137,990	11,702,151
FY1979	604	7,357,205	3,473,819	1,234,290	12,065,305	0	8,661,852	125,000	20,852,157
FY1980	619	8,119,770	3,634,336	1,519,380	13,273,486	$1,432,182	6,932,813	875,816	22,514,297
FY1981	624	9,058,240	4,435,738	2,447,325	15,941,303	1,859,810	21,881,390	191,780	39,874,283
FY1982	705	10,819,403	2,919,053	2,174,000	15,912,456	2,154,839	0	258,000	18,325,295
FY1983	953	12,810,655	4,400,651	2,511,435	19,722,741	2,066,132	8,555,100	300,000	30,643,973
FY1984	953	15,317,835	4,084,814	2,069,434	21,472,083	2,387,430	10,426,970	300,000	34,586,483
FY1985	1,058	17,430,365	4,289,055	2,172,906	23,892,326	2,400,000	0	200,000	26,492,326
FY1986	1,151	19,435,613	4,503,508	2,281,551	26,220,672	2,500,000	0	100,000	28,820,672

Source "Corrections Briefing Document: *Guthrie v. Evans* Lawsuit at Georgia State Prison" (Atlanta: Georgia Department of Corrections, 1982). Note that the figures for FY1984–FY1986 are estimates made in 1982.

dants (and the state of Georgia), exclusive of legal fees, was probably $249,656,383.00 over ten fiscal years (see table 5.1).

The fees involved in the court litigation of *Guthrie* included court filing fees, transcription and legal stenographic fees, plaintiffs' counsel fees, fees of court- and plaintiff-appointed expert witnesses, fees of court-appointed special masters and special monitors, travel expenses incurred by defendants' counsel, and extensive copying costs. The fees of defendants' counsel are not available, since the Georgia Attorney General's Office did not charge a fee of the defendant state. However, the involvement of several assistant attorneys general made legal and court costs to the defendant state substantial, even if not billed. The plaintiffs' counsel, the Legal Defense Fund, settled for 1972–79 attorneys fees of $650,000, although they documented $1,421,209 in expenses and fees through December 1979. Legal fees in the budget summaries prepared by Department of Corrections totaled $2,666,061 but do not include the final payments to (1) the Legal Defense Fund from 1980 to 1985 (est. $100,000); (2) Georgia Legal Services, Inc., from 1978 to 1986 (est. $3,300,000); and (3) special monitor Nathan's fees and expenses in 1982 (est. $600,000). These additional costs may have pushed the total costs of legal fees, excluding defendants' counsel costs, to over $6,666,061 for the fiscal years 1976 through 1987.

During this period of litigation, the cost of caring for inmates at GSP rose dramatically. This was at least partly due to spiraling inflation in the 1970s and early 1980s, which affected all Georgia correctional institutions. The average cost at all Georgia correctional institutions, including GSP, per inmate per day, went from nearly seven dollars in FY1972 to over thirty-one dollars by FY1985.[24] However, costs at GSP soared past this average rate of increase. From an average cost per inmate per day of six dollars in FY1972 (below the state average), GSP came to average nearly seventy dollars by FY1985, or more than double the state average of about thirty-one dollars. The differences in cost may be attributed to the mandates required by the remedial decrees in *Guthrie* but not directed at other Georgia correctional institutions. However, many key decision makers noted that these mandates were implemented at all other Georgia prisons and correctional officials maintained that all appropriate requirements of conditions and procedures in *Guthrie* were implemented at all facilities and not just GSP. There is, however, considerable controversy on this point.

The dramatic change in cost per inmate at GSP may be due to circumstances peculiar to the maximum security changes at GSP and to more general technological changes in prisons. From FY1972 to 1978, GSP was simply the largest prison in the state and housed the greatest number of inmates.[25] As the violence at GSP became more dramatic in the mid 1970s, and as decisions were made to tighten security, the number of inmates was drastically reduced. By FY1985, GSP had only 800 inmates and over 1,150 guards. Also, the latest technological devices for maximum security prisons were installed. This required new expertise in operations and also contributed to a decrease in inmate population. This reduction of inmates, then, accompanied by increases in guard, dietary, medical, mental health, and other personnel, contributed to increased costs at GSP. In addition, the maximum security monitoring devices installed throughout the prison involved new technologies that were expensive to acquire and maintain.

Did Judge Alaimo effect these budget changes in *Guthrie*? Cases comparable to *Guthrie* imply that judges may have some authority to order state funding to reform state institutions by threat of contempt citation or other equitable remedies (e.g., *Newman v. Alabama*, M.D. Ala., 1979). Similarly, others strongly imply that judges have the actual power to direct budgetary decisons.[26] With the exception of court costs and attorneys fees, however, Judge Alaimo never expressly ordered that state funds be appropriated for any items. All state capital and non–capital expenditures related to *Guthrie* were based on remedial decrees derived from negotiated stipulations of all parties and simply approved for the case record by the judge. To say, then, that the court "ordered" these changes is simply to note that Judge Alaimo formally approved the stipulations and consent decrees of both parties. Of course, the state of Georgia balked when ordered to pay over seventy thousand dollars in legal fees to the unpopular federal monitor, Vincent Nathan.[27] And the state was ordered to pay the plaintiffs' attorney fees for Sanford Bishop, the Legal Defense Fund, and Georgia Legal Services. But even these fees were arrived at after negotiated stipulations by all parties. The judge never used his equitable powers to order state funding for items other than these court costs.

Ramifications of the Remedial Litigation in *Guthrie*

In legal/remedial aspects, *Guthrie* is truly an exemplary case because so many alternative remedial strategies were incorporated in
its fourteen years. Like many prison institutional reform cases,
Guthrie began as an in forma pauperis brief by inmates seeking
class action status against the state for unconstitutional prison
conditions and practices. Also like these cases, *Guthrie* was resolved by the use of equitable remedies such as court-approved
consent decrees and stipulations. *Guthrie* included certain alternatives to civil litigation, specifically mediation, improved legal assistance to inmates, and inmate grievance procedures. Judge Alaimo
used the contempt citation once to enforce remedial decrees and
threatened to use receivership or other punitive measures if compliance was not achieved quickly. Special masters were appointed,
as was a special monitor, to assist the judge in overseeing the case.

Unlike many institutional reform cases, however, the decisions in
Guthrie were never appealed to a higher court. Judge Alaimo and
Governor Busbee were reputed to have agreed to settle the case
rather than continue to litigate to appeal. One can only speculate
on the "deal" between the governor and the judge, but there is some
indication that the arrangement gave the state more input in the
formulation of the remedial decrees in the case. The settlement of
the case by court-approved consent decrees and stipulations might
not have been possible had the state pursued full civil trial and
appeal. Although all key decision makers agreed that the case took
far too long to settle, all at GSP seemed content with the result. It
may be that Judge Alaimo foresaw that the state would not have
made long-lasting changes had he mandated them by judicial order
alone.

Although all parties to the *Guthrie* case appeared satisfied with
Judge Alaimo and the results, they were *not* in agreement during
the process of remedy formulation. The key decision makers disputed nearly each aspect of every consent decree and stipulation in
lengthy and intense negotiation sessions. In these negotiation sessions, extending intermittently from 1977 through 1985, defendants' counsel complained that the remedial decrees exceeded minimum constitutional standards. In the final analysis, however, the

defendant state stood behind the provisions of every order as its assented word.

How did plaintiff and defendant conceptions of the remedies enacted in *Guthrie* relate to the three theories of rights outlined at the beginning of this chapter? None of the key decision makers seemed to define an a priori or universally agreed on set of principles. Rather, the rights in *Guthrie* grew from an initial complaint that listed seven basic issues to over twenty-five hundred separate remedies relating to specific aspects of the inmates' lives at GSP (e.g., the temperature of various hot-food items by plus or minus ten degrees). In fact, these items were described and considered as "rights" in the aforementioned final analysis. Additionally, these remedial rights were culled from the plaintiffs' counsel in the process of negotiation, and not from concrete violations of specific rights by the defendants. Although the original complaint alluded to specific infractions of inmates' rights, the litigation was not limited to these infractions. Instead, the key decision makers tried to put the entire institution in constitutional terms, regardless of whether this involved a complaint of specific violations of rights.

Finally, the rights enumerated in *Guthrie* were not abstracted or deduced from value statements found in the U.S. Constitution or Supreme Court decisions. Rather, each seemed to relate inductively to a comparison between facts found elsewhere and at GSP. These facts were gathered by key decision makers in large part from the experiences of court-appointed experts who testified on proper prison sanitation, diet, security systems, and the like. The key decision makers in *Guthrie*, then, did not authoritatively apply the judicial opinions found in comparable appellate decisions or specific prison remedial decrees from other states. Nor did they agree to precisely what these facts meant or how they applied to *Guthrie*. Indeed, they never quite agreed on what constituted a constitutional prison but uniformly referred to the dynamic, changing nature of constitutional conditions and practices related to confinement. In the process, certain rights were modified and compromised to reach an appropriate strategy for the maximum security prison. In the end, however, nearly all key decision makers agreed that GSP was a maximum security prison that complied minimally with constitutional standards.

The practice of rights in *Guthrie*, then, suggested that key decision makers thought of inmates' rights as a "half-understood, half-hunch" set of behaviors that were not authoritatively directed by policy outcomes or by previous judicial opinions. Judge Alaimo did not singularly discover or announce basic constitutional principles to direct the outcome of the case or exercise power over participants to shape a policy direction and outcome. Instead, he participated with other key decision makers who fiercely disputed, but ultimately agreed upon a set of specific procedures and conditions for the day-to-day operation of Reidsville.

Guthrie, then, was not driven by the substance (principles), nature (specified or process), or authoritative will (policy) embedded in any of its remedial decrees. Rather, the remedial decrees served as a shorthand for the hard-won consent and stipulations negotiated by the parties. The social practice of rights embedded in the persons and personalities of the key decision makers, more than any other variable, seemed to "drive" the litigation to its ultimate resolution.

This does not imply that other theories about the nature of rights are irrelevant. It only suggests that the behavior of rights in *Guthrie* was not driven by a perception of rights as either principle or policy. Rather, this study of *Guthrie* reveals that practitioners focused their attention on the structure and practical physical details in renovating GSP, the "state of the art" in maximum security prison facilities, and regulations copied from other prison systems. In the final analysis, the remedial decrees as crafted and implemented were justified by their persuasiveness to all parties, who consented to, stipulated to, or approved them. The key decision makers in *Guthrie* closed the dispute by reference to a practice of maximum security prison operations modeled on other successful designs and advocated by experts for such institutions.

Conclusion

To return to the two central questions we posed at the outset, let us briefly summarize the practical and theoretical ramifications of the institutional reform litigation in question. Practically, GSP was transformed by negotiated consent decrees and stipulations into a constitutional prison. In more concrete terms, the overcrowded, run-down, violent, and poorly managed maximum security prison was rebuilt and restructured into the modern, single-cell, relatively safe, ACA-accredited institution it is today.

In contrast to the more pathological studies of institutional reform litigation that highlight the failures of federal court intervention, this case study illustrates the salutary impact of one federal court's involvement in state administration. To be sure, Judge Alaimo did not act in imperial judicial fashion, harshly imposing his will on reluctant and recalcitrant state officials. GSP was transformed by negotiated consent decrees and stipulations, and not by a single judicial mandate. This relative success suggests that institutions are more likely to be permanently changed by an approach that is not adversarial in the typical trial sense of the term. This assumes, of course, that consensus does emerge during the extended process of negotiation and that the institutions have or receive the necessary wherewithal to implement the specified reforms. Obviously, these assumptions cannot be taken for granted and indeed may override the aforementioned potential of the litigation strategy exemplified in *Guthrie.*

This study of the *Guthrie* litigation raises two interesting theoretical issues related to the nature and theory of rights. As explained earlier, the lists of remedies that were outlined in the course of *Guthrie v. Evans* and that prevailed at its conclusion in 1986 totaled approximately twenty-five hundred specific items. These ranged from single-cell provisions to the temperature of meat served at meals. As explained earlier, these remedies did not develop out of a preconceived concept of prisoner or prison rights, nor were they mandated in a judicially crafted corrections policy. Rather they emerged in the course of the extended litigation.

During and at the close of the litigation, many of the participants referred to these specific remedies as "rights"; indeed, in the final analysis these specific remedies were regarded as essential to the prevailing concept of a "constitutional prison." If the *Guthrie* consent decree is used as a model in other states (and there is already some evidence that it will be), then this confusion of remedies and rights may well carry over into the general arena of correctional law. In this sense, the litigation and its resulting solution will have ramifications that go beyond the confines of Reidsville.

In the general legal order, rights are understood as meaningful when they are made real in the detail of specific remedies. In the *Guthrie* litigation, however, particular remedies seemed to assume a life and identity of their own and, to some degree, to carry the status more typically reserved to the broader concept of rights. Although all participants in the litigation agreed that their ultimate aim was the structure and operation of a constitutional prison, not all would agree that inmates have a right to a specific meat temperature. Yet specific remedies were frequently interpreted as essential to the right to a constitutional prison and were included with little or no discrimination as to lesser or greater importance.

This confusion of remedy and right has been observed by other students of institutional reform or extended-impact litigation. In 1981, for example, the *Harvard Law Review* noted that "[t]he tendency in complex enforcement is for remedies to become part of the substantive law, as 'rights' in themselves, or more generally, as the normative criteria by which a system's lawfulness is judged."[28] In a more recent work, Low and Jeffries explore this relationship between right and remedy and argue that in prison reform litigation, courts strive to give meaning to the Eighth Amendment right against cruel and unusual punishment or, more specifically, conditions of imprisonment.[29] As Low and Jeffries explain, this right is typically set at a high level of abstraction with the result that over time remedies assume an identity of their own and are asserted independently of the initial umbrella right.[30]

To some degree this confusion of remedy with right at the trial level evokes the blurring of right and privilege at the appellate level. In frequently cited decisions (e.g., *Goldberg v. Kelley* on the civil side and *Morrissey v. Brewer* on the criminal), the Supreme Court expanded the concept of right and the corresponding due process provisions. Along with other developments in law and society, these seem to represent an expansion of the concept of right with the result that it is sometimes difficult to distinguish it from privilege.

With regard to the theoretical ramification, it is possible to argue that appellate courts in blurring the distinction between right and privilege have operated out of a set of principles that they regard as preconceived or that they have preferred. In short, they have approached constitutional lawmaking as a Judge Hercules or Judge Herbert. Dworkin's rights theory or the more policy-focused interpretations, then, may help to explain constitutional decision making in the appellate arena. In the trial court arena, especially in those cases that do not proceed to trial, the social practice theory of rights seems to offer more potential. As previously outlined, the *Guthrie* case offers a good illustration as the final list of over twenty-five hundred remedies/rights evolved over the course of the fourteen-year litigation while the participants struggled to come to terms with the demands of a constitutional prison.

In summary, the theoretical lessons of the Guthrie case, albeit limited by the single-case focus, may prove to be more far reaching than the substantial practical changes that took place at Reidsville. If trial courts continue to identify remedies with rights, and if these remedies/rights are crafted in the slow, sometimes tortuous, and lengthy negotiations illustrated by *Guthrie*, constitutional theorists will have to struggle not only with an expansive blurring of the concept of right but also with the possibility that different theories are necessary to illuminate constitutionally related decision making at the trial and appellate levels.

Notes

1. Lon L. Fuller, "The Forms and Limits of Adjudication," *Harvard Law Review* 92 (1978), 353–409.
2. Stuart A. Scheingold, *The Politics of Rights: Lawyers, Public Policy, and Political Change* (New Haven: Yale University Press, 1974).
3. Ronald Dworkin, *Taking Rights Seriously* (Cambridge: Harvard University Press, 1978); and Ronald Dworkin, *A Matter of Principle* (Cambridge: Harvard University Press, 1985).
4. John Rawls, *A Theory of Justice* (Cambridge: Belknap Press, 1971).
5. Dworkin, *A Matter of Principle.*
6. David A. J. Richards, "Rules, Policies, and Neutral Principles: The Search for Legitimacy in Common Law and Constitutional Adjudication," *Georgia Law Review* 11 (1977), 1069–1114.
7. Dworkin, *Taking Rights Seriously*, p. 345.
8. Richard E. Flathman, *The Practice of Rights* (Cambridge, Eng.: Cambridge University Press, 1976), pp. 6, 17.
9. Ellen Joan Pollock, "Q: What's a Toledo Lawyer Doing in a Georgia Prison? A: Running It," *The American Lawyer* 5 (1983), 97–99.
10. Marc R. Levinson, "Special Masters: Engineers of Court-Ordered Reform," *Corrections Magazine* 8 (1982), 6–18.

11. Robert F. Kennedy, Jr., *Judge Frank M. Johnson, Jr.: A Biography* (New York: G. P. Putnam's Sons, 1978).
12. Tinsley E. Yarbrough, *Judge Frank M. Johnson and Human Rights in Alabama* (University: University of Alabama Press, 1981).
13. Colin S. Diver, "The Judge as Political Powerbroker: Superintending Structural Change in Public Institutions," *Virginia Law Review* 65 (1979), 43–106.
14. David M. Trubeck, Joel B. Grossman, William L. F. Felstiner, Herbert M. Kritzer, and Austin Sarat, *Civil Litigation Research Project Final Report*, 3rd ed. (Madison, Wisc.: Disputes Processing Research Program, 1987).
15. Chinyelu Lumumba, "Greetings Friend: What Happened to Guthrie Suit," *Clearinghouse on Georgia Prisons and Jails* (January 4, 1979), 1.
16. Anonymous, "Prison Union Notes," Georgia State Prison (January 5, 1978).
17. Fuller, *The Forms and Limits of Adjudication*, op. cit.
18. David H. Rosenbloom, "The Judicialization of Public Administration and the Ungoverning of the United States," presented at the annual meeting of the American Society for Public Administration, New York, 1983.
19. Comment, "Enforcement of Judicial Financing Orders: Constitutional Rights in Search of a Remedy," *Georgetown Law Journal* 59 (1970), 393.
20. Linda Harriman and Jeffrey D. Straussman, "Do Judges Determine Budget Decisions? Federal Court Decisions in Prison Reform and State Spending for Corrections," *Public Administration Review* 43 (1983) 343–51.
21. George E. Hale, "Federal Courts and the State Budgetary Process," *Administration and Society* 11 (1979), 357–68.
22. Kathryn Moss, "The Catalytic Effect of a Federal Court Decision on a State Legislature," *Law and Society Review* 19 (1985) 147–57; William A. Taggart, "The Impact of Court-Ordered Prison Reform on State Expenditures for Corrections," presented at the annual meeting of the Academcy of Criminal Justice Science, Orlando, Florida, 1986.
23. *Florida Times Union*, June 6, 1985 and Atlanta *Constitution*, June 27, 1985.
24. *Annual Report of the Georgia Department of Offender Rehabilitation* (Atlanta: Department of Offender Rehabilitation, 1972–85).
25. Ibid.
26. Harriman and Straussman, "Do Judges Determine Budget Decisions;" Hale, "Federal Courts and the State Budgetary Process."

27. Ellen Joan Pollock, "Q: What's a Toledo Lawyer Doing in a Georgia Prison? A: Running It."

28. Note, "Complex Enforcement: Unconstitutional Prison Conditions," *Harvard Law Review* 94 (1981), 626–46.

29. Peter W. Low and John Calvin Jeffries, Jr., *Civil Rights Actions: Section 1983 and Related Statutes* (Westbury, N.Y.: Foundation Press, 1988).

30. Ibid., p. 682.

6

When Intervention Works: Judge Morris E. Lasker and New York City Jails

TED S. STOREY

In 1970 inmates in New York City's most decrepit jail, known as the Tombs, filed a class action suit against New York City alleging that they were being held in unconstitutional conditions of confinement. Nineteen years later, all but one of New York City's pretrial detention facilities remained under the supervision of the federal court and subject to consent decrees. The purpose of this chapter is to chronicle and evaluate the impact of the federal court's intervention on the city's correctional system.[1]

The Pre-Intervention Setting

In 1966 John V. Lindsay was beginning the first of his two terms as mayor of New York City. That same year, George F. McGrath was appointed commissioner of correction by Mayor Lindsay. McGrath replaced the respected and legendary Anna M. Kross, who had retired after presiding over the Department of Correction for twelve years. McGrath took over a jail system that was comprised of nine separate correctional facilities designed to house a total of about 7,400 inmates.[2] When McGrath was sworn in, the jails were already ailing as the inmate population was 10,338—some 40 percent over the system's rated capacity.[3]

McGrath, as head of the New York City Department of Correction (DOC), had primary control over the city's correctional complex. As a political appointee, he was formally answerable only to the mayor. McGrath was a basically humane and progressive-minded "jails man." But his ability to manage the system as he wished was severely limited.

As in most big cities, jails in New York City received little political and financial support. Historically, jails had been last on the city's public agenda and were used as a human dumping ground. In essence, the jail system's "clients" consisted of citizens detained or incarcerated for crimes, many of them poor, drug-dependent, and mentally ill "problem people" whom the city's law enforcement, social welfare, and mental health agencies would not, or could not, handle.

Over the years, however, the city's jail system did attract the attention and support of a few state and local policymakers. In the 1960s, for example, State Senator John R. Dunne was a strong ally of the city's jail system. In 1967 Dunne became chairman of the Senate Committee on Penal Institutions.[4] But neither his involvement, nor that of the few other well-placed champions of improving the quality of life inside the city's jails, was sufficient to raise corrections from its historic "no-priority" status.

Conditions behind bars in New York City worsened rapidly after McGrath became commissioner. When McGrath was appointed commissioner, Lindsay gave him a mandate to bring the jail population under control. In 1968 McGrath embarked the DOC on a major jail construction program which cost about seventy-three million dollars. The construction program added two major facilities and expanded an existing facility. Construction for the first facility began in 1968. The construction program netted the city about 1,800 additional beds when the final phase was completed in

1972.[5] Meanwhile, however, by 1969 the city's jails were bursting with about 14,000 inmates in facilities designed to hold 7,993.[6]

The worst of the city's jails was the Manhattan House of Detention for Men (MHD), which was built in the complex housing Manhattan's criminal courts as well as the DOC's headquarters. MHD, beter known as the Tombs, in 1969 held an average of 2,000 men in facilities designed for 925.[7] The Tombs was so overcrowded that about half of its inmates were being housed three men to a one-person cell.[8] A survey, taken by a Manhattan congressman, Edward I. Koch,[9] revealed that the third man in a cell had to sleep on the cement floor; nine out of ten times he did not even get a mattress or a blanket until after a few days, and many had to wait a week. A large portion of the survey's respondents also complained about the presence of rats, roaches, and body lice as well as a severe shortage of soap.[10] The survey findings led jail supporters to use the rallying cry "One man, one mattress."[11]

Koch, of course, could not have foreseen that ten years later similar though less harsh complaints would be directed at his administration. The problems at the Tombs and the rest of the system did not suddenly appear in 1970, and the findings were not news to McGrath and the DOC. Despite the severe problems facing the DOC, including a 30 percent population increase, its fifty-million-dollar operating budget was cut by about 5 percent in 1969.[12]

The city had already sought and obtained some help from the state in easing its overcrowding problems. In 1968 the New York State Legislature, in an effort to help the city, enacted a law authorizing the state commissioner of correction to lease space in state prisons to counties or cities for housing sentenced male inmates.[13] In contrast to the city, the state's prison population was substantially under capacity. State facilities had about seven thousand vacancies that could be used to alleviate the city's overcrowded facilities.[14] The city already had been transferring sentenced women inmates to state facilities since 1966. In August 1969 the state agreed to take one thousand city-sentenced misdemeanants into its prison system.[15]

Although the August 1969 transfer of inmates provided relief to the city's jails, it proved only temporary as the jail population in late fall again rose to nearly fourteen thousand. In November, the State Senate's Committee on Penal Institutions issued a report assailing the jails of New York City and upstate New York. The report, based on a nine-month inquiry, said "intense overcrowding, inadequate personnel and poorly designed facilities have resulted in turning detention facilities into settings less humane than our public zoos."[16] A month later the committee's chairman, Senator John R. Dunne, met with Mayor Lindsay and Commissioner McGrath to discuss ways of alleviating the crisis.

In an atmosphere of crisis, Dunne, Lindsay, and McGrath met. Senator Dunne agreed to urge the state to take twenty-five hundred additional city inmates as soon as possible. Dunne also promised to work on legislation that would transfer responsibility to the state for all city-sentenced prisoners, that is, misdemeanants as well as felons. In return for Dunne's assistance, McGrath promised to immediately initiate an intensive search for additional short-term detention facilities within the city.[17] The only effort in that direction McGrath and his department made was inspection of the one facility that was specifically proposed at the meeting. DOC found the facility unacceptable and did not look any further. DOC seemed unable to take the initiative in solving its own problems. A State Senate report later characterized McGrath's response to the December City Hall emergency meeting as "inadequate, and [it] demonstrated a serious lack of concern for the problem. . . . Response to that meeting appeared typical of the priority correction matters received in New York City."[18]

The city's inability to effect meaningful reform in the jails was not a new problem. Traditionally, corrections was a third-class citizen in the hierarchy of city government, which is why quasi-independent oversight organizations were developed to act as a check and a conscience on the city's treatment of inmates. On the state level, the Commission of Correction had the power and duty to visit and inspect all local and state correctional facilities.[19] Specifically, the commission had statutory power to "[c]lose any jail . . . which is unsafe, unsanitary or . . . which has not adhered to or complied with the rules or regulations promulgated . . . by the state commission of correction."[20] Additionally, under section 48 of the Correctional Law, the commission could request the commissioner of correction to apply for an order from the state supreme court[21] directing an institution to remedy any item not meeting minimum standards.

Despite periodic reports by the commission citing the over-crowded conditions in the city's jail system, and specifically conditions in the Tombs, which did not meet state minimum standards, the commission did not use its statutory powers. The commission's reports dismissed the substandard conditions as necessary incidents of overcrowding. Later, the Senate committee report on the Tombs riots found that the commission had "been lax in its responsibility by failing to utilize the powers it possessed to compel the City to correct the overcrowding and inhumane conditions in its institutions."[22]

Commissioner McGrath and Mayor Lindsay also received criticism from the New York City Board of Correction. The Board of Correction is an unsalaried public body appointed by the mayor and has statutory authority to visit the city's jails.[23] It was intended to serve as an independent citizen's oversight organization to ensure the interests of inmates were being served by the city. For over ten years prior to the litigation, the board urged the mayors of New York, in often elaborate and detailed annual reports, to place a high priority on finding solutions to the overcrowding problem.[24] However, in 1967 McGrath spoke in favor of dismantling the board because it interfered with his department. Venting his frustrations from the board's criticism of DOC, McGrath said: "The City Charter provides for a built-in board to frustrate a city function. . . . [T]hese are citizens with no expertise. The city is full of people who are running around with badges and shields interfering with the orderly process of government. . . . [I]t's abominable."[25] Mayor Lindsay, although more subtle with his criticism, seemed to agree with McGrath about the board.

Consequently, Lindsay and McGrath continued to ignore the board's repeated warnings about potentially explosive conditions in the jails. In a letter to the major dated February 16, 1970, the board stated: "Once again your attention is directed to our previous reports, many of whose recommendations remain valid and still await implementation. As you are aware, the problem of over-crowding continues to be consistently high, undesirable and dangerous."[26] Six months later the jails erupted into riots. In fact, only three weeks before the August disturbances at the Tombs, a representative of another oversight organization, the Correctional Association of New York, met with McGrath to advise him about conditions inside the Tombs. The Correctional Association had received confidential information concerning a buildup of tension among inmates, and at this meeting McGrath was warned of the possibility of trouble at the Tombs.[27]

One of the few warnings or threats the city did listen to was that of the Correction Officers' Benevolent Association. In the summer of 1969 the union warned the city of dangerous conditions at the jails, but the warnings at first went unheeded. In February 1970, however, as conditions deteriorated, union members initiated what became an occasional informational picket at City Hall and also threatened a work slowdown.[28] As one corrections administrator said, "The correction officers were not looking for a raise in pay, they were not looking for more time off, they were not looking for any privileges—all they wanted was to improve the conditions in the prisons."[29] In response to the union's protests, the city began working with the courts in an effort to speed up the time it took to process or dispose of cases.

The union's action reflected best, perhaps, the failure of the political process to respond to the jail crisis. This ironic twist in the political process was noted perceptively in a New York *Times* editorial: "[I]t is a bizarre reflection on the democratic system that a group of unionized municipal employees had to come to the edge of an illegal action under the Taylor no-strike law to impel the community to take this much-needed step toward improved law enforcement."[30] While "bizarre," it was also indicative of the way New York City would handle the jail situation throughout the first decade of the litigation that was to come.

On the morning of August 10, 1970, inmates at the Tombs overpowered guards supervising breakfast and secured control of the ninth floor. Five guards were held for eight hours. The crisis ended when inmates were allowed to present their grievances to the press and the Mayor's Office, and when Commissioner McGrath pledged that no reprisals would be taken against them. The list of grievances included charges of brutality, racism, bad food, overcrowding, and lengthy pretrial detention time.[31] McGrath responded to the charges: "The ironic thing is that most of what they say I have said many times over the past months. . . . The institution is abominably overcrowded."[32] The day the siege began, the Tombs housed 1,992 men—more than twice its official capacity.

The jail was so understaffed that many of the guards were working sixteen-hour days.

Leo C. Zeferetti, president of the Correction Officers Benevolent Association, complained that the guards felt as victimized as the inmates by crowded and unsanitary conditions at the Tombs. The guards were frustrated by a staff shortage and a scaled-down training program for new guards. Said one guard: "For weeks we've been telling the wardens that something was going to happen. . . . But nothing was ever done. In a way, this whole thing has a good side. Now the public is aware of how bad the situation is inside."[33] A New York *Times* editorial recognized the guards' complaints as validating inmates' grievances but noted, "The trouble is that no basic reform ever follows the official recognition of the long train of abuses. . . ."[34] But this time inmates asked the federal court to intervene and order reform, so the city could not let more promises of corrections reform fade away.

One month after the riots at the Tombs, on September 10, 1970, New York City's Legal Aid Society (LAS) filed a class action in federal court on behalf of pretrial detainees at the Tombs, who made up more than 90 percent of its population. The lawsuit was not filed in direct response to the August riots; rather, it had been in the planning stages since March.[35] Within a thirty-day period, corrections in New York City became a high-profile subject and its third-class standing moved up a notch. In October inmates in the Brooklyn and Queens jails, as well as the Tombs, erupted into riots more severe and widespread than the August disturbances, and once again corrections was in the headlines. The restrictive measures and brutality used against the inmates at the Queens House of Detention following the October riots caused LAS in November 1970 to file a class action on behalf of the Queens inmates.[36]

The Intervention: Trials and Tribulations

The Tombs lawsuit originally was known as *Rhem v. McGrath*, but when McGrath was replaced as commissioner by Benjamin Malcolm in January 1972, the case became known as *Rhem v. Malcolm*.[37] *Rhem* was only the first of many lawsuits LAS would file on behalf of pretrial detainees in New York City's correctional system. Eventually six other actions were filed on behalf of detainees in the system's major facilities.[38] In 1979, after consent decrees were signed for each action, the cases were consolidated under the supervision of Judge Morris Lasker in New York's Southern District. Until then, each was treated as a separate action, and two were even in separate jurisdictions as both Queens and Brooklyn are in the Eastern District of New York, whereas Manhattan and the Bronx are in the Southern District.[39]

During the time between the filing of *Rhem* in 1970 and the signing of the consent decrees in 1979, the litigation went through many phases. Three different mayoral administrations held office during this period, and each handled the litigation differently.

Under Lindsay, the DOC's budget was increased, and it was given a mandate to increase inmate programs to help ease confinement conditions and stress. Benjamin Malcolm was hired from the State Parole Department to be executive first deputy to Commissioner McGrath; he was responsible for implementing new inmate programs. A little over a year later, in January 1972, Malcolm replaced McGrath as commissioner of correction.[40] However, while some substantive improvements were made at the Tombs and other facilities, many of the improvements reported to the court were merely cosmetic.[41]

Late in the summer of 1972 Judge Morris E. Lasker was drawn as presiding judge for the *Rhem* trial. He had been a federal judge in the district court for almost four years and was known to be concerned with prison issues. This boded well for the plaintiffs. LAS attorney Joel Berger recalled, "From the moment Lasker was drawn as the judge for our trial, the City was very anxious to talk to us real quick."[42] At LAS's first meeting, the city was represented by its top lawyer, corporation counsel Norman Redlich,[43] by the mayor's counsel Michael Dontzin, and by the city's lead litigation attorney. At that first meeting, Berger got the message that the city wanted to talk and did not want to go to trial.

As a result of the negotiations, in January 1973, just before trial, plaintiffs and the city entered into a stipulation of settlement in regard to some issues raised in the *Rhem* complaint, including overcrowding, unsanitary conditions, and inadequate medical care.[44] Berger thought it was particularly fortunate that they were able to talk the city into settling some of the lawsuit but letting the rest go to trial. It made the trial more manageable and yet still allowed the inmates to legitimate their cause through the courts.

Plaintiffs' general legal complaints were similar to those in other jail litigation being argued around the country at that time. They argued that their incarceration at the Tombs "(1) violates due process because, as unconvicted detainees, they are entitled to but are not being held under the least restrictive conditions necessary to assure . . . appearance at trial; (2) violates the equal protection clause because . . . they are held in undeniably harsher conditions than convicted prisoners and (3) violates the Eighth Amendment, because those conditions . . . constitute cruel and unusual punishment."[45] The city contended that it was necessary for the detainees to be held in maximum security and therefore the conditions, given the character of the Tombs, were constitutionally justified.[46] In January 1974 Lasker ruled in favor of the inmates on all points.[47]

The year after the decision was a tumultuous one. Abraham Beame was just beginning his term as mayor of New York when Lasker's decision came down, and nobody knew what to expect from Beame. There had been a general feeling that Lindsay was concerned with the jail problem and that the people involved with Lindsay's administration had a strong sense of civic duty. But according to Berger, "That spirit did not exist during the Beame years. I suspect that if Lindsay had remained mayor for a third term, the next four years would have been different with respect to corrections, notwithstanding the budget crisis. The Beame administration was really hostile towards corrections."[48] Benjamin Malcolm concurred with Berger. Malcolm thought that if Lindsay had stayed on as mayor after 1974, Lindsay would have settled *Rhem.*

There was also a significant change in the corporation counsel when Beame took office. Adrian Burke was Beame's first corporation counsel and W. Bernard Richland succeeded Burke shortly into Beame's term. The corporation counsel suffered a decrease in funding and support and the office declined severely during Beame's term.[49] Under Beame, the corporation counsel did not have the same support and influence as Redlich did under Lindsay. Malcolm was one of the few top officials to survive the transition from Lindsay to Beame. But as Malcolm recalled, "I wasn't even Beame's first choice for Commissioner, but community pressure made him reappoint me." As a result, Malcolm felt he had absolutely no mandate to carry out *Rhem* or anything else at DOC.[50]

At the beginning, Lasker did not have any particular philosophical approach to the *Rhem* litigation. If anything, his approach was pragmatic. He was concerned mainly with concentrating on the particular complaints and legal issues, most of which were fairly new at the time. Lasker's views on the allocation of political responsibility and the role of the court developed gradually and with experience. But even as he wrote the first *Rhem* opinion, Lasker's views began to take shape. Basically, Lasker believed that such litigations as *Rhem* intruded on political decision making, but he also thought that the court had a clear duty to act when there were deprivations of constitutional rights. Lasker later reflected, "The legislature and executive are without question better equipped to handle these matters. They have more power, funds, and experience."[51]

Although many courts do try to fashion specific remedies in institutional reform cases, Judge Lasker did not. Lasker wanted to demonstrate that he did not view the court's role as that of a policymaker, and he took care to distinguish the court's role from the city government's role in supervising the jails. Lasker wrote that the state of affairs at the jail existed because the public through its government had not assumed its responsibilities: "Courts are the agency which must enforce the execution of public responsibilities when other branches fail to do so: 'courts sit not to supervise prisons but to enforce the constitutional rights of all "persons," including prisoners' (*Cruz v. Beto*, 405 U.S. 319 [1972])."[52] Lasker, in a later opinion, repeated that quote from *Cruz* to emphasize that he did not want to tell the city how to run its jails, but he just wanted to ensure that the jails were being run within constitutional limits.

After the *Rhem* decision, the city took an even more adversarial and hostile approach toward the litigation. The reason for this hard-line stance can be attributed to several factors. First, Beame took office the same month *Rhem* came down and his administration had no interest in the city's jails. Also, the city's nationally publicized fiscal problems began approaching crisis proportions, and the fiscal crisis became not just a top priority but the only priority. Finally, the attorneys handling the case in the corporation counsel's office, and one in particular, strongly believed in the principle they were defending. They seemed to believe that Judge Lasker was interfering with the authority of the administration and that the jails were in adequate condition.[53]

The Beame administration's approach to city services during the fiscal crisis stressed survival. Corrections was at the bottom of any agenda. Beame's administration ignored both the consent decree signed by Lindsay and Lasker's orders in *Rhem*. According to Benjamin Malcolm, the city's decision to stonewall was based on the fact that there was no money:

> Their standard phrase was, "Ben, we ain't got no money." For example: I had a block of money to enlarge the kitchen at the Tombs. I went to Deputy Mayor Cavanagh and said that I would like to switch this money and use it to begin contact visits. He asked where I got the money, and I said it was in my budget. He said that he would rather give it to the sanitation department than the prisons. I wouldn't say they were insensitive, but I would say that it just wasn't one of their priorities. It never was the whole time. . . . Even when things did not cost much, Beame was unresponsive.[54]

Malcolm thought it was deplorable that the consent decree was ignored by the administration: "Lasker could have had us all in contempt, but being the compassionate person he is, he did not."[55]

Donald Tobias was an assistant corporation counsel who worked primarily on the jail cases during this time, and his view of the city's strategy during the Beame administration was different from that of Malcolm. Tobias said the city did not stonewall but rather it handled the litigation as any law department would: it was aggressive and fought every order of the judge because Lasker was going too far.[56] "[The] federal judiciary was well meaning, but it did not have expertise to make specific regulations. It should have been done by elected officials. . . . It wasn't a question of the City condoning inhumane conditions, but it was a question of who was best suited to deal with the jails."[57] The fiscal crisis did create pressures for the litigation, including a pared-down legal team. However, according to Tobias, the city never argued that the fiscal crisis was a defense to unconstitutional conditions.[58] Joel Berger complained that Tobias and the corporation counsel never understood that after the Second Circuit affirmed Lasker's decision the lawyers' work was done, the legal issues were over with, and it was time to comply with the court.[59]

LAS responded to the city's stonewalling by picking up the pace of the litigation. LAS lawyers put as much pressure on the city as they could, because LAS felt the city would get a break anyway because of the fiscal crisis. Berger recalled: "We tried to put a full court press on the City. . . . I got complaints from City officials, formally and informally, that we should ease off the City, that we are all in this together, and that if the City goes bankrupt, things will be even worse for everyone, including the inmates."[60] Berger, though, is convinced that if it were not for the litigation, conditions in the jails during the fiscal crisis would have descended to a level below what they were during the 1970 riots. According to Berger, "They would have strangled the Department of Correction."[61]

In a July 1974 memorandum, six months after his decision was handed down, Judge Lasker summed up the city's lack of cooperation: "The history of the case . . . has been one of frustration largely caused by the City defendant's delay and the absence or incompleteness of reports or plans of performance which they were ordered to submit. . . ."[62] Four years had passed since the riots at the Tombs, and its dismal conditions still existed. Lasker ordered the Tombs to be closed in thirty days unless the city produced a comprehensive plan for immediate elimination of the unconstitutional conditions there.[63] In Fall 1974 the city appealed Judge Lasker's order to close the Tombs to the Second Circuit, which quickly affirmed Lasker's decision.[64]

A week after the Second Circuit's decision, on November 15, 1974, the city announced that instead of making improvements, it would close the Tombs. Lasker was surprised: "I didn't realize how much the City was stonewalling until even after I issued the order to comply or close down the Tombs. . . . I fully thought they would comply."[65] Lasker did not regret his decision, but he wished the city had acted sooner to remodel the Tombs. Lasker noted, "It lay idle for years and could have been used by the City if they put some money into it. But that was during the fiscal crisis, and they weren't about to spend a nickel on a jail then."[66]

The Tombs was officially shut down on December 20, 1974, more than four years after *Rhem v. Malcolm* was first filed.[67] The remaining inmates, numbering almost four hundred, were transferred to the House of Detention for Men (HDM) on Rikers Island. The case, however, did not close along with the Tombs. Unfortunately, but not unexpectedly, conditions at HDM were not much better than at the Tombs. Accordingly, after a motion for relief by the plaintiffs, followed by several days of hearings and a couple of court visits to HDM, Judge Lasker held that plaintiffs transferred from the Tombs were entitled to the same constitutional standard pronounced in *Rhem* wherever they were confined.[68] This decision was soon affirmed by the Second Circuit.[69]

When LAS learned that the city would follow Lasker's orders only for the *Rhem* inmates transferred from the Tombs, it filed *Benjamin v. Malcolm*[70] in June 1975 on behalf of all detainees housed at HDM. As in *Rhem*, the complaint in *Benjamin* alleged that the conditions under which plaintiffs were being held were constitutionally impermissible.[71] It cited decrepit physical conditions in the cells and common areas, overcrowding, lack of decent sanitation, unbearable noise levels, obstacles to visiting by detainees' families and attorneys, inadequate recreational facilities, excessive idleness and in-cell time, and inadequate food service.

The jail situation grew extremely tense following the closing of the Tombs and the filing of *Benjamin*. In 1975 New York City's fiscal crisis reached its apex as the city was on the brink of bankruptcy. HDM on Rikers Island was overcrowded, and the city kept a preliminary injunction for relief at HDM tied up on appeal during the summer of 1975 for as long as it could.[72] In fall 1975 inmates at HDM rioted; it was one of the worst inmate riots New York City had seen. Inmates took over seven of the eight cellblocks at HDM and took hostages. Malcolm and his men negotiated through the night. Lasker came out to Rikers during the night and talked to the inmates at their request. Malcolm eventually settled with the inmates and was able to avoid bloodshed. But the following morning Malcolm's officers walked out and demanded to meet with him. The officers thought Malcolm had given in to the inmates: "One officer stepped up and asked me if the decisions were made by me, the Board of Corrections or the Judge. I said that they were all mine and they went back to work. The day after we had a meeting at City Hall and an officer invited Beame out to Rikers."[73] It was the first and last time he visited.[74]

The circumstances surrounding the Rikers Island riot represented the nadir of the jail litigation and the state of corrections in New York City. After filing *Benjamin* in June, LAS sought a preliminary injunction that would confer the same rights on the *Benjamin* inmates as the *Rhem* inmates were receiving at HDM: single-celling, contact visits, and so on. Although the cells at HDM were the same size as the cells at the Tombs, and despite a Second Circuit opinion affirming single-celling orders and contact visits, the city strenuously opposed LAS's motion, and Donald Tobias requested and was granted extra time to prepare a brief in opposition. Meanwhile, as the city delayed implementation of court-ordered restrictions on HDM, inmates were shifted into HDM to avoid court orders at other facilities. Thomas Murray, a twenty-six-year veteran of DOC and currently its chief of operations, remembers the months before and after the riot: "It was the worst three months of my career. . . . We knew it was going to blow."[75]

Berger and his successor, Michael Mushlin, also knew HDM was volatile, which is why they were angry with the city for causing the delays and frustrated with Judge Lasker for allowing the delays. According to Mushlin, "By shifting inmates to [HDM] to avoid court orders, DOC was not only acting unethically, they were also being administratively irresponsible, and it brought them a riot."[76] The city's opposition to the HDM injunction was qualitatively different from its defense in the Tombs litigation. At the time of the Tombs litigation, appropriate conditions of confinement, including single-celling, were still open questions. But once the Second Circuit affirmed the lower court's single-celling orders and other minimum standards, the city had an obligation to make good. Said Mushlin, "The effect of the City's [opposition] motions was to create unjustified delay of the implementation of people's constitutional rights, and the City knew it."[77]

Lasker hesitated to push the city too quickly toward reform. He always tried to respond to the parties, especially the city, in a judicious manner. In most instances Lasker proceeded as if the parties were operating in good faith. When Tobias asked the judge for more time to prepare his opposition brief, Lasker gave Tobias the benefit of the doubt. However, when Lasker finally heard Tobias's arguments, he was shocked and rhetorically asked Tobias,

"Are you telling me that the men housed at [HDM] are smaller than the men at the other institutions?"[78] While Lasker's policy of patience may have had some adverse short-term affects, such as contributing to the Rikers Island riot, in the long term it was successful in maintaining a proper balance between the court and executive while effecting reform in the city's jails. At the time, Berger thought Lasker made some mistakes in allowing the city's delays. But looking back, Berger noted: "Lasker was going slow in the way he was implementing things, but he wasn't cutting back on substance. . . . Today, I realize he steered us through the budget crisis very successfully."[79]

After the riots, the tone of the litigation became less contentious. A key factor in this shift was a major reduction in the inmate population. As Malcolm put it: "For some strange reason [the] population began to nosedive. We went from that peak of 14,000 down to about 7,600 by the time I left in 1978."[80] Also, as Joel Berger noted, after the HDM riot, things became a little less politicized. Berger described the period as the beginning of the more friendly, less adversarial climate that developed when Koch took office.

Berger and Malcolm also became more friendly, perhaps because it became more apparent to both that they were on the same side. At the beginning of the litigation, Malcolm appeared sympathetic in private conversations with LAS but then would file papers that were contrary to what he had said privately.[81] Malcolm later said that in the beginning of the litigation he thought Lasker was going too far, but as the litigation progressed, his "early view of Lasker as a judge overstepping his boundary changed to that of a judge who had the guts and courage to stand up and keep the system in line."[82]

In this less adversarial atmosphere, *Benjamin* went to trial. The trial continued for about three weeks in October 1976 and then concluded in spring 1977. While Lasker deliberated, Ed Koch was elected mayor of New York City, and his administration took office in January 1978. Koch's administration brought a new approach to the jail litigation; its policy was to attempt to dispose of the issues raised in the litigations by negotiation or settlement. The parties, in this new spirit of reconciliation, requested Lasker to withhold determination of issues pending in *Benjamin* as well as other related cases. An order incorporating an agreement to negotiate was entered in March 1978.[83]

From Intervention to Compliance

When Koch's administration took office in 1978, the jail litigation went from an adversarial, arms-length process to a more friendly and open relationship among the contending parties. Koch brought an air of optimism and action to the jail litigation, and as a congressman he had already shown his support for jail reform. On Christmas day before he took office, Koch went out to Rikers Island to share a holiday meal with corrections officers and inmates as a show of his support and concern. In a March 1978 speech to New York City's Bar Association, Koch reemphasized his pledge to resolve the city's correctional problems: "The previous City administration took a contentious stance on this litigation despite federal rulings and did not even respond to what were indisputably justifiable demands. My administration has adopted a different posture. We accept our responsibility for maintaining jails that are humane and meet constitutional requirements. . . . No longer will representatives of this City stonewall in defense of inhumane conditions.[84] A strong mandate was thus delivered to settle the litigation and create a humane correctional system.

Koch appointed Allen G. Schwartz corporation counsel and asked Schwartz both to rebuild the severely weakened Office of the Corporation Counsel and to settle the jail litigation.[85] Koch also created the office of deputy mayor for criminal justice and appointed Herbert Sturz to the post. Sturz was the founder and president of the Vera Institute of Justice and had a strong record of innovation in the criminal justice area. While Beame was still mayor Benjamin Malcolm had resigned as commissioner of correction to become a member of the Federal Parole Board appointed by President Carter. Koch appointed prominent attorney Arthur Liman to head a task force to find a new commissioner, and subsequently William Ciuros, a deputy commissioner in the state corrections system, was appointed commissioner. Unfortunately, Ciuros turned out to be a poor choice and lasted only nineteen months.[86]

The shift to a less adversarial atmosphere in the litigation was also aided by new faces at LAS. Joel Berger, who had from the beginning headed LAS's corrections litigation efforts, left LAS in March 1977 to join the NAACP Legal Defense Fund. Berger was not necessarily responsible for the litigation's extremely adversarial tone, but new faces made reconciliation easier. Michael Mushlin, who had worked with Berger for over five years, took over as project director. Allen Schwartz asked Leonard Koerner, who had been head of all commercial litigation for the corporation counsel, to take over the jail cases.

The city entered into negotiations with LAS as a tripartite team representing three different branches of the city government. Koerner was the lead negotiator and represented the corporation counsel. DOC was represented by legal counsel Mark Rosen, and he was sometimes backed up by people from the operations unit of DOC. The parties met in the office of Deputy Mayor Sturz, who was represented by his assistant Ellen Schall. Mushlin and Theodore Katz, then Mushlin's deputy and eventually his successor, were the primary negotiators for LAS.

At first the city, especially DOC, took a fairly straightforward approach to the negotiations. Mushlin remembers that at the beginning DOC had no idea what it wanted and there seemed to be a lack of clarity in its position.[87] LAS would draft a proposal for a provision and DOC would reject it without offering a counterproposal.[88] Because this attitude seemed to be taking the negotiations nowhere, Ellen Schall began taking a more active role: "My job was to help them [DOC] formulate what they wanted. Corrections knew they didn't want what LAS wanted, but they were not articulate about what they wanted."[89] Not only was DOC unable to articulate what it wanted, but it was not unified either. Apparently, what Commissioner Ciuros wanted was not always what his counsel Mark Rosen wanted or what his wardens wanted.[90] LAS's goal was to make the decrees as specific as would reasonably be appropriate. While LAS did not want to take away appropriate levels of discretion from DOC, LAS thought general provisions would merely cause more litigation.[91] It was, of course, precisely the detail of the consent decrees that DOC later resented.

The consent decrees were completed in fall 1978, just six months after the negotiations began. The consent decree for each institution was a detailed fifty-page document which covered over thirty provisions. That these long and detailed agreements were negotiated in such a short time was a testament to the desire of all parties to put their hostilities aside and begin reforming the system. The provisions covered areas including laundry facilities, possession and receipt of publications, procedures for cell searches, attorney visits inmate council participation, due process and programs for detainees in high security categories, environmental health, law library, and lock-in/lock-out time.[92] In the consent decree, the inmates had a very strong document which detailed most aspects of their living conditions. For example, the inmates (who also passed agreement on the decree) could go directly to the posted document and under "Linens and Bedding" find they were supposed to have at least two sheets, one towel, one pillow, one pillow case, one mattress with cover, and sufficient blankets to provide comfort and warmth.[93]

The consent decrees, however, seemed to be tainted from the beginning. Usually, one advantage of a consent decree is that both sides mutually agreed to the provisions. Mutual participation and consent can incite willingness in both parties to work at fulfilling the provisions. Although the city was represented by three different executive branches, DOC was the true defendant as far as the settlement talks were concerned since DOC was expected to implement the decrees. DOC, however, did not fight hard to have a say in what the policy would be, and when the policy was determined, DOC did not fight hard to manage its direction. One reason was that dealing with lawyers was foreign to corrections administrators, which led to distrust and hesitancy to agree to written documents. DOC also seemed to resent the involvement of Sturz and Schall, especially given their backgrounds—Sturz came from the Vera Institute and Schall had been an LAS attorney (but not associated with the jail litigations) for over six years. More important, there was no leadership at DOC on the settlement issue. Much of the blame must be placed on Commissioner Ciuros.

Ciuros started out at a disadvantage because he was unfamiliar with the city correctional system and in particular with the history of the litigation. If Ciuros had served through the Beame years as Malcolm did, he might have welcomed the negotiations as a wonderful opportunity to finally begin cleaning up the system. Instead, Ciuros seemed to treat the settlement talks as a nuisance. Upon taking office, Ciuros never even sought from Malcolm background information on the jail litigation or on any other problems Malcolm had encountered when commissioner. Instead of taking the lead during negotiations, Ciuros stayed in the background and became visible only at the end after the basic provisions were agreed upon.[94] In fact, it was said that Ciuros's lack of initiative was another reason for such detailed consent decrees: "Ciuros neither understood nor supported doing anything about these issues, and in the end, he was led by the nose and was explained to in detail what he was supposed to do, and that was worked into the consent decrees rather than by any other way."[95]

Rather than taking the initiative during the settlement talks, DOC representatives put themselves in a victim's stance and claimed they were backed into the decree. Just before the decree was to be signed, DOC balked, charging that its representatives had never really seen the consent decree or, alternatively, that they were forced into agreeing with its provisions. In response, Sturz and Schall wrote a memo to the mayor documenting DOC's involvement in the negotiations.[96] When the decree finally was signed, it was a document DOC, ultimately responsible for implementation, wanted no part of.

DOC overestimated its ability to achieve compliance and set up an unrealistic timetable. LAS encouraged a short timetable because its lawyers thought that a deadline too far in the distance encourages bureaucratic complacency.[97] Most of the provisions of the consent decree required compliance within eighteen to twenty-four months. Even a well-run system could not implement all the substantial changes required in that time frame. The unrealistic schedule for compliance merely served to aggravate institutional resistance to the decree.

The cost of implementing the consent decree was an acknowledged concern during settlement talks. Koerner was in constant communication with the Office of Management and Budget (OMB), which was ultimately responsible for allocating money needed to comply with the decree. Sometimes someone from OMB even attended the negotiations. OMB is notoriously tight with budget allocations, but with Mayor Koch's mandate, Koerner was able to extract promises from OMB to cover implementation costs. When DOC later sought approval of its budget, however, it had difficulty obtaining sufficient funds from OMB. In particular, DOC needed to hire the hundreds of new officers required for compliance purposes, and OMB needed a push to give more money. Sturz,

Schwartz, and Koerner did the pushing by using the litigation as leverage to get more money. As Koerner put it, "The court was a motivator for budget increases."[98] An ancillary consequence of the fact that the litigation drove budget decisions was that OMB developed a contentious relationship with DOC because OMB was frustrated in not being able to go through the normal process of engaging an agency over its needs.

In summer 1979 Benjamin Ward replaced Ciuros as commissioner of corrections. Ward inherited not only the consent decrees but also a rising inmate population and a court-imposed population cap, first on HDM and eventually on the whole system. Ward became commissioner before DOC had forged a decree compliance plan. When Schall briefed Ward and his deputy commissioner, Mark Corrigan, on the decree, Schall ended up with an offer to work for DOC: "He told me that if I was so smart for having negotiated them, then why don't I join DOC and help implement them, and eventually I accepted."[99] According to Schall, Ward did have a desire to comply, and Schall was hired for her knowledge of the decrees as well as her ability to adeptly handle LAS. It is also possible that Ward may have viewed Schall as a sympathizer with LAS, and he may have figured that if he left some of the responsibility of compliance with Schall, he could keep LAS away from him a while longer.

In fall 1979 Ellen Schall became deputy commissioner of legal policy and program services at DOC. Schall's job was to monitor DOC's compliance efforts and represent DOC in court. When Schall began, she knew little about how to implement organizational change. Schall also found herself trying to effect reform in an archaic and entrenched bureaucracy; it was practically an impossible task, especially for her: "I felt resistance. I was a woman; I was young; I was white, a lawyer, liberal, an ex-Legal Aid lawyer. All of that mattered. And I got painted into a corner as a reformer."[100] Ward wavered in his support of the decrees. Sometimes he was behind them, but then there were moments when he thought they were "the most paternalistic set of interference he had ever seen from a bunch of liberal Legal Aid lawyers."[101] Schall recalled:

> The fact that he had these mixed feelings must have gotten communicated to the organization. That's not an organization that had a very

sophisticated view of change or leadership or management. So, it believed in its para-military way: you put out an order and things would
happen. But that's just not true. So they put out an order that would say
pay attention to X, and people would pay attention to X for about
twenty minutes, until there was a second order to pay attention to Y,
and people would switch to Y for another twenty minutes.[102]

While there clearly was resistance to the decree in DOC, it was not
uniform. Instead, there were pockets of resistance and pockets of
acceptance.

Jackie McMickens, who succeeded Ward as commissioner of
DOC in 1984, was chief of operations under both Ciuros and Ward,
and the burden of implementation fell to her. According to
McMickens, it was not until Ward became commissioner that an
implementation program was put into place.[103] However, it was
very difficult for the uniformed officers to accept the decrees.
Corrections workers tend to dislike and distrust administrative
change, and in the New York City system changes came quickly.
Schall felt that one of the primary reasons for DOC's failure to
break down staff resistance was its inability to educate and explain
why the changes were good for staff: "We failed to get across the
notion that courts intervene only when corrections fail. Corrections
was really twenty years behind a lot of law enforcement agencies in
its policies, and the courts were in the middle of correction's business across the country for a reason. We didn't put it into a context
that made it possible for people to buy in, understand, or go along
with."[104] According to Thomas Murray, a twenty-six-year veteran
of DOC and currently DOC's chief of operations: "In the beginning
we resisted a lot of the change because [we] had the idea that we
were not there to make inmates comfortable but to make them
uncomfortable."[105] But even when implementation is approached
correctly, changing the attitudes and routines of officers can be a
difficult and long process.

LAS applied continuous pressure on DOC to keep the implementation process working. Usually they tried to informally push
DOC ahead on compliance issues; however, both parties soon
began to realize that they could not continue in this informal
manner. In 1981 LAS filed a contempt motion and requested that
Judge Lasker appoint a special master to take over or monitor the

implementation process. According to Mushlin, one reason LAS waited so long before requesting the court to appoint a master was that he and his staff believed that plaintiffs' counsel has more power in absence of a master.[106] Commissioner Ward, however, refused to have anything to do with a master.

In 1982 Ellen Schall (before leaving DOC to become commissioner of juvenile justice) and Jackie McMickens worked out a compromise with LAS which resulted in the creation of the Office of Compliance Consultants (OCC). Technically, OCC is not a creature of the court. Rather, it is an independent monitoring unit created by New York City and LAS. The director of OCC is Kenneth Schoen, a former commissioner of corrections of Minnesota and now the program director for the Justice Program of the Edna McConnell Clarke Foundation. Schoen was well known and respected by both parties, which not only made it easier for the parties to agree to create OCC but also facilitated the growth of their trust in OCC. Schoen is not involved with OCC on a daily basis but acts more as an adviser and public spokesman.

OCC's daily operations are run by a supervisor and a staff of two field workers who regularly visit the facilities. The first supervisor was Kathryn Monaco, an attorney from New Mexico who had experience in corrections. She was with OCC for two years and was succeeded by Michael D. Cleary in 1984. Cleary had been a staff member of the Board of Corrections for ten years before coming to OCC. OCC was set up so that its two staff members would always come from DOC—one from its civilian division and one from its uniform division. The only reason LAS agreed to this arrangement was because the city insisted on it, and Schoen, who agreed with the city, assured LAS that the staff would not be biased. To allay LAS's fears, very specific language was put into the OCC agreement mandating that Schoen's staff selections be approved by LAS, that the staff be responsible only to Schoen, and that after six months, if Schoen found that the staff did not have sufficient objective fact-finding authority, they could be replaced by non-DOC staff. LAS has interviewed all of the staff candidates Schoen has considered.[107]

This arrangement has been very successful. When OCC staff members visit the facilities, they are not treated as outsiders, and yet they are objective and critical of DOC while on the job. Because they are employees of DOC, they know how the department operates. It is difficult for DOC to hide things from them, and they know how much to expect from DOC. These OCC staff members have also been accepted back into DOC with promotions. OCC's budget is paid for by the city, and its 1987 budget was about $225,000.[108]

Besides settling the inmate lawsuits, Mayor Koch wanted to reopen the Tombs, which had been closed since December 1974. It was decided that the only way to satisfy the standards set by Lasker in *Rhem* was to completely gut the Tombs and rebuild it from the inside out. Construction began in 1979, and four years later in November 1983 the Tombs finally reopened. The forty-two-million-dollar renovation of the Tombs transformed it into one of the most humane and efficient jails in the country. At the time of the riots in 1970 the Tombs housed about two thousand men in a facility designed for nine hundred men. The new Tombs was designed to house fewer than five hundred men and is divided into three self-contained modules, or "minijails," each with a library, classrooms, a commissary, a nurse's station, a television area, and an indoor gym.[109] Its module and direct supervision design has been a model for jails around the country.[110] The successful renovation of the Tombs was a testament to the Koch administration's desire to remedy the wrongs of the past administrations and to the plaintiffs' and Judge Lasker's determination to make New York City meet its responsibilities.

From Litigation to Bureaucratic Politics

When OCC was set up in 1982, it marked the beginning of a new era for corrections in New York City. The battle over jail reform has moved away from the courts and toward the political arena. The court still is involved and the parties still use the court when all other channels fail, but the difference is that there are other channels and they normally do not fail. OCC has become one of the primary vehicles through which the parties communicate and work out their differences over implementation. Furthermore, the parties themselves do not necessarily operate like regular private or public litigants; rather, they have become more like public agencies fighting out policy issues in a fashion somewhat similar to any political battle between conflicting New York City agencies and constituencies.

Soon after LAS began to get involved with corrections litigation it created the Prisoners' Rights Project (PRP) as an organ to handle the suits. Initially PRP was funded with federal grants, but it soon was funded by the city as a separate line on the budget of LAS's Criminal Appeals Bureau, and the city has continued to fund it ever since. The city has never used funding as a bargaining chip. As the current chief attorney for PRP, Theodore Katz, stated: "The City recognizes that our office plays an important role in relieving pressure in the system, and when pressure builds up in jails and prisons, there develops conflagration which serves nobody's interest."[111] Furthermore, the city has probably saved a significant sum of money by funding its opponents through an organization like LAS, because other attorneys would most likely have received court-ordered fees at rates higher than the salaries PRP attorneys receive (PRP does not seek attorneys' fees from the city).

There is much stability and continuity at PRP. Joel Berger, its first project director, was there for about seven years; his successor, Michael Mushlin, was also there for about seven years, three years as director; and Katz has been at PRP for over eleven years and has been project director for about eight years. According to Katz, PRP has become recognized as part of the city decision-making process, largely because of the force of the consent decrees, the experience and institutional memory of PRP attorneys, and their reputation for competence and responsible conduct in negotiations and litigation. Generally, relations between PRP and the city (DOC and corporation counsel) are good. The parties are much more intent on working things out informally, and therefore PRP does not need to go to court every time it sees a violation. As Katz stated, "The whole process of OCC is a testament to the fact that there is cooperation going on between the parties."[112] This new process of dialogue and negotiation through OCC has likewise shifted the role of the lawyers at PRP. Said Katz, "[T]here is a feeling of being both lawyer and bureaucrat."

DOC did not truly become mobilized or focused until OCC put pressure on it to move implementation forward. DOC still has problems with leadership at the top and an antiquated bureaucracy which has not yet been able to internalize provisions of the consent decrees. However, DOC is no longer merely a reactive or passive party, nor does it always wait for ultimatums from the court. DOC leaders seem sincerely interested in maintaining compliance. Although they often fumble in their compliance effort, it is not necessarily for lack of effort but sometimes because of the inadequacy of their bureaucracy.

The motor that drives this new dialogue between the city and those representing the inmates' interests is OCC. OCC operates not only as a monitor but also as a catalyst to the whole implementation process. Staff members approach their work methodically and deal with the consent decree provision by provision. OCC begins evaluating compliance with a consent decree provision by interpreting what is required of DOC then measuring the progress DOC has made. For example, if the issue is telephone service, OCC begins by counting and checking each telephone in each detention facility. OCC staffers submit a questionnaire to all inmates in regard to phone service. OCC then follows up with a preliminary report stating the status of compliance. The preliminary report also offers recommendations.

The parties, PRP and DOC, are then given an opportunity to respond to OCC's preliminary findings, after which there is a series of meetings where the parties attempt to resolve any differences. DOC is then expected to draft a departmental directive addressing the implementation provisions. After OCC and PRP respond to the directive and more compromises are made, DOC is expected to implement the directive. OCC monitors progress and makes suggestions along the way. Disengagement of the provision from the decree is the final goal. At present, not a single provision has been disengaged.

Progress toward compliance has been particularly slow, even by New York City standards. Progress, however, has not been slow because of the type of political resistance the inmates faced in the 1970s. Instead, the inmates are faced with bureaucratic resistance and the inherent administrative complexities of correctional reform. DOC spends more money per inmate than any other correction agency in the country, but, according to OCC supervisor Michael Cleary, DOC suffers from a classic case of bureaucratic inertia.[113] DOC waits for OCC to go out and check on compliance, but it never takes the initiative. This inertia has been fed by top leadership changes. Benjamin Ward left DOC in 1984 to become police commissioner, and he was replaced by Jackie McMickens. Just three years later, McMickens was forced out as commissioner and replaced by Richard Koehler; the latter, who resigned in 1989, barely lasted two years.

Over the last few years, OCC has taken an even greater leadership role in the implementation process because DOC has been delinquent in its responsibilities.[114] Initially, when drafts of OCC's quarterly progress reports to Judge Lasker were sent out to DOC for comment, the agency's reactions were mostly negative and highly defensive. OCC responded by phrasing its criticisms in the draft reports more gently. Nevertheless, officials at DOC felt that OCC had too little patience and did not fully understand the difficulties DOC faced.[115] According to McMickens, when DOC managed to meet only half a target, OCC would report it to Judge Lasker as not having met the target. DOC officials felt that they received little credit for vigorous if imperfect compliance efforts. Thomas Murray observed: "With the number of people we have to service and the uncertainty in this environment, it is tough walking around thinking you can't make a mistake."[116]

However, despite these conflicts, OCC has managed to keep PRP and DOC in continuous and constructive dialogue. This dialogue between the parties could be compared to an interagency process. It includes negotiation and compromise between interested parties. The process is flexible and has the capacity to experiment and to allow DOC to prove itself. OCC and PRP are able to act as a check on DOC if it begins to deviate from its agreements. Most importantly, the inmates are provided with access to and a voice in this political and bureaucratic process through the mechanism of OCC. The process has not always been effective or efficient, but that is the nature of government in New York City.

Progress has also been affected by a severe overcrowding problem. During the 1980s the inmate population rose from under eight thousand to over eighteen thousand inmates. Pretrial detainees now make up about three-fourths of the inmate population. Systemwide caps have been imposed on DOC and they are monitored by the court, the Board of Corrections, and the State Commission on Corrections. In fall 1983 overcrowding was so severe that DOC was unable to keep the population under the imposed limit. Under pressure from the court to reduce the jail population, Mayor Koch and Commissioner Ward ordered pretrial detainees to be released from city facilities on no bail or 10 percent bail in order to bring the inmate population under the cap. In two weeks over six hundred pretrial detainees were released.

The inmate release politicized the overcrowding issue to the detriment of decree issues. Overcrowding affects all aspects of quality of confinement, but issues dealt with in the decrees, such as sanitation and classification, are no less important. The overcrowding issue has assumed greater urgency than compliance with the consent decrees. After the inmate release, Mayor Koch swore never to let that happen again, and thus the mayor created a new mandate for corrections. The city was going to build its way out of this crisis. This policy of reducing overcrowding by building more jails was publicized after the inmate release, but it was a policy the city had been following since 1980, though perhaps ineffectively.

While OMB continuously fought with DOC over how jails would be staffed and serviced and generally discounted DOC's operating budget requirements,[117] the capital budget was a different story, as there was never a doubt that more jails would be built. Both Mayor Koch and his deputy and then head of OMB, Paul Dickstein, strongly believed that building more jails was the only appropriate response to overcrowding. As a result, money flowed freely for new construction of both permanent and temporary facilities. The only problem the city had—a problem most cities always have—was actually getting the jails built.

The inmate release made it more politically feasible for the mayor to increase capital expenditures for corrections. A new jail building program would add 3,896 new cells and dorm beds over the next five years, increasing citywide capacity from 10,100 to almost 14,000 beds. In lobbying for his plan, the mayor, using the prisoner release program as leverage, was quoted as saying: "I am faced with the choice of releasing prisoners into city streets or taking scarce capital dollars from other programs to build more jails. . . . The only real and the only responsible choice is to build more jails."[118] Three weeks later the New York City Board of Estimate approved the allotment of $277 million for the mayor's plan to build nearly 4,000 new jail spaces.

Since 1983 New York City has spent over half a billion dollars in capital funds trying to build its way out of its overcrowding problems. The DOC bureaucracy, antiquated before the consent decrees, has been pushed to administer departmental growth in two directions—its physical capacity and conditions within. As a result of DOC's building program, the sheer size of the department has doubled. Over 40 percent of DOC's correctional officers have less than two years of experience.[119] While DOC has been experiencing this substantial growth, it has also been expected to comply with the consent decrees. DOC has struggled to create an effective bureaucracy to deal with compliance as the size of the department has grown so substantially and quickly.

DOC was grappling with overcrowding problems in 1970 when the court became involved; it still is. But litigation and the presence of the court have enhanced the political standing of corrections in New York City. DOC may not get everything it wants, but neither do most agencies in New York City. In the aftermath of the Tombs riots, a New York *Times* editorial on corrections reform asked, "Does anyone in authority care—enough?"[120] Now as a result of the court's intervention, not only do more people care, but better safeguards are in place to ensure that they care enough.

Conclusion

Almost two decades have passed since the first lawsuit was filed, and all of New York City's pretrial detention facilities, except the Tombs, are still under supervision of the federal court. Today there are over eighteen thousand inmates in New York City's jails, and over thirteen thousand of them are pretrial detainees. Rikers Island, with over eleven thousand inmates housed on it, may be the largest penal colony in the world. DOC is completing a half-billion-dollar building program and is still struggling to meet the demand for jail space. Although it has taken a long time and much is unfinished, significant positive reforms have been implemented in these pretrial detention facilities. Conditions, programs, and services for inmates have improved tremendously since 1970, but they have not kept pace with the inmate population.

The Tombs, once an embarrassment to the city, is now hailed as one of the most humane detention facilities in the country. Inmate services still suffer in some areas, but in general they are 100 percent better than they were before the lawsuits, as good food, showers, clean bedding, and recreation are no longer rarities to most inmates. There are also educational programs for inmates where there had been none. Largely as a result of these improvements, there has not been a major inmate riot since 1975.

Although it has happened slowly, there has also been a change in attitudes among the correctional officers and administrators. During the 1980s officers grew to understand that improvements in jail conditions defuse inmate tensions and make their job easier.

But while officers have begun to internalize some of the values underlying the consent decrees, this process started much too late. DOC has reached full compliance in only a few areas, and it has been a struggle for PRP and OCC to pressure DOC to maintain compliance. Just recently, in a lawsuit on behalf of inmates in Rikers Island's primary facility for sentenced inmates, Judge Lasker found that the violence and brutality endured by inmates at the hands of other inmates and correctional officers constituted cruel and unusual punishment.[121]

Nevertheless, parties on both sides of the litigation agree that, absent the court's intervention and the firm stewardship of Judge Lasker, pretrial detainees in New York City would still be suffering inhumane conditions. Despite the rocky history of the litigation, intervention by the court has improved substantially the quality of life inside New York City's jails.[122]

Notes

1. Research for this study was generously funded by the Daniel and Florence Guggenheim Foundation.
2. New York *Times*, February 19, 1967, p. 53, col. 2.
3. Ibid., August 16, 1969, p. 56, col. 3.
4. Since he was first elected to the State Senate, Dunne, a liberal Republican, concentrated on the issue of penal reform, even though the issue was not important to his constituents in Nassau County (Long Island). As chairman of the committee, Dunne earned a reputation as a crusader against poor prison conditions and frequently

was criticized for his outspokenness. Ibid., August 18, 1970, p. 18, col. 4.

5. Construction for a new Rikers Island Women's House of Detention, known as the Correction Institution for Women (CIW), began in April 1968; the facility was operating by 1971. It provided 679 single-occupancy cells with a built-in capacity for expansion to 900 single-occupancy cells. But it did not add beds to the system, since it was replacing the 700-bed Greenwich Village women's facility. The project cost twenty-four million dollars. The city began building a new Adolescent Remand Center on Rikers Island in April 1969. It was ready for occupancy by 1972 and provided an additional 1,080 single-occupancy cells. Total cost was forty-five million dollars. In February 1969 the city began constructing an addition to the Correction Institution for Men (CIM) on Rikers Island. It provided 768 new single-occupancy cells at a cost of four million dollars. It was completed by 1971. Ibid., August 23, 1970, p. 29, col. 1.

6. Ibid., February 18, 1970, p. 1, col. 6.

7. Ibid., November 10, 1969, p. 30, col. 1.

8. The standard cell was six feet wide, seven feet nine inches long, and seven feet ten inches high.

9. Then U.S. representative for the seventeenth Congressional District in Manhattan.

10. New York *Times*, April 8, 1970, p. 45, col. 7. The survey was conducted in early February 1970 with the permission of Commissioner McGrath. In all likelihood, the conditions at the Tombs had been that way for at least two years and not much better even before that, as the Tombs was overcrowded ever since it opened.

11. Interview with Joel Berger, former project director for Prisoners' Rights Project of the Legal Aid Society.

12. New York *Times*, August 18, 1969, p. 18, col. 4.

13. New York State Senate Committee on Crime and Correction, *The Tombs Disturbances: A Report*, October 5, 1970, p. 9 (hereinafter cited as *Tombs Disturbances*). The new law enacted was section 6-g of the State Correctional law.

14. New York *Times*, August 18, 1969, p. 18, col. 4.

15. Ibid., August 16, 1969, p. 56, col. 3.

16. Quoted in New York *Times*, November 10, 1969, p. 30, col. 1.

17. *Tombs Disturbances*, p. 9.

18. Ibid., p. 12.

19. Section 46 of New York Correctional Law.

20. Ibid.

21. In New York, the supreme court is a trial-level court.

22. *Tombs Disturbances*, p. 6.

23. The appointment process and the board's powers were changed in an effort to strengthen the board in a 1975 amendment to the City Charter.

24. *Tombs Disturbances*, p. 6.

25. New York *Times*, December 14, 1967, p. 68, col. 3.

26. *Tombs Disturbances*, p. 6.

27. Ibid., 7.

28. New York *Times*, February 18, 1970, p. 1, col. 6.

29. *Tombs Disturbances*, p. 7.

30. New York *Times*, February 19, 1970, p. 46, col. 2.

31. Ibid., August 11, 1970, p. 1, col. 1.

32. Ibid.

33. Ibid., August 13, 1970, p. 24, col. 3.

34. Ibid., p. 32, col. 1. A week later, another editorial added this: "In one decade after another, official bodies have criticized the overcrowding in the Tombs and all the conditions that contribute to that disgraceful congestion. Promises of reform are made—and forgotten. Today the Tombs has twice as many prisoners as it was built to hold. By shining light into the cellblocks after the disturbances there, Senator Dunne has exposed official shortcomings that more than ever demand correction. But does anyone in authority care—enough?" New York *Times*, August 20, 1970, p. 29, col. 1.

35. It had also been suggested that LAS brought the suit in response to inmate complaints made during the riots about the quality of legal representation they received from LAS's criminal defense division. But, in fact, that division had nothing to do with the lawsuit.

36. The Queens case, *Valvano v. Malcolm*, 520 F.2d 392 (1975), was filed to protect the outspoken inmates from brutality by corrections officers but soon became a full-blown conditions of confinement lawsuit under Federal Judge Orrin G. Judd in New York's Eastern District. In fact, *Valvano* went to trial before *Rhem*.

37. *Rhem v. Malcolm*, 371 F. Supp. 594 (1974). The four named plaintiffs were inmates Joel Berger and his collegues interviewed and who they thought would make good witnesses if still around at trial. LAS wanted the lead name to be unique, catchy, and something they could live with for a while, and they thought Rhem was the best of the four. The four names were James Rhem, Robert Freely, Leo Robinson, and Eugene Nixon. This is how most of the lead names were chosen. In *Valvano* there was not much choice because Mr. Valvano was so outspoken. For a while Berger tried using names like "Detainees of

Brooklyn House of Detention," but his staff liked using the catchy names better. Berger interview.

38. *Benjamin v. Malcolm*, House of Detention for Men; *Forts v. Malcolm*, Correctional Institution for Women; *Ambrose v. Malcolm*, Bronx House of Detention; *Maldonado v. Ciuros*, Adolescent Remand Center; *Detainees of the Brooklyn House of Detention for Men v. Malcolm; Valvano v. Malcolm*, Queens House of Detention for Men.

39. "People have asked why didn't we sue the whole system at the beginning instead of just the Tombs. We were just feeling our way through. We didn't know how much we would get to. Ultimately, we did want to get for the other facilities what we were trying to get at the Tombs. Now looking back, I think we should have followed *Rhem* with a citywide suit rather than just with *Benjamin*. But even so, the Brooklyn and Queens cases were underway, and we had drawn Judge Judd who also was concerned with the prisons." Berger interview.

40. Malcolm was also the city's first black commissioner of correction.

41. Interview with Benjamin Malcolm, former New York City commissioner of correction, July 29, 1987. This was also borne out in Judge Lasker's trial opinion. *Rhem v. Malcolm*, 371 F. Supp. 594, 597 (1974).

42. Berger interview.

43. Subsequently dean at New York University Law School.

44. A consent decree enforcing the stipulation was entered by Judge Lasker August 2, 1973. *Rhem*, 371 F. Supp. 594, 597 (1974).

45. Ibid., p. 600.

46. Ibid.

47. Ibid.

48. Berger interview. More of Berger on the Beame administration: "Things improved a little bit towards the end of the Beame administration when John Zuccotti replaced Mr. Cavanaugh as Deputy Mayor, and during that same period Peter Tufo began his tenure with the BOC. Most of Beame's administration was a real disaster. I know the Board of Correction was very disappointed with the City. Many felt that Lasker in *Rhem* had created a tremendous opportunity to begin salvaging the jails without additional litigation."

49. Malcolm interview; Berger interview; interview with Donald Tobias, former assistant corporation counsel, July 27, 1987.

50. Malcolm interview.

51. Interview with Federal District Judge Morris Lasker, July 8, 1987.

52. *Rhem*, 371 F. Supp. 594, 636.

53. Tobias interview.
54. Malcolm interview.
55. Ibid.
56. But Tobias also blamed Berger and LAS for being too adversarial: "One of the major problems with maintaining progress in the case was that we were trying to achieve reform within an adversary context. Berger was not trying to improve conditions for the inmates; rather, he was trying to win a victory. LAS was not going to settle for less than the letter of the order—absolute victory—because they were dealing in an adversary context. They were not dealing in a business context where businessmen get together and usually a compromise is best for everybody. This was the most frustrating part of the whole case. Yet, LAS blamed the City for acting as an adversary rather than helping the process along. But it was LAS's hard-line stance which forced the City into an adversarial role." Tobias interview.
57. Ibid.
58. The city did feel, however, that in a fiscal crisis the judge should heed the limits of his office a little more closely and that the city's arguments should have been given a little more weight.
59. Telephone interview with Joel Berger, October 31, 1988.
60. Berger interview.
61. Ibid.
62. *Rhem v. Malcolm*, 377 F. Supp. 995, 996 (1975).
63. Ibid., p. 1000.
64. *Rhem v. Malcolm*, 507 F.2d 333, 340 (2d Cir. 1974).
65. Lasker interview.
66. Ibid.
67. Note that Judge Lasker did not order the Tombs to be closed; rather, it was the city's decision to close the Tombs.
68. *Rhem v. Malcolm*, 389 F. Supp. 964, 966 (1974).
69. *Rhem v. Malcolm*, 527 F.2d 1041 (2d Cir. 1975).
70. James Benjamin, an inmate at HDM, was chosen name plaintiff as a play on Correction Commissioner Benjamin Malcolm's name.
71. *Benjamin v. Malcolm*, 495 F. Supp. 1357, 1359 (1980).
72. *Rhem* 527 F.2d 1041 (2d Cir. 1975).
73. Malcolm interview. The correction officers were also bitter because Bronx D.A. Mario Merola, who had jurisdiction of Rikers Island, granted immunity to all inmates involved in the riots as part of the settlement.
74. "One of the things I advised Koch on before he took office was to get out to the institutions early on and show your face; show the officers you care and show the inmates you care. And he did; he went out on

Christmas before he took office and had dinner with them." Malcolm interview.
75. Interview with Thomas W. Murray, chief of operations at DOC, July 30, 1987.
76. Interview with Michael Mushlin, former project director for Prisoners' Rights Project of LAS, July 28, 1987.
77. Ibid.
78. Ibid.
79. Berger interview.
80. Malcolm interview.
81. Berger interview.
82. Malcolm interview.
83. *Benjamin v. Malcolm*, 495 F. Supp. 1357, 1359 (1980).
84. Edward I. Koch, "Critical Issues in Criminal Justice," *The Record of the Association of the Bar of the City of New York*, 33, no. 4 (April 1978), 187, 194.
85. After taking office, Schwartz asked for an emergency appropriation of $5.4 million to hire an additional 116 lawyers, and he received it despite financial pressures on the city. Ibid.
86. Liman had consulted with Malcolm, and Malcolm was surprised they selected Ciuros: "He was a man whose image got in his way. He was . . . known throughout the country and wore a uniform with lots of braids and what not on it. . . . Ciuros came from the State system, and while he had a background in prisons, he knew nothing about the City system." Malcolm interview.
87. Mushlin interview.
88. Interview with Ellen Schall, former deputy commissioner of correction and current commissioner of juvenile justice in New York City, July 14, 1987.
89. Ibid.
90. Ibid.
91. Mushlin interview.
92. *Benjamin v. Malcolm*, Stipulation for Entry of Partial Final Judgment, November 29, 1978.
93. Ibid., p. 9.
94. Schall interview; Mushlin interview.
95. Interview with Monte Kurs, former deputy criminal justice coordinator, former counsel to deputy mayor of operations, deputy commissioner of division of public structures in Department of General Services, July 30, 1987.
96. Schall interview.
97. Mushlin interview.

98. Interivew with Leonard Koerner, Chief Assistant Corporation Counsel, July 16, 1987.
99. Schall interview.
100. Ibid.
101. Ibid.
102. Ibid.
103. Interview with Jackie McMickens, former commissioner of correction, July 31, 1987.
104. Schall interview.
105. Interview with Thomas W. Murray, chief of operations at DOC, July 30, 1987.
106. Mushlin interview.
107. Letter from Theordore H. Katz, December 28, 1988.
108. Interview with Michael D. Cleary, supervisor for Office of Compliance Consultants, July 1, 1987.
109. New York *Times*, October 17, 1983.
110. See National Institute of Justice Construction Bulletin: *Cost Savings in New Generation Jails* (July 1988).
111. Interview with Theodore Katz, project director of Prisoners' Rights Project of LAS, June 9, 1987.
112. Ibid.
113. Cleary interview.
114. OCC Progress Report to Judge Lasker, April 1–July 31, 1986.
115. McMickens interview; Murray interview.
116. Murray interview.
117. Kurs interview; McMickens interview.
118. New York *Times*, December 10, 1983, p. 1, col. 1.
119. Cleary interview; Murray interview.
120. New York *Times*, August 20, 1970, p. 29, col. 1.
121. *Fisher v. Koehler.*
122. Note that the jail situation is dynamic and the names and numbers are subject to change.

7

The Rule of Law, Disciplinary Practices, and Rahway State Prison: A Case Study in Judicial Intervention and Social Control

EDWARD E. RHINE

In classic studies by Gresham Sykes, Richard Cloward, and others, it was found that prison officials governed largely by entering into informal bargains with inmates.[1] Well into the 1960s, prison officials could rely on a shared convict code of conduct and tacit cooperative arrangements with inmate leaders to ensure a modicum of order and stability behind bars.

Recent studies indicate that informal accommodations and trade-offs between inmates and staff remain a key tool of prison gover-

The views presented herein are those of the author and are not those of the Administrative Office of the Courts or the Judiciary of New Jersey.

nance.[2] Today, however, prison officials are more likely than they were in the "Big House" era to rely on formal mechanisms of social control as well. These mechanisms include all-encompassing institutional rules and regulations, official rewards and privileges, assignment to different classification statuses, and an ever-expanding continuum of punitive sanctions.[3] It is through the prison's disciplinary system that institutional rules are enforced, classification statuses are changed, and punitive sanctions are imposed.

The disciplinary system serves as the foundation of social control in the contemporary prison. Moreover, it is here that the shift from informal to formal social control is most discernible. Until recently, prison officials had unlimited discretion to summarily enforce the myriad rules and regulations and to punish inmates without regard to innocence or guilt.[4] However, during the 1970s federal courts in a number of states (e.g., New York, California, Illinois) began handing down decisions requiring that due process be provided during prison disciplinary proceedings. Though these rulings were often cautious in tone and modest in scope, they established the principle that disciplinary practices and procedures had to be governed by rational decision-making criteria to ensure procedural fairness.

In 1974 the Supreme Court issued its "landmark" disciplinary decision, *Wolff v. McDonnell.* Declaring that there "is no iron curtain drawn between the constitution and the prisons of this country,"[5] *Wolff* set forth what due process rights were to be made available to inmates involved in disciplinary hearings that might result in a grievous loss (e.g., forfeiture of commutation time).

Since *Wolff* was decided it has become evident that inmates must be afforded some though not all of the requisites of due process prior to the imposition of disciplinary sanctions. What is not as apparent is how prison disciplinary systems actually operate and with what effects within the constraints of procedural due process.[6]

This chapter addresses this issue by discussing the implementation and impact of *Wolff* and of a 1975 New Jersey Supreme Court decision, *Avant v. Clifford* (67 N.J. 496), on the disciplinary system at Rahway State Prison. My findings are drawn primarily from field observations made in 1979–80, supplemented by documentary material and data highlighting major changes and developments since the completion of the original research.[7] I offer the Rahway experience as a window on the capacity of the rule of law to effectively mediate the endemic tension between prison officials' interest in maximum social control and an inmate's interest in being protected against arbitrary and capricious interference with the "liberty" that remains even in confinement.[8] Due process law seeks to reconcile or balance the competing interests at stake through the provision of procedural safeguards that protect inmates while simultaneously providing prison officials with the discretion necessary to ensure institutional order and control. An understanding of how this occurs relates directly to the benefits and limitations of judicial reform in this vital area of correctional administration.

Prison Discipline and Due Process: Two Supreme Courts Respond

Before the dawn of judicial intervention, prison administrators had plenary power over those in their charge. Despite frequent prodding, state and federal courts refused to review the merits of litigation dealing with the internal operation of the prison. This policy, often referred to as the "hands-off" doctrine, effectively insulated correctional officials from accountability through judicial review.[9] Although the unqualified acceptance of the hands-off doctrine began to show signs of erosion in several areas (e.g., access to the courts) during the mid to late 1960s, until the early 1970s there was a complete absence of procedural due process with respect to prison discipline.[10]

A central justification underlying the judiciary's reluctance to intervene was its fear that doing so would undermine institutional order and control.[11] In its caution, the judiciary recognized what prison officials had long taken for granted: disciplinary practices resulting in the threat or imposition of punitive sanctions supported a rule-regimented, authoritarian order inside prison walls. To allow prisoners the right to challenge the disciplinary system would grant them the right to question the very legitimacy of the prison's central method of governance.[12]

Nonetheless, in the early 1970s federal courts began issuing rulings addressing prison disciplinary practices. In the decisions that followed, the major issue the courts focused on was the procedure by which the guilt or innocence of inmates accused of institutional infractions was determined.[13] Although several of the rulings considered other issues, each sought to resolve what due process guarantees were constitutionally mandated prior to the imposition of disciplinary sanctions. However, it was not until the Supreme Court responded in *Wolff v. McDonnell* (1974) that the procedural requirements governing prison discipline were given constitutional definition.

On June 26, 1974, the Supreme Court decided *Wolff v. McDonnell*. The question the Court addressed was not whether prisoners retained due process protections per se but "whether the protections of the due process clause extend[ed] to proceedings in which prisoners may be confined in a disciplinary cell or lose good-time credits."[14]

In its ruling the Court asserted that whereas a prisoner's rights "may be diminished by the needs and exigencies of the institutional environment, a prisoner is not wholly stripped of constitutional protections when he is imprisoned for crime."[15] At the same time, it cautioned that "prison disciplinary proceedings are not part of a criminal prosecution, and the full panoply of rights due a defendant in such proceedings does not apply."[16] In the Court's view, due process in prison discipline called for such guarantees as were necessary to achieve "a mutual accommodation between institutional needs and objectives and the provisions of the Constitution that are of general application."[17]

In striking the balance required by due process, the Court declined to adopt the full range of procedures suggested in earlier decisions.[18] Instead, it ruled that the following elements of due process must be afforded to inmates involved in prison disciplinary proceedings:[19]

> 1. Advance written notice of the charges against the prisoner must be given to him at least twenty-four hours prior to his appearance before the disciplinary board. This will "give the charged party a chance to marshall the facts in his defense and to clarify what the charges are, in fact."
> 2. There must be a written statement by the fact-finders "as to the evidence relied on and reasons for the disciplinary action." This requirement will help "to insure that the administration, faced with

possible scrutiny by state officials and the public, and perhaps even the courts . . . will act fairly."

3. The inmate facing disciplinary proceedings "should be allowed to call witnesses and present documentary evidence in his defense when permitting him to do so will not be unduly hazardous to institutional safety or correctional goals." However, "prison officials must have the necessary discretion to keep the hearing within reasonable limits and to refuse to call witnesses that may create a risk of reprisal or undermine authority."

4. Counsel substitute (either staff or, where permitted, a fellow inmate) should be allowed where an illiterate inmate is involved, or where the complexity of the issue makes it unlikely that the inmate will be able to collect and present the evidence necessary for an adequate comprehension of the case.

5. The prison disciplinary board must be impartial. The disciplinary measures which are imposed must not "be rendered capriciously or in the nature of retaliation or revenge."

Wolff pertains to prison discipline and "serious misconduct" only. The procedures mandated by the decision are not required for the imposition of lesser penalties, such as loss of privileges.[20]

Shortly after *Wolff*, the New Jersey Supreme Court handed down a comprehensive ruling on due process and prison discipline in *Avant v. Clifford* (1975). *Avant* was originally instituted following a "Thanksgiving Day riot" at Rahway State Prison on November 25, 1971. Subsequent to this disturbance, the suspected rioters were summarily transferred to the Yardville Youth Reception and Correction Center and placed in administrative segregation. The inmates filed suit, claiming that their transfer without a hearing was contrary to due process.

In judging whether the state's disciplinary Standards comported with the requirements of procedural due process,[21] the court applied both a federal due process yardstick and New Jersey's "fairness and rightness" norm.[22] While affirming much of the Higher Court's opinion in *Wolff*, the New Jersey Supreme Court interpreted the state's "fairness and rightness" norm to mandate additional protections.[23] In addition, the Court examined the specificity of the acts prohibited in the institutions and the range of sanctions which could be imposed, and it found both to be constitutionally acceptable.

Wolff v. McDonnell and *Avant v. Clifford* represent major rulings delineating those elements of due process that must be provided to inmates caught up in prison disciplinary proceedings.[24] Both decisions refer only to "serious violations," and both accept that where inmates are potentially subject to some form of "grievous loss," their interest in due process has "real substance" and is protected by the "liberty" clause of the Fourteenth Amendment. While each ruling seeks to achieve a reasonable balance between correctional goals and inmate rights, the larger objective, as *Avant* notes, is to "strike down arbitrary action and administrative abuse and to ensure procedural fairness in the administrative process."[25] In nearly identical language, *Wolff* states that "the touchstone of due process is protection of the individual against arbitrary action of government."[26] Together, these rulings endeavor to place procedural restraints on the exercise of official discretion and to foster impartiality in the decision-making process.

How these rulings have been implemented and the extent of their impact on the disciplinary system at Rahway State Prison will be addressed in the sections that follow.

Wolff, *Avant*, and the Disciplinary System at Rahway State Prison (1979)

In 1979 Rahway State Prison was the largest of the institutions within New Jersey's adult prison complex, housing approximately 37 percent of the total inmate population. During the fiscal year ending June 30, 1979, of the 1,315 average daily prisoners at Rahway 1,070 (81%) were confined inside the walls and 245 (19%) were housed in one of the three minimum custody camps.

During the summer of 1979 inmate life at Rahway was characterized by rule-governed regimentation. As part of the system of formal social control, numerous institutional rules and regulations determined inmate movement, custody status, possessions, privileges, work assignments, and more. Moreover, a comprehensive listing of sixty-six prohibited acts, along with a broad range of punitive sanctions, defined and enforced the outer limits of acceptable inmate behavior.[27] While inmate compliance with the rules was generally forthcoming, ultimately order was maintained and inmate cooperation secured by the demonstrated willingness of prison officials to employ varying degrees of force whenever necessary. The imposition of coercive sanctions is, in fact, the sine qua non of prison social control. At Rahway it was most visibly manifest on a day-to-day basis in the operation of the disciplinary system referred to as "courtline."

In 1979 there were four stages to Rahway's disciplinary system. The stages began the moment an inmate was given a disciplinary *charge*, continued through an *investigation* of the charge on to a courtline *hearing*, concluding with an *appeal*. At different points along the way, an inmate was entitled to a number of due process rights—rights aimed at achieving fairness and impartiality in the outcome. These stages, and the various decisions associated with them, are discussed next.

Disciplinary Charges

Rule enforcement is a continuous activity within the institution. Officers, regardless of where they work, are expected to maintain constant surveillance over the inmates in their areas. If an inmate commits a prohibited act, the officer is expected to file a disciplinary report. Yet, aside from serious infractions where such reports are almost always submitted, an officer is able to exercise considerable discretion in deciding whether or not to write a disciplinary report. Given the plethora of rules covering prisoner behavior, an officer could choose to spend most of each shift writing disciplinary charges. Although most officers at Rahway did not pursue this line of action, the number of charges written was nonetheless quite high. During 1979 alone, 2,690 charges were adjudicated on courtline. Although the volume shifts from one year to the next, from April 1976 through 1979 the disciplinary hearing officers decided a total of 10,675 charges, averaging 237.2 per month.[28]

Data gathered from the daily disposition sheets for July through September 1979 illustrate the types of charges that resulted in disciplinary action. During these three months 693 disciplinary hearings were held at Rahway involving 895 charges; 716 charges were disposed of at 534 courtline hearings, while 179 infractions were decided at 159 unit hearings.[29] Hence, 80 percent of all institutional violations cited and 77 percent of all disciplinary hearings involved courtline.

In terms of the inmates, 39.4 percent ($N = 421$) of the population received at least one charge, which means that 60.6 percent ($N = 649$) remained charge-free. All told, 305 inmates received one or two charges only, while 97 others were given anywhere from three to five violations, and 19 inmates received six charges or more. More generally, 19.5 percent ($N = 209$) of the prisoner population was accused of committing 76.3 percent ($N = 683$) of the infractions resulting in a disciplinary hearing. These figures indicate that while a majority of inmates were not charged at all, of those who were, a rather small number accounted for a disproportionate share of the total.

Tables 7.1 and 7.2 list the types of charges referred to courtline between July and September 1979. Of the 716 infractions, 522, or 73 percent, were nonasterisk offenses, and 194, or 27 percent, were asterisk violations. When table 7.1 is considered alone, two of the charges stand apart from all the rest: refusing to obey an order of any staff member ($N = 158$) and being in an unauthorized area ($N = 152$). The first charge ordinarily involves minor incidents such as an inmate's refusing to show an officer his I.D. card when told to do so or hanging a curtain the full length of his cell, thereby obstructing a "wing-cop's" view.

Inmates are given "out of place" charges for being in a wing or tier where they do not house, or being in any other area of the prison without a pass authorizing them to be there. For the most part, nonasterisk offenses fall under the category of order-maintenance violations, violations that are sanctioned mainly to preserve some measure of routine order and control on a day-to-day basis.

As table 7.2 illustrates, asterisk charges appeared on courtline far less often than nonasterisk offenses. The most frequent of these, conduct which disrupts or interferes with the security or orderly running of the institution ($N = 59$), is also the least precise. One prisoner was given this charge for pushing other inmates in the strip-frisk room following contact visits. Another inmate received this charge, also known as a ".306," when, after being denied permission to leave the wing, he shoved his way through a barrier door as the officer opened it to enable a social worker to pass through.

TABLE 7.1. Nonasterisk Charges Referred to Courtline at Rahway State Prison, July–September 1979

Type of Violation	F	%
Refusing to obey an order of any staff member	158	30.3
Being in an unauthorized area	152	29.1
Possession of anything not authorized for retention or receipt by the inmate and not issued to him through regular institutional channels	24	4.6
Fighting with another person	23	4.4
Using abusive or obscene language to a staff member	17	3.3
Failing to stand count	16	3.1
Unexcused absence from work or any assignment	15	2.9
Refusing to work or to accept a program assignment	14	2.7
Lying or providing a false statement to a staff member	13	2.5
Unauthorized use of mail or telephone	11	2.1
Violating a condition of any community release program	10	1.9
Engaging in sexual acts with others	9	1.7
Possession of property belonging to another person	9	1.7
Interfering with the taking of count	8	1.5
Correspondence or conduct with a visitor in violation of regulations	7	1.3
Destroying, altering, or damaging government property or the property of another person	6	1.1
Unauthorized contacts with the public	5	1.0
Indecent exposure	3	0.6
Failing to perform work as instructed by a staff member	3	0.6
Gambling	3	0.6
Making sexual proposals or threats to another	2	0.4
Tampering with or blocking any locking device	2	0.4
Possession of money or currency ($50.00 or less) without specific authorization	2	0.4
Possessing any staff member's clothing and/or equipment	2	0.4
Failure to follow safety or sanitation regulations	2	0.4
Malingering, feigning an illness	1	0.2
Counterfeiting, forging, or unauthorized reproduction of any document, article of identification, money, security, or official paper	1	0.2

TABLE 7.1   (*continued*)

Type of Violation	F	%
Using any equipment or machinery which is not specifically authorized	1	0.2
Being unsanitary or untidy: failing to keep one's person and one's quarters in accordance with posted standards	1	0.2
Tatooing or self-mutilation	1	0.2
Giving money or anything of value to, or accepting money or anything of value from an inmate, or member of his family, or his friend	1	0.2
	$N = 522$	100.0

The most serious asterisk violations involve aggressive or threatening inmate actions against others. When compared with both asterisk and nonasterisk infractions disposed of on courtline, these types of charges accounted for roughly 10 percent of the total. However, as will be shown later, when they did occur they were severely sanctioned. To prison officials they represented actions that had the potential to jeopardize institutional security and/or the physical safety of both staff and inmates. One sign of their perceived seriousness was that all asterisk charges (with but two exceptions) were referred to courtline instead of a unit hearing.

Before disciplinary reports were actually processed, they were first reviewed by the centerkeeper to see if all the necessary information was filled out by the charging officer. He then decided if the inmate was to be placed in prehearing detention,[30] "layed in" (confined to his cell), or allowed to remain in general population pending a hearing. Finally, the centerkeeper was responsible for seeing that a notice of the charge was delivered to the inmate.

Adequate notice of a disciplinary violation is essential not only to inform an inmate of the charge against him but to enable him to prepare a defense. According to the Standards (254.262), unless there were "exceptional circumstances" a copy of the report was to be delivered to an inmate no later than forty-eight hours after the violation and at least twenty-four hours prior to his hearing. Notice is the first point in the disciplinary system where the due process

TABLE 7.2. Asterisk Charges Referred to Courtline at
Rahway State Prison, July–September 1979

Type of Violation	F	%
Conduct which disrupts or interferes with the security or orderly running of the institution	59	30.4
Threatening another with bodily harm or with any offense against his person or his property	33	17.0
Possession, introduction, or use of any narcotic paraphernalia, drugs, or intoxicants not prescribed for the individual by the medical staff	25	13.0
Stealing (theft)	20	10.3
Assaulting any person	17	8.8
Possession or introduction of a gun, firearm, weapon, sharpened instrument, knife, or unauthorized tool	11	5.7
Assaulting any person with a weapon	8	4.1
Escape	8	4.1
Misuse of authorized medication	6	3.1
Extortion, blackmail, protection: demanding or receiving money or anything of value in return for protection against others, to avoid bodily harm, or under threat of informing	1	0.5
Attempting or planning escape	1	0.5
Possession or introduction of any explosive or any ammunition	1	0.5
Encouraging others to riot	1	0.5
Engaging in, or encouraging, a group demonstration	1	0.5
Encouraging others to refuse to work or participation in work stoppage	1	0.5
Attempting to commit any of the above acts preceded by an asterisk, aiding another person to commit any such act, or making plans to commit such acts shall be considered the same as a commission of the act itself	1	0.5
	N = 194	100.0

provisions of *Wolff* and *Avant* are applicable. In the overwhelming majority of charges, these provisions were satisfied in practice.

A review of 704 courtline reports revealed not a single instance where a prisoner was found guilty of an offense for which he never received notice of the charge. In 96 percent ($N = 678$) of the charges, a copy of the disciplinary report was delivered within forty-eight hours of incident, often sooner. In 97 percent ($N = 685$) of the charges, the twenty-four hour requirement was likewise met.

An important aspect of the proceeding is the notice form itself. In 1979 an inmate at Rahway received a carbon copy of the original disciplinary report which included, among other things, his name, number, wing and job assignment, the prohibited act, a description of the alleged infraction, the place of the offense, and the name of the charging officer. When properly filled out, the report form provided the inmate with an adequate amount of information from which to prepare a defense.

Investigation by the Control Unit[31]

Before a disciplinary charge was actually forwarded to courtline, it was assigned to an officer from the control unit for investigation. In contrast to *Wolff* and *Avant*, which were silent on this issue, the Standards at that time mandated that certain minimum procedures had to be followed in conducting such investigations.[32]

At Rahway an inmate received a copy of the charge before the investigative stage began. During the original field work most of the nonsupervisory officers in the control unit were assigned to do investigations. The procedure they usually followed was to locate the inmate, read him the charge, and obtain his version of the incident. This part of the investigation generally lasted only a minute or two. Occasionally the officers also asked the inmate if he had any witnesses he wished to call to courtline, or if he wanted to be represented by counsel substitute. There was, however, no consistency here. Whether or not these questions were posed depended on the thoroughness of individual investigators.[33]

An important and final task that the investigators performed was to provide the disciplinary hearing officer with a recommendation on the charge. They did not tell the hearing officer what sanction to impose. Rather, they simply noted if the charge had merit and if it should therefore be upheld. Data on the relationship between the investigators' recommendations (which they did not always make) and the outcome on courtline are revealing.

In 120 charges, or 79 percent of the time, the investigator recommended that the inmate be found guilty, while in another 32 charges, or 21 percent of the total, the recommendation was one of not guilty. The extent of agreement and disagreement between the hearing officer and the investigator replicates these percentages. Thus, the hearing officer agreed with the investigator's conclusions in 79 percent of the charges and disagreed in the other 21 percent. With respect to the latter, when the hearing officer did not agree with the investigator, with but four exceptions, he ruled in the inmate's favor.

The investigations often provided the hearing officer with information over and beyond that contained in the disciplinary report, and they exerted an influence over the outcome on courtline. It was an influence that was not visible to an inmate, for he never received a copy of the investigation. Nonetheless, although the investigative phase was crucial in the disciplinary system, the most consequential phase took place when an inmate appeared on courtline.

Courtline Hearings

During the period of field work, when inmates referred to "courtline" it was the hearing itself and the possibility of sanctions that they had in mind. Courtline hearings were usually held three or four days a week. On any given day up to 20 charges were adjudicated by the hearing officer, though ordinarily the number was less than this. Recall that during the three months in question, 716 charges were decided at 534 courtline hearings. Of these proceedings, 77 percent ($N = 410$) involved the disposition of one charge; the remaining 23 percent ($N = 124$) involved cases with two charges or more. (The number of hearings equals the number of cases.)

The length of the hearings observed varied considerably, ranging from just under two minutes to nearly ninety minutes. All but four of these hearings lasted twenty-seven minutes or less. The average amount of time spent on a case was nine minutes.

The normal format followed at courtline began as soon as the inmate escorted by a security officer entered the hearing room. Once the inmate was seated the hearing officer read him the charge, obtained his plea, and asked for his explanation of the incident. (In 130 hearings for which data were gathered, 76.9 percent of the inmates pled not guilty, while 23.1 percent admitted their guilt.) If the inmate did not request representation, witnesses, or confrontation/cross-examination, the hearing officer asked the inmate to leave the room while he reached a decision. This process generally took no more than several minutes. If the inmate was found guilty, he was told of the sanction and provided with a carbon copy of the adjudication form, explaining the evidence relied on and the reason for the action taken. At this point the inmate was also informed of his right to appeal the decision and the procedures he had to follow to do so.

In a majority of cases the courtline hearings were routine affairs involving only a review of the charging officer's report, the investigator's report and recommendation, the inmate's testimony, several questions by the hearing officer, and a decision. An example of such a case, involving an asterisk violation, is presented next.

Case 013

Charge: Stealing
Investigator's Recommendation: Charge should be upheld
Inmate Plea: Not Guilty
   On the disciplinary report the officer wrote: "While frisking the outgoing laundry detail I removed from inmate V's swag laundry a jacket belonging to Greystone State Hospital. This item . . . was unauthorized to leave the laundry. Thus this charge."
   The hearing officer read this report to inmate V., along with the investigator's report, and asked him what he had to say about the offense. V. stated that he was pressing another inmate's jacket, but when he came upstairs no inmate would claim it. Expressing concern about remaining charge-free, V. said "I know the marks '(for GSH).' Do you think I would've put it openly over my arm?"
   The hearing officer told inmate V. that his explanation made sense. V.'s disciplinary card [which the hearing officer had before him as he did in all cases] showed this to be his first charge in seven months at Rahway.
   After deliberating for several minutes, the hearing officer found V. guilty, but in view of his good disciplinary record he gave him a suspended sentence. V. was advised of his right to appeal.
Sanction: 15 days Loss of Privileges—Suspended
Evidence Relied On: Officer's Report
Reason for Sanction: First Offense
Length of Hearing: 6 minutes

In contrast, the following case involved a very common nonasterisk violation.

Case 037

Charge: Refusing to Obey an Order of any Staff Member
Investigator's Recommendation: Charge should be upheld
Inmate Plea: Not Guilty
   On the disciplinary report the officer wrote: "at 10:30 P.M., I did tell inmate A. to remove the curtain on his cell door. At approximately 2:30 A.M., while making a check of the wing, I saw that A. had not removed the curtain from his door."
   When questioned by the hearing officer, Inmate A. explained that he works at night. That night when he came in he went to sleep. He did not hear the officer tell him to take the curtain down. Then he added: "I'm guilty for having the curtain up, but I'm not guilty for having refused to obey his [the officer's] order to take it down."
   A. was found guilty of the charge, told of the sanction, and advised of his right to appeal.
Sanction: 7 days loss of Privileges
Evidence Relied On: Officer's Report
Reason for Sanction: To ensure compliance with institutional rules
Length of Hearing: 4 minutes

The format of most courtline hearings adhered rather closely to these cases, but on a number of occasions it did not. This is because inmates, under certain circumstances, are entitled to the due process guarantees of witnesses and representation. Nonetheless, it is up to the hearing officers to interpret and apply these rights in individual cases. How they went about these tasks will be discussed shortly. For now it is important to note that at the outset of courtline, the first thing the hearing officers checked for was compliance with a seven-day time limit, itself a due process guarantee.

The Seven-Day Hearing Requirement

If an inmate remained in general population pending courtline, he had to receive a hearing within one week unless there were "exceptional circumstances, unavoidable delays, or reasonable postponements" (Standards 254.270). If the seventh day fell on a Saturday, Sunday, or holiday, the hearing was to be convened on the first day following the weekend or holiday. The extent of compliance with this provision is assessed next.

Exactly 482 (85.3%) of the charges were held within seven days. Another 11 charges (2%) were not; these were recorded by the hearing officers as violations of due process. Three charges, not disposed of within the necessary time frame, resulted in a not guilty finding, even though they were really violations of due process. Finally, 69 charges (12.2% of the total) were not heard on time through a variety of "exceptional circumstances" or "reasonable postponements." In most of these charges an initial hearing was held within the time frame, but a decision was "deferred" so the hearing officer could gather additional information (e.g., witnesses' statements), further review the evidence, or await the results of lab tests. Postponements here worked in favor of the inmates as often as they worked against them. Thirteen charges were adjudicated after an escapee was returned to custody, and for five charges the seventh day fell on a weekend. Thus, with respect to this provision, compliance was substantial.[34]

Representation (or Counsel Substitute)

Under certain conditions an inmate is entitled to representation at his disciplinary hearing. This protection must be extended whenever an inmate is illiterate or unable to collect and present evidence on his own behalf. At Rahway, substitute counsel was provided by the Prisoners' Legal Association, though other prisoner groups sometimes fulfilled this function. Staff members were not employed as representatives.

From July through September 1979, most (78.6%) of the inmates who appeared on courtline did not request representation, although 113 (21.4%) did. Of the latter, 85 (75.2%) received it, and 28 (24.8%) did not. Substitute counsel was permitted by the hearing officers for one of three reasons: (1) the inmate was charged with an asterisk violation and/or multiple offenses; (2) he was confined in prehearing detention at the time of his hearing; or (3) he was considered illiterate and unable to understand the charge(s) against him.

The reasons for denying counsel substitute were just the reverse of those for permitting it. In the twenty-eight cases where the inmate's request for representation was turned down, the hearing officers invariably cited two reasons: (1) the inmate was not confined in prehearing detention at the time of his hearing; and (2) he was considered literate and capable of understanding the charges against him. (Nonetheless, in three of these cases the inmate was charged with at least one asterisk offense for which he was found guilty.)

Counsel substitute, when granted, was to be given time to speak with the inmate and prepare a defense. At Rahway there was no established procedure whereby this provision was implemented consistently in practice. Sometimes there was ample opportunity to prepare a defense; on other occasions the representative was called down and met with the inmate for the first time during courtline. Although the input of substitute counsel was often limited to brief remarks in the hearings that were observed, in several cases the representative served as a full-fledged advocate. The case presented next is an example of such advocacy. Atypical in many respects, it offers an illustration of a hearing characterized by the provision of nearly total due process.

Case 122

Charge: Threatening another with bodily harm, or with any offense against his person or his property (1 count); Extortion, blackmail, protection (1 count); Unauthorized use of mail or telephone (2 counts)

Investigator's Recommendation: "Extortion" and "Unauthorized use of mail or telephone" should be upheld; nothing else recorded

Inmate Plea: Not Guilty (to all four charges)

For three out of the four charges (excluding one of the telephone charges) the officer submitted the same disciplinary report. According to this officer, "from 12-12-78 to the present there have been a series of collect phone calls placed to various cities and towns all over the state to innocent residents. These various calls consisted of threats/sexual proposals, extortive demands. On each resident's phone bill the call indicated that the phone call originally came from 2-Up (a housing dormitory). An intensive investigation has been

conducted by this writer to ascertain the inmate placing these calls.
. . . On July 11, 1979, at approx. 12:33 P.M. inmate E. placed a collect call to a resident living in Belmar, N.J. Saying it was collect from "John" the resident in Belmar accepted the call because she has a brother named John." Inmate E. went on to state "I have your brother John here w/me because he owes me money, and if you ever want to see him again you'd better answer these questions: Do you have a boyfriend? Do you and your boyfriend have sex? Do you suck your boyfriend's cock? Does your boyfriend eat you out? Are you wearing underwear? What color is your hair? Play with yourself?" On the above date, and approximate time, officer M. observed inmate E. on the telephone.

Inmate E. entered the hearing room with his representative from the Prisoners' Legal Association. A request by the latter to tape record the proceeding was turned down by the hearing officer who said that he would enter any statements into the written record if either man asked him to do so.

The representative then said that they had a witness who would testify that inmate E. was not on the phone at the time of the phone call. The hearing officer replied that if the issue came up later he would consider their request then. Neither side returned to this issue.

Three motions were introduced by the representative, each of which was read by the hearing officer, and recorded. He seemed to accept one of the motions saying that the evidence sustained at best one charge, that the others were repetitive.

The hearing officer then read aloud the investigator's report, an operations report, and a letter from the complainant. When asked for a statement E. said that he had been instructed by his attorney [outside the prison] to remain silent. The hearing officer replied that while a negative inference could be drawn from his silence, all the evidence would be considered.

The representative next requested to confront and cross-examine the wing officer who observed the calls. The officer was summoned to the hearing, and once again stated that he had observed inmate E. on the phone the day of the incident. He also said that he worked two shifts that day, and that he noted the number and time of all calls made by E. The representative questioned the accuracy of the times recorded by the officer.

The hearing officer brought the proceeding to a close, and after reviewing the evidence, found E. not guilty on one of the phone charges, and dismissed the extortion charge as repetitive. He told E. and his representative that he wanted more time to evaluate the remaining charges. The next day he dismissed the other phone charges, and found E. guilty of the charge involving threatening another.

Sanction: 15 days Lockup; Administrative Segregation for 1 year; Loss of 365 days Commutation Time; Refer to Prosecutor.

Evidence Relied On: "Officer's testimony"; "substantial evidence that threat occurred"; "E. makes no statement in refutation."

Reason for Action Taken: Wing telephones exist to enable inmates to retain closer ties with family and friends and to exercise a measure of independence in taking care of personal business. Because these phones are unmonitored they create tremendous potential for abuse and therefore impose a heavy responsibility on inmates to use them legitimately. This incident represents a major abuse of the phone privilege for illegal purposes, and to threaten/harass/embarrass citizens. Such acts must be punished and deterred. E., by his action, has shown an inability to function in an environment which grants him some measure of freedom of actions and exacts in turn inmate self-discipline. Therefore, the close supervision of Administrative Segregation is more than warranted. Man's prior disciplinary record supports this conclusion.

Length of Hearing: 66 minutes.[35]

Witnesses

According to *Wolff*, inmates may call witnesses who are "necessary for a proper understanding of the case . . . [and] . . . reasonably available," and whose appearance will not be "unduly hazardous to institutional safety or correctional goals."[36] Most (80.2%) of the inmates who appeared on courtline did not request witnesses. Of the 104 inmates who did, 91.4 percent ($N = 95$) had their request granted. However, in 55.8 percent ($N = 58$) of these cases written statements were used in place of oral testimony. Witnesses appeared in person in only 25.9 percent ($N = 27$) of the cases. They were denied outright 8.7 percent ($N = 9$) of the time. In the remaining ten cases, more than one witness was permitted, but at the same time, at least one witness was also denied.

Inmates' requests for witnesses were turned down for one of four reasons. "Irrelevance" was recorded on the adjudication form, meaning that the witness in question did not have direct firsthand knowledge of the incident. Second, the request was denied either because the witnesses' names were not given to the investigator or because the inmate did not request them during an earlier hearing. This reflects the hearing officers' belief that in the interim between the investigation and the hearing, or between an initial appearance and a subsequent appearance, witnesses' testimony may be "arranged." Although they are not openly skeptical about the truthfulness of inmate witnesses, the hearing officers are sensitive to what they feel are subtle institutional pressures to support a fellow inmate. As one hearing officer stated during the original field work:

> It may happen all the time that witnesses are arranged. In confinement a guy has to protect himself and he will respond to those circumstances, especially if he is pressured. More often than being blatant the pressure is more subtle, indirect. For example, an inmate may say to another inmate: "You didn't hear me threaten that officer did you?" And the inmate will agree to say that he didn't hear any threat in order to avoid a confrontation.

Third, witnesses were not allowed after it was determined that they were not "reasonably available" (e.g., in one case an inmate requested an officer who was on vacation). Finally, witnesses were denied as repetitive, though whenever this happened the inmate in question received other witnesses.

Witnesses on courtline were not always other inmates. In forty-six of the cases, officers and/or staff members provided statements, often along with inmate testimony. Aside from comments serving to clarify the incident (e.g., who said what to whom), in a number of instances their testimony supported the inmate's version of the incident. Nonetheless, officers like inmates are vulnerable to institutional pressures—in this case, not to side with inmates against other officers.

In most instances where a single witness was permitted, his testimony was brief, lasting no more than a minute or two. But this was not always so, especially when two or more witnesses offered oral testimony. In the case described next, the inmate received a very serious assault charge. At his hearing (held in prehearing detention), he was granted counsel substitute and six witnesses (three inmates and three officers), all of whom testified in person. Although this case once again represents an exception to the rule, in contrast to Case 122, it demonstrates the potential importance of this particular due process guarantee.[37]

Case 091

Charge: Assaulting any person with a weapon
Investigator's Recommendation: ?
Inmate Plea: Not Guilty

This case represents the most serious assault by one inmate against another during the period field work was carried out at Rahway. Inmate B. was charged with entering the cell of another inmate, and beating him in the face with a lock held in a stocking. Severe injuries resulted. As the suspected assailant B. was put in prehearing detention, but released the following day. An investigation of the incident was concluded ten days later at which time B. was charged with the infraction and returned to "double-lock." The disciplinary charge relied solely on the word of an inmate informant.

B. was permitted representation and witnesses. When the proceeding began, the hearing officer summarized the contents of the confidential report, and told B. that his review of the report was "preliminary, not final." When asked for his statement, B. admitted arguing loudly with inmate K. (who was injured) the evening before the assault took place. But he denied committing the act. He claimed he went to the messhall the morning of the assault, and returned to his wing with a cup of coffee. At that point, B. says an alarm went off, and all inmates were locked in their cells.

Three inmate witnesses were then brought into the hearing. One of them testified that B. left the wing when the doors were opened for breakfast, and returned with coffee. This witness, and the other two inmate witnesses, said they were all sitting there with B. when the alarm sounded.

The next witness was B.'s wing officer. He stated the time he unlocked the wing, and recalled that he locked the wing back up eight minutes later when the alarm went off. At the suggestion of the representative, a second officer was called. This officer controlled the entrance to the tier when inmate K. was assaulted. He said he did not recall B. coming in on the morning of the incident, but added that it was only his second day on the job.

The testimony of a third officer was gathered later in the day by the hearing officer. This officer said he saw B. in the messhall the morning of the assault.

The hearing lasted approximately fifty minutes. The hearing officer found B. not guilty of the charge based on the witnesses' combined testimony. On the adjudication form under evidence relied on he wrote "testimony of three officers establishes man was seen in messhall during eight minutes or so he was out of the wing, and was not seen by one right wing officer."

Confrontation and Cross-Examination

Although inmates do not have a constitutional right to confront and cross-examine adverse witnesses, in accordance with *Avant*, the Standards state that it was to "be provided in such instances where . . . the hearing officer deems it necessary for an adequate presentation of the evidence, particularly when serious issues of credibility are involved" (254.274). If it was denied, the hearing officers had to record the reason for the denial.

In practice, the hearing officers regarded confrontation and cross-examination (C/CE) as a matter over which they had complete discretion. In a training film, one of the hearing officers referred to C/CE as a "sticky thing," "not usually done." Out of 527 inmates for which information was available, 95 percent ($N = 501$) did not ask for C/CE. The 5 percent who did totaled 26 inmates; of these, 23 were granted their request. There was no pattern to this rather surprising figure, though 16 of the cases involved asterisk and/or multiple charges. The other 8 cases involved single non-asterisk violations.

An overview of how often inmates received one or more of the three due process protections discussed thus far (representation, witnesses, and confrontation/cross-examination) is provided in table 7.3. The table also compares the relationship between the provision of these rights and the outcome (guilty or not guilty) on courtline. During the three months in question, there were no cases of an inmate receiving all three of these rights within the context of a single hearing. In terms of the total sample ($N = 534$), 370 inmates (69.3%) did not request or were denied these protections, while 164 (30.7%) were granted at least one of them ($N = 125$) and 39 (7.3%) were granted two.

Clearly, of all the due process protections, being permitted to call a witness is associated most often with a not guilty outcome on courtline. By itself or in combination with representation, it is associated with a significantly higher percentage of not guilty findings than any of the other options (64.5% and 41.7%, respectively). Neither representation nor C/CE seems to be strongly related to a

TABLE 7.3. Major Due Process Rights by Outcome on Courtline, July–September 1979

| | Due Process Right | | | | | | | |
Outcome	No Due Process	C/CE Only	Witnesses Only	Witnesses and C/CE	Representation Only	Representation and C/CE	Representation and Witnesses	Total (%)
Not guilty	93 (25.1%)	0	40 (64.5%)	2 (22.2%)	10 (18.2%)	0	10 (41.7%)	155 (29.0)
Guilty	277 (74.9%)	8 (100.0%)	22 (35.5%)	7 (77.8%)	45 (81.8%)	6 (100.0%)	14 (58.3%)	379 (71.0)
Total (%)	379 (69.3)	8 (1.5)	62 (11.6)	9 (1.7)	55 (10.3)	6 (1.1)	24 (4.5)	534 (100.0)

Note: $p < .000$.

not guilty outcome, in each instance falling below the not guilty percentage for inmates receiving no due process. Only when it is provided along with witnesses does C/CE show any association with a not guilty finding at all.

While table 7.3 does not control for a number of other variables that might affect the outcome (e.g., an inmate's admission of guilt), it does offer evidence of the comparative importance of these protections on courtline. In view of its general lack of relationship to not guilty verdicts on courtline, the provision of C/CE appears to be a token gesture. On the other hand, the presence of witnesses is a crucial determinant of the outcome. As will be shown later, in cases where the testimony of witnesses proved decisive, it was usually the testimony of an officer as opposed to that of an inmate.[38]

Dispositions

The hearing officers in 1979 had a wide range of dispositions available to them, including both nonpunitive options and punitive sanctions. Moreover, for any given charge, they could impose more than one penalty. Because of this the number ($N = 914$) of dispositions handed down on courtline between July and September 1979 is higher than the total number of charges ($N = 716$).

Table 7.4 shows how often each disposition was used. The most frequent punitive sanction was lockup, or solitary confinement. It was imposed 191 (21%) times for periods ranging from two to fifteen days. There were no instances where an inmate was held in lockup for a period of time beyond the maximum permitted by the disciplinary Standards. The next most common punishment, a suspended sentence, was handed out 114 times, accounting for 12.5 percent of the total.

Numerous factors influenced the severity of the sanction(s), but one important determinant was the charge itself. Both asterisk and nonasterisk infractions were often sanctioned by a period of lockup. Although the former were dealt with more harshly than the latter, the severest sanctions imposed by the hearing officers were for charges involving violence (or the threat of violence) and escape (usually from minimum security honor camps).

Various combinations of sanctions were handed down on courtline.[39] However, as the number of sanctions exceeds the number of

TABLE 7.4.   Courtline Dispositions at Rahway State Prison
July–September 1979

Type of Disposition	F	%
Not guilty	210	23.0
Lockup	191	20.9
Suspended sentence	114	12.5
Refer to Classification Committee for housing or job change or for urine monitoring	77	8.4
Loss of commutation time	48	5.3
Concurrent sentence	48	5.3
Dismissed as repetitive	43	4.7
Transfer to administrative segregation, or Vroom Readjustment Unit, or Trenton State Prison	41	4.5
Loss of privileges	31	3.4
Reprimand	25	2.7
Revert to maximum security status	20	2.2
Violation of due process	15	1.6
Refer to prosecutor	15	1.6
Loss of contact visits	9	1.0
Vacate and impose suspended sentence	8	0.9
Restitution	7	0.8
Idle status	6	0.6
Dismissed as disciplinary action	6	0.6
	$N = 914$	100.0

charges, the issue of innocence or guilt by charge is obscured. This issue may be resolved by assigning one of two outcomes to a given charge: guilty or not guilty. When this is done, of the total number ($N = 716$) of charges, 38 percent fall into the not guilty and 62 percent into the guilty category. If these charges are then divided into their designated asterisk ($N = 194$) and nonasterisk ($N = 522$) categories, 36.6 percent of the nonasterisk charges were adjudicated not guilty and 63.4 percent, guilty. For asterisk charges 43 percent ended in a not guilty decision, while 57 percent resulted in a finding of guilty. Hence, a higher percentage of asterisk than nonasterisk violations were found not guilty on courtline.

The final issue to be considered is perhaps the most important. Of all the inmates who appeared on courtline ($N = 534$), how many were found guilty and how many not guilty? This issue is itself obscured by the figures just presented in that an inmate may be acquitted on one charge and found guilty of another in the same hearing. When cases are considered apart from charges, it turns out that 29 percent ($N = 155$) of the inmates were found not guilty while 71 percent ($N = 379$) were adjudicated guilty.

The fact that no sanction was imposed on a fair number of charges (especially asterisk violations) suggests that during the field work courtline proceedings were not oriented toward a simple decision as to what sanction to impose, and nothing more. Rather, there appears to have been an effort to evaluate an inmate's innocence or guilt. However, when cases are examined, it is also apparent that when an inmate appeared on courtline he was more likely to be found guilty than not guilty of a charge.[40]

Evidence Relied on and Reason(s) for Any Actions Taken

In 1979 the Standards (254.275) stated that an inmate could be found guilty of a disciplinary charge only if there was "substantial evidence" pointing to his involvement in the incident or "reasonable cause" to believe that his actions represented a danger to those around him. One of the hearing officers defined these requirements in the following way. In order to find a person guilty in a criminal trial the level of evidence must be beyond a reasonable doubt. This, he felt, equalled "95% certainty or above." For the same finding in a civil case, the necessary level of evidence drops to a preponderance of probability, or "roughly 66% certainty." Within the prison setting, the evidentiary level drops even further, to "51% certainty." As both hearing officers acknowledged, the level of evidence required to convict was "very low."

In their adjudication of charges on courtline, the hearing officers considered a wide array of evidence, including the charging officer's report, an inmate's admission of guilt, self-incriminating inmate testimony, the investigative report, other staff or officer statements (e.g., operations reports), witnesses' testimony, confidential information, and lab tests. Table 7.5 presents the frequency with which a given type of evidence was cited by the hearing officer in finding an inmate guilty.

The charging officer's report, either by itself or supported by other types of information (mainly operations reports filed by other officers), was considered sufficient to convict in 74 percent ($N = 322$) of the charges. Where they relied on the disciplinary report alone, the hearing officers cited to a significant degree what they called the "theory of vested interest." According to this theory, if, after all the evidence has been reviewed, the case comes down to the officer's word against the inmate's, the weight of credibility lies entirely with the former. The inmate has a stronger vested interest in lying, and in getting his lie accepted, for he stands to suffer adversely if he is found guilty, whereas the officer has no such interest. Commenting on this theory, a hearing officer noted, "Frankly, if there is a conflict in testimony between an inmate and an officer, and that is all I have to rely on, I will side with the officer and find the inmate guilty."

As it works out, such "conflict" is not all the hearing officers "have to rely on." Inmates admitted their guilt in 115 charges. In 15 of these charges, their admission was coupled with other evidence. In another 38 charges the inmate's testimony was considered self-incriminating (though in 31 of these charges the disciplinary report was also cited). When the hearing officers found an inmate guilty of an institutional infraction they relied on four basic types of evidence: the charging officer's report, other staff or officer statements, an inmate's admission of guilt, and self-incriminating inmate testimony.

In finding an inmate not guilty of a disciplinary charge, the hearing officers most often recorded only that the "evidence was insufficient," or "there was reasonable doubt." These comments, which do not really proclaim the inmate innocent of the violation, were listed for ninety charges. The next most frequently cited type of evidence was the investigator's report. By itself ($N = 55$) or along with other evidence ($N = 16$) it was used to find an inmate not guilty of a charge more often than guilty. The third and final type of evidence most often considered was the testimony of a witness ($N = 44$). Recall that both inmates and officers (or staff members) served as witnesses on courtline. However, not once in forty-four

TABLE 7.5. Type of Evidence Relied On by the Hearing Officers in Finding an Inmate Guilty of a Disciplinary Charge on Courtline July–September 1979

Type of Evidence Cited by Charge	F	%	More Than One Type of Evidence Cited by Charge	F	%
Officer's report	209	47.7	Officer's report plus other staff or officer statements	54	12.3
Inmate admits guilt	100	22.8	Officer's report plus inmate testimony self-incriminating	31	7.1
Other staff or officer statements	0	0	Officer's report plus inmate admits guilt	11	2.5
Inmate testimony self-incriminating	7	1.6	Officer's report plus investigator's report	7	1.6
Investigator's report	2	0.5	Officer's report plus field or lab test	5	1.1
Field or lab test	0	0	Inmate admits guilt plus other staff or officer statements	2	0.5
Confidential information	3	0.7	Inmate admits guilt plus field test	2	0.5
Total charges/evidence = 438			Other (three types of evidence cited)	5	1.1

charges was the testimony of an inmate witness recorded under "evidence relied on" as the reason for a finding of not guilty. Although the names and/or statements of inmates and officers often appeared together as witnesses, it was the testimony of the latter that was recorded as the evidentiary basis for the decision.

The hearing officers are expected to state the reasons for the sanctions they impose and to include them on the adjudication form that is given to the inmate. Their reasons, in fact, fall under seven different headings: deterrence, the disciplinary record of the inmate, maintaining order and security, ensuring compliance with an officer's order, the serious nature of the violation, job related, and a miscellaneous category of "other."

In relation to the total number of times each appeared under "reason for sanction(s) imposed," deterrence was first ($N = 171$), with the inmate's disciplinary record following closely ($N = 161$). More often than not, reference was made to a good record ($N = 125$) rather than a poor one ($N = 36$). With some frequency, the hearing officers cited order maintenance and the importance of ensuring compliance with institutional rules or an officer's order ($N = 65$). The very serious nature of a violation (and/or its potential for triggering a major disturbance) was recorded somewhat less frequently ($N = 58$). Job-related reasons (which generally involve clashes between inmates and work supervisors) were listed only sixteen times.[41]

Appeal

At the conclusion of courtline, if he was found guilty, the inmate was told that he had twenty-four hours to appeal the decision. All sanctions were automatically suspended during this period. If the inmate chose to appeal, the suspension remained in effect until the matter was resolved.

Once an appeal was submitted, it was returned to the control unit where it was assigned to a social worker for further investigation. Following the investigation the appeal was returned to the control unit where it was reviewed by a supervisor, who, in turn, made a recommendation and forwarded it to the superintendent's office for a final decision.

A number of inmates never bothered to file an appeal because they were found not guilty. Excluding the not guilty category ($N = 154$), 56 percent ($N = 210$) of the inmates who were convicted did not submit an appeal, whereas 44 percent ($N = 168$) did. The appeals outcomes that were available for the second group ($N = 164$) indicate that the courtline sanction was modified in 38 cases and left unchanged in 126 cases. Hence, given only those cases where an inmate found guilty filed an appeal, the decision of the hearing officer was upheld 77 percent of the time and altered in some way 23 percent of the time.

In eleven of the thirty-eight cases where the superintendent changed the courtline penalty, administrative segregation, referral to the prosecutor, or forfeiture of commutation time was dropped altogether. A six-month sentence to "ad seg" was removed in two of these cases. In two others, referrals for 60 to 90 days were dropped. With respect to commutation time, 180-day forfeitures were twice rescinded, while in two other cases, 60 days were restored. Thus, in some instances significant reductions were made in courtline sanctions.

Reductions in the remaining cases ($N = 27$) ranged from subtracting several days from a loss of privileges to changing a ten-day lockup penalty to a suspended sentence. In other instances a fraction of forfeited good time or contact visiting time was restored. Finally, in two cases involving single nonasterisk violations, a courtline finding of guilty was reduced to not guilty.

The reasons for the superintendent's decisions were not recorded. Nonetheless, interviews with officers from the control unit indicate that changes were made in a courtline disposition for one of four reasons. First, a violation of due process was uncovered during the social worker's investigation. Second, a sanction was modified because it was considered too severe in relation to the infraction. Most of the superintendent's decisions appear to have involved reductions of this kind. Third, the superintendent simply relied on the recommendation from the control supervisor. The fourth and final reason involved reducing an inmate's sanction in exchange for information on the whereabouts of drugs, "hooch," or weapons in the institution—a form of reciprocity which the control officers argued served to prevent more serious incidents from occurring.

Judicial Intervention and the Bureaucratization of Prison Discipline

It has been fifteen years since the Supreme Court decided *Wolff*, fourteen years since the ruling in *Avant*. The seminal decisions affecting prisoners' rights are apparently behind us, yet inmates continue to file suits and the courts continue to intervene, albeit with increased deference to prison administrators.[42] Within this context, Rahway State Prison serves as an important case study insofar as its disciplinary system generally accorded inmates the due process to which they were entitled. This section and the next will summarize the more salient findings from the original research, highlight several significant developments since that time, and offer an assessment of the value and limitations of due process law acting in a mediating capacity at Rahway State Prison.

Clearly, major changes have been made in the Standards governing inmate discipline as a result of *Wolff* and *Avant*. Although formal disciplinary Standards had been promulgated prior to these rulings,[43] substantial revisions and modifications were introduced in direct response to these decisions.[44] Since then further changes have been made providing even greater codification and specificity with respect to disciplinary practices and procedures.[45]

As a result of developments triggered by *Wolff* and even more so *Avant*, the disciplinary Standards are both comprehensive and detailed in their procedural requirements. They are also legalistic in substance, often reproducing the language used in *Wolff* and *Avant*. More important, they are fully responsive to the requisites of due process, in some instances going well beyond what is required by these decisions (e.g., investigations and appeals).

If only by virtue of their breadth and specificity, the post-*Avant* Standards have reduced the margin of institutional control and autonomy over the disciplinary system. However, the Department of Corrections actively oversees compliance with the disciplinary Standards through its Hearing Officer Program. The significance of this program will be discussed shortly. For now it is sufficient to note that at Rahway these developments have fostered a notable bureaucratization of disciplinary practices and procedures.

In contrast to the situation before *Wolff* and *Avant*, where disciplinary practices were loosely structured and characterized by substantial if not unreviewable discretion, the disciplinary system now is much more formal, rational, and legal in structure. The disciplinary system at Rahway is characterized by a set of uniform procedures and a rational decision-making process for adjudicating inmate violators.

Nonetheless, the system of social control, and courtline in particular, serves as the foundation for maintaining institutional order and for gaining at least passive inmate compliance with the rules. Inmate life is characterized by rule-governed regimentation. In addition to myriad institutional rules and regulations, inmates are expected to comply at all times with seventy-nine officially prohibited acts. This list of proscribed acts provides considerable definition with respect to the kinds of behaviors that constitute a disciplinary violation. However, as a consequence of the increase in specificity, the listing of asterisk–nonasterisk violations more than doubled since 1973.

This growth in the number of prohibited acts is important in terms of rule enforcement within the institution. At Rahway an officer's most essential tool of control is "writing up" an inmate for a disciplinary violation. Among other functions, submitting disciplinary charges contributes to the maintenance of internal order and sustains the authority of the officer over the inmate. But rule enforcement alone is sufficient neither to ensure a modicum of order and control nor to secure prisoner compliance with the rules. Prisoner compliance is secured and order is sustained ultimately through the operation of courtline.

Courtline represents the sine qua non of social control at Rahway, for it is the primary mechanism whereby punitive sanctions are imposed. However, the fact that the disciplinary system is now more formal in structure and legalistic in operation does not mean that it is any more fair, especially if prison officials are able to adhere to the trappings of due process and then summarily punish inmates without regard to innocence or guilt.[46] This is, in fact, the very tension that the rule of law in the guise of procedural due process attempts to mediate. How effective it is in doing so goes to the very heart of the judiciary's capacity to intervene and enhance the fair treatment of inmates within a maximum security prison.

The Rule of Law and Social Control
at Rahway State Prison

It is important to note that due process law does not directly challenge the legitimacy of the prisons' power structure or prison officials' use of discretion to maintain institutional order and control. Rather, it challenges the arbitrary and summary application of this power and the exercise of discretion in the absence of accountability. It does so by requiring prison officials to follow a sequence of steps before sanctioning an inmate for misconduct. In its emphasis on procedural formality, due process law mandates the creation of an adjudicatory system which, through a series of safeguards posted at different points along the way, is designed to provide inmate offenders with fair and impartial treatment. These safeguards are also intended to place meaningful restraints on those charged with enforcing institutional rules. This is, in fact, the main value of due process law.

As a consequence of *Wolff* and *Avant*, the disciplinary process relies on a variety of written forms[47] while the procedures are governed by the due process safeguards pertaining to time limits and the requirement that reason(s) be provided for any actions that are taken (e.g., the denial of counsel substitute) or sanctions that are handed down. These safeguards place some checks on the exercise of official discretion and simultaneously ensure some accountability for the decisions that are made. To their consternation, officers now find that poorly written or vaguely worded disciplinary charges may result in a finding of not guilty.[48] When the procedural time limits are exceeded without reasonable justification, a charge may be dismissed as a violation of due process. The hearing officers know that prisoners who feel they have been treated unfairly may file a lawsuit against them or pursue some other remedy, subjecting their decisions to subsequent and outside review.[49] Although there are limits to this accountability, the fact that it exists at all is sufficient to ensure that prison officials go through the motions of fairness when it comes to the adjudication of disciplinary cases. At Rahway the most important official is the hearing officer and the most critical stage the courtline hearing.

Much of the value of due process is either realized or compromised during the course of a disciplinary hearing. Within this context, fairness and impartiality are realized to the extent that the hearing is oriented toward fact-finding, the disinterested determination of an inmate's innocence or guilt, and the provision of a meaningful opportunity to present a defense. These ideals are compromised if the hearing becomes merely a forum wherein the primary issue to resolve is what disposition to impose.

During the original field work, courtline hearings were obviously concerned with what sanctions to impose in those cases where the hearing officer found an inmate guilty of a disciplinary violation. However, in contrast to several studies which suggest that prison disciplinary proceedings are, in fact, primarily dispositional in nature,[50] courtline hearings were not concerned solely with what sanction to impose. The majority of the disciplinary charges referred to courtline involved relatively minor, nonasterisk violations. Moreover, as many of the prisoners who appeared on courtline did so with one or two nonasterisk charges, a large percentage of the courtline hearings were routine and did not involve the presence of, or a request for, witnesses or counsel substitute. Where there is a commitment to fact-finding, and to the impartial evaluation of an inmate's innocence or guilt, this commitment should be manifest in a certain percentage of not guilty findings. It is thus significant that the most frequent courtline disposition (with respect to charges) was a finding of not guilty.[51] Perhaps of more importance, the not guilty percentage for the more serious asterisk violations was slightly higher than for the less serious, nonasterisk charges. Among other things, this indicates that courtline hearings were not singularly oriented toward what sanction to impose, and nothing more. Some emphasis was placed on the objective determination of the facts and an impartial assessment of the innocence or guilt of an inmate accused of committing an institutional infraction.[52]

This emphasis was especially apparent in the small number of cases where an inmate received a serious asterisk charge or some combination of nonasterisk and asterisk violations. In these types of cases the adjudicative process on courtline became quite formal and deliberate in nature. The hearing officer usually granted an inmate's request for witnesses, counsel substitute, or C/CE (though never all three within the span of a single hearing). The inmate was given ample opportunity to fully contest the charge(s) in a hearing that sometimes lasted over an hour. Before reaching a decision, the hearing officer reviewed whatever evidence was available concerning the incident, usually going over it together with the accused. While most of the inmates in these cases were eventually found guilty, this was not always so.

A case was presented earlier (Case 091) involving a very serious assault by one prisoner on another. An inmate was eventually charged with the assault based on confidential information supplied by an inmate informant. Given the seriousness of the incident and the presence of a confidential report, it was apparent at the outset of the hearing that the onus was on the accused to prove that he was innocent. In the absence of procedural due process, this inmate would have been given a summary hearing and then sanctioned severely. Instead, he received a lengthy hearing during which he was permitted the assistance of counsel substitute and the opportunity to call six witnesses (including both officers and inmates) to corroborate his version of events. As a result, he was able to establish reasonable doubt that he was, in fact, the assailant. A series of evidential insertions that were allowed because of due process gradually accumulated, one on top of the other, and challenged the veracity of the confidential report. This case illustrates that if the procedural safeguards associated with due process are permitted during the course of a disciplinary hearing, they offer an opportunity for an inmate to establish his innocence, if he is in fact innocent.

Although there are notable limitations associated with due process safeguards, in combination their presence at Rahway has resulted in a shift in the balance of power—both symbolic and real—between keeper and kept. Inmates have certain due process rights which prison officials are obliged to respect. An inmate's guilt can no longer be taken for granted. Rather, the fact that he is alleged to have committed an institutional infraction must be proven. Nonetheless, although restrictions have been placed on the discretion of prison officials to discipline inmates, the overall impact and thus the mediating value of due process is blunted by several factors: the need to assume the good-faith efforts on the part of prison officials, especially the hearing officers, the volume of disciplinary charges that are processed at any given time, and, perhaps most important, the social and organizational dynamics of a maximum security prison. Each of these factors will be discussed in turn.

Conclusion: Fairness and Discipline

Several studies have concluded that without a commitment to fairness on the part of prison administrators, due process law will have little impact on the outcome of a disciplinary proceeding.[53] As Jacobs points out:[54]

> While the courts might be able to impose a form of decision making on the prison, they are not in a position to overturn substantive decisions. . . . By necessity the courts must assume the good faith of the administration . . . unless the administration itself acts in good faith and assumes a responsibility to supervise the fairness of the process, inmates are essentially little better off than before, and without a remedy unless, of course, the administration completely fails to follow the required procedures.

Providing, albeit unintended, support for Jacobs, one of the hearing officers acknowledged that "absent a sense of fair play by prison authorities the [disciplinary] system reduces to one of form over substance."

At Rahway there was a discernible—if matter of fact—recognition that inmates were entitled to fairness on courtline, that they could not be treated as they had been prior to *Wolff* and *Avant*. This recognition extended from the superintendent down to prison staff and even to some of the officers. The hearing officers themselves seemed to be committed, at least in most instances, to giving a prisoner a fair shake. One indicator of this was found in their willingness to grant most inmates who requested it the assistance of representation, witnesses, or even C/CE. Nonetheless, this attitude of fairness is firmly rooted within and tempered by a set of taken-for-granted institutional assumptions regarding the centrality of maintaining order and the manipulative character of the prisoner population. This is not to say that fairness is not realized on courtline but to argue that it is realized only within the context of these assumptions. These assumptions will be discussed in a moment. For now it is necessary to consider a feature of the disciplinary system that by itself compromises the mediating value of due process.

Each month at Rahway an astounding number of disciplinary charges are referred to courtline.[55] Although a small percentage of prisoners are responsible for a disproportionate share of this total, which means that the actual number of cases disposed of on court-line is less than the number of charges, even the number of hearings held each month is quite high. In either event, given that the majority of prisoners referred to courtline contest their charge(s), the volume of disciplinary traffic by itself is sufficient to prevent the provision of full due process (i.e., witnesses, representation, and C/CE) in each and every case. The hearing officer system of adjudication is not equipped to extend full due process on a continuing basis to all inmates who receive formal hearings, even if the hearing officers themselves were committed to doing so.

Recall that during the original field work 75 to 95 percent of the prisoners who appeared on courtline did not ask for counsel substitute, witnesses, or C/CE. In those instances where just two out of three of these safeguards were provided, the hearing often turned into a rather lengthy affair, sometimes resulting in postponements so that more witnesses might be called or additional evidence gathered. If even a small number of those inmates who did not request any of the aforementioned safeguards had actually done so, one of two outcomes would have developed: either their requests would have been granted, leading to longer hearings and more delays, or, more likely, their requests would have been denied with much more frequency. This indicates that the amount of due process provided at Rahway depended on the fact that a significant number of inmates did not bother to ask for it. However, the sheer number of charges processed is not the only factor that compromises the effectiveness of the rule of law.

As various commentators have shown, the fundamental feature of the prison's social structure is the castelike distinction that is maintained between the prisoners on the one hand and prison officials on the other.[56] Rahway is no exception to this. Although there is to be found some occasional bantering between inmates and officers, there is also a good deal of open hostility, antagonism, and mutual mistrust. Social distance between keeper and kept is not only considered desirable—it is enforced.

At Rahway, as in other maximum security prisons, this castelike distinction carries with it a set of assumptions regarding the inmate population. By virtue of the role they occupy within the social organization of the prison, inmates are regarded as highly manipulative and exploitative. They are viewed as predatory in behavior and thus ever willing, if given an opportunity, to break institutional rules either for personal gain or simply to "beat the system." The consequence is that their word is open to serious question. When these assumptions are joined with the "theory of vested interest," the result is that prisoners have a serious credibility problem when they appear on courtline.

As far as prison officials are concerned, the theory of vested interest merely reflects institutional common sense. Because an inmate who receives a charge is liable to be punished if he is found guilty, he has a strong vested interest in lying to avoid this outcome. The charging officer has no such interest and will not, under normal circumstances, lie or fabricate an incident in reporting a disciplinary violation. This theory becomes particularly influential whenever a courtline hearing reduces to a swearing contest between the reporting staff member and the accused inmate. In such cases, the theory dictates that credibility lies with the former.

Clearly, inmates who receive disciplinary reports confront a serious credibility problem in attempting to prove their innocence. However, not only does the accused inmate's role within the prison community undermine the value of his testimony, but it also places limits on the value of calling inmate witnesses whose word is similarly suspect. At Rahway, prison officials place little value on the testimony of an inmate witness because they believe that informal pressures are placed on such witnesses to support the accused. This seeming lack of credibility is revealed in the finding that not once did the courtline testimony recorded as the evidentiary basis for a not guilty finding cite another inmate's name.

The fact that the assumptions discussed herein exert an influence over the adjudication of disciplinary infractions at Rahway is not surprising; other studies have reported similar findings.[57] However, what these other studies all too often fail to consider is that within the prison setting these assumptions make sense.[58] And it is because they make sense that the mediating value of due process law is seriously compromised. As a consequence of these assumptions, the burden of responsibility shifts to the accused inmate to show that he is in fact not guilty of a disciplinary charge. The presumption of innocence does not follow an inmate into a disciplinary hearing. Given their commitment to fairness, the hearing officers at Rahway usually provided an inmate with an opportunity to establish his innocence. At best, this is what prison officials' commitment to fairness in the disciplinary process ultimately means: procedural safeguards give the inmate a chance to prove his innocence within the context of taken-for-granted assumptions that render his efforts to do so difficult but by no means impossible.

Notes

1. Richard A. Cloward et al., *Theoretical Studies in Social Organization of the Prison* (New York: Social Science Research Council, 1960); Gresham M. Sykes, *The Society of Captives* (Princeton, N.J.: Princeton University Press, 1958).
2. Leo Carroll, *Hacks, Blacks, and Cons* (Lexington, Mass.: Lexington Books, 1974); Robert Johnson, *Hard Time: Understanding and Reforming the Prison* (Monterey, Calif.: Brooks/Cole, 1987).
3. Erik O. Wright, *The Politics of Punishment* (New York: Harper & Row, 1973); Ronald Berkman, *Opening the Gates: The Rise of the Prisoner's Movement* (Lexington, Mass.: Lexington Books, 1979); John Irwin, *Prisons in Turmoil* (Boston: Little, Brown, 1980); James B. Jacobs, *Stateville: The Penitentiary in Mass Society* (Chicago: University of Chicago Press, 1977); John J. DiIulio, Jr., *Governing Prisons: A Comparative Study of Correctional Management* (New York: The Free Press, 1987).
4. Philip J. Hirschkop and Michael A. Milleman, "The Unconstitutionality of Prison Life," *Virginia Law Review* 55 (1969), 795–839; David F. Greenberg and Fay Stender, "The Prison as a Lawless Agency," *Buffalo Law Review* 21 (1972), 799–838; Ronald L. Goldfarb and Linda R. Singer, *After Conviction* (New York: Simon and Schuster, 1973); Gordon Hawkins, *The Prison* (Chicago: University of Chicago Press, 1976); Gennaro F. Vito and Judith H. Kaci, "Hands On or Hands Off? The Use of Judicial Intervention to Establish Prisoners' Rights: An Examination of Sostre and Other Prisoner Suits," in *Coping with Imprisonment*, ed. Nicolette Parisi (Beverly Hills, Calif.: Sage, 1982), pp. 79–100; Barbara Knight and Stephen T. Early, Jr., *Prisoners Rights in America* (Chicago: Nelson-Hall, 1986).
5. *Wolff v. McDonnell*, 418 U.S. 539 (1974), pp. 555–56.
6. A surprising number of studies have been conducted in recent years addressing prison disciplinary practices and, to a lesser extent, the impact of due process on these practices. Some of the more salient studies include Harvard Center for Criminal Justice, "Judicial Inter-

vention in Prison Discipline," *Journal of Criminal Law, Criminology, and Police Science* 63 (1972), 200–228; Donald P. Baker et al., "Judicial Intervention in Corrections: The California Experience—An Empirical Study," *UCLA Law Review* 20 (1973), 452–575; Timothy J. Flanagan, "Discretion in the Prison Justice System: A Study of Sentencing in Institutional Disciplinary Proceedings," *Journal of Research in Crime and Delinquency* 19 (1982), 216–37; Bruce R. Jacob and K. M. Sharma, "Disciplinary and Punitive Transfer Decisions and Due Process Values in the American Correctional System," *Stetson Law Review* 12 (1982), 1–134; James W. Marquart and Ben M. Crouch, "Judicial Reform and Prisoner Control: The Impact of *Ruiz v. Estelle* on a Texas Penitentiary," *Law and Society Review* 19 (1985), 557–86; Lynn S. Branham, "Implementing and Ignoring the Dictates of the Supreme Court: A Comparative Study of Michigan and Illinois Prison Disciplinary Proceedings," *New England Journal on Criminal and Civil Confinement* 12 (1986), 197–328; Michael Mandel, "The Legalization of Prison Discipline," *Crime and Social Justice* 26 (1986), 79–94; N. E. Schafer, "Discretion, Due Process, and the Prison Discipline Committee," *Criminal Justice Review* 11 (1986), 37–46; and Jim Thomas et al., "Exacting Control Through Disciplinary Hearings" (unpublished paper, Department of Sociology, Northern Illinois University, Dekalb, 1989). Several of these studies argue that the presence of procedural due process in the prison setting has resulted in a shift in the balance of power between keeper and kept; others conclude that it has not limited significantly prison officials' discretion or control. This issue will be considered in the final section of this chapter.

7. This chapter draws heavily on research conducted by the author for his doctoral dissertation; see Edward E. Rhine, "Law, Social Control and Due Process in a Maximum Security Prison" (doctoral diss., Rutgers University, 1981). Additional interviews and documentary material obtained covering the period 1980–88 supplement the earlier research and identify salient developments affecting the disciplinary system at Rahway State Prison during this time.

8. David Trubek, "Complexity and Contradiction in the Legal Order: Balbus and the Challenge of Critical Social Thought about Law," *Law and Society Review* 11 (1977), 528–69.

9. "Beyond the Ken of the Courts: A Critique of Judicial Refusal to Review the Complaints of Convicts," *Yale Law Journal* 72 (1963), 506–58.

10. The decline of the "hands-off" doctrine and the consequent redefinition of the prisoners' status represent a decisive turning point in the history of corrections, a development far more significant than the sum

total of court decisions affecting prison administration. For incisive analyses of this topic, see James B. Jacobs, *New Perspectives on Imprisonment* (Ithaca, N.Y.: Cornell University Press, 1983); and Jim Thomas, *Prisoner Litigation: The Paradox of the Jailhouse Lawyer* (Totowa, N.J.: Rowman and Littlefield, 1988).

11. Other rationales were also used. First, it was argued that the administration of a prison system was an executive, not a judicial, function. Second, the courts avoided active intervention, claiming they lacked expertise in complex matters of prison administration. Third, the recognition and enforcement of prisoners' rights would require that they appropriate or reallocate funds, a legislative function. For an excellent analysis of these and other rationales underlying the "hands-off" doctrine, see "Beyond the Ken of the Courts" and Kenneth C. Haas, "Judicial Politics and Correctional Reform: An Analysis of the Decline of the "Hands-Off" Doctrine," *Detroit College of Law Review* 4 (1977), 795–831.

12. Charles Silberman, *Criminal Violence, Criminal Justice* (New York: Random House, 1978).

13. *Morris v. Travisono*, 310 F. Supp. 857 (D. R.I. 1970); *Sostre v. Rockefeller*, 312 F. Supp. 863 (S.D. N.Y. 1971); *Clutchette v. Procunier*, 328 F. Supp. 767 (N.D. Cal. 1971); and *Landman v. Royster*, 333 F. Supp. 621 (E.D. Va. 1971).

14. Thomas W. Ross, "Constitutional Law—Procedural Due Process in Prison Disciplinary Proceedings—The Supreme Court Responds," *North Carolina Law Review* 53 (1975), 796. :

15. Ibid., p. 555.

16. Ibid., p. 556.

17. Ibid.

18. These decisions, *Goldberg v. Kelly*, 397 U.S. 254 (1970), *Morrissey v. Brewer*, 408 U.S. 471 (1972), and *Gagnon v. Scarpelli*, 411 U.S. 778 (1973), dealt, respectively, with welfare termination and parole and probation revocation. Together they established that due process was a flexible concept whose requisites were shaped by the weight of competing interests involved in a given dispute.

19. In its reasoning the Court made use of two interrelated arguments. On the one hand, it observed that "prison disciplinary proceedings take place in a closed, tightly controlled environment peopled by those who have chosen to violate the criminal law" (p. 561). Moreover, this environment is characterized by "unremitting tension" between guards and prisoners. "Frustration, resentment, and despair are commonplace" (p. 562). Thus the imposition of disciplinary sanctions in this setting necessarily involves confrontations between inmates and prison

authorities. On the other hand, such proceedings may also advance the rehabilitative goals of the institution by fostering change in "the behavior and value systems of prison inmates sufficiently to permit them to live within the law when they are released" (pp. 562–63). The dual interests of the state in maintaining order and security within the institution while at the same time promoting rehabilitative objectives led the Court to decide against "encasing disciplinary procedures in an inflexible constitutional straightjacket that would necessarily call for adversary proceedings typical of the criminal trial" (p. 563). In an early review of *Wolff*, Richard C. Hand *Analysis of the Effects of "Wolff vs. McDonnell" on Prison Disciplinary Practices and Procedures* [Washington, D.C.: Resource Center on Correctional Law and Legal Services, 1974]) argued that "at every critical juncture the state prison officials' need to have discretion was seen to outweigh the asserted interest of the prisoner in having a particular procedural protection" (p. 50).

20. Furthermore, *Wolff* specifically stated that an inmate did not have a constitutional right to (1) confrontation and cross-examination of adverse witnesses, a matter left to the "sound discretion of prison officials," or to (2) retained or appointed counsel. With regard to the former, the Court felt that confrontation and cross-examination would, if allowed as a matter of course, create the potential for disruption and reprisal. In terms of the latter, the Court cited *Gagnon*, saying that the "insertion of counsel into the disciplinary process would inevitably give the proceedings a more adversary cast and reduce their utility as a means to further correctional goals" (p. 570).

21. *Avant* was decided on June 23, 1975. As the court itself remarked, it shaped its opinion to deal with the newly revised disciplinary Standards promulgated by the New Jersey Division of Correction and Parole on March 20, 1975. These Standards (hereinafter cited as Standards) constituted the procedural rules governing the operation of the disciplinary system in each of the state's prisons at that time.

22. This "norm" has often been utilized to require a quantum of rights greater than that provided under the federal Constitution. See "Prisoners' Rights—New Jersey Fairness and Rightness Standard—Procedural Requirements for Prison Disciplinary Hearings," *Rutgers Law Review* 29 (1976), 720–54.

23. These protections included the following provisions:

a. To ensure an "impartial tribunal" the Adjustment Committee must be composed of one correctional officer, an institutional staff member, and a "qualified" third member drawn from noncorrectional personnel. According to the Standards, disciplinary hearings may be conducted either by the

The Rule of Law, Disciplinary Practices, and Rahway State Prison 215

Adjustment Committee or by a single hearing officer. When and if the single hearing officer technique is implemented, he or she should be assigned from the central office instead of coming from within the institution itself.

b. Under ordinary circumstances, the inmate is entitled to a hearing within one week of the alleged violation. If he is confined in prehearing detention, absent exceptional circumstances, a hearing should be held within seventy-two hours of the violation.

c. Confrontation and cross-examination should be provided to an inmate where the Adjustment Committee considers it necessary for an adequate presentation of the evidence, particularly where serious issues of credibility are involved. Where the committee deems confrontation and cross-examination unnecessary, the reasons for such denial should be recorded and made available to the inmate.

d. The committee must state its reason(s) for refusing to call a witness, and in the statement of disposition, it must indicate the reason(s) for refusing to disclose any items of evidence.

e. In terms of the level of evidence required, disciplinary action may not be taken except where there is "substantial evidence" to support the inmate's involvement or "reasonable cause" to believe that the inmate's behavior constituted a danger to other persons, property, security, or the orderly running of the institution.

f. In the event that an inmate might be subject to criminal prosecution for the same act that represents a disciplinary violation, he must be informed of his right to remain silent and be provided with "use immunity" for any testimony given at the hearing. Use immunity means that neither his testimony nor any evidence derived therefrom may be used against him in a subsequent criminal proceeding.

24. Since *Wolff*, the Supreme Court has handed down a number of decisions with significant implications for prison discipline and due process. These decisions include: *Baxter v. Palmigiano*, 96 S.Ct. 1551 (1976); *Meachum v. Fano*, 427 U.S. 215 (1976); *Montanye v. Haymes*, 427 U.S. 236 (1976); *Wright v. Enomoto*, 462 F. Supp. 397 (N.D. Cal. 1976), *aff'd*, 434 U.S. 1052 (1978); *Hewitt v. Helms*, 459 U.S. 460 (1983); and *Ponte v. Real*, 105 S.Ct. 2192 (1985).
25. *Avant*, p. 520.
26. Ibid., p. 555.
27. The listing of prohibited acts was promulgated in the Department of Corrections Standard 251.263. Inmates received the listing of prohibited acts in an inmate handbook on discipline which they obtained upon reception into the prison system.
28. When *Avant* was decided, the New Jersey Supreme Court alluded to the possibility of using a single hearing officer on courtline in place of the Adjustment Committee. Subsequent to *Avant*, the Department of Corrections received funding to develop a hearing officer program.

Two hearing officers were hired by the department in 1976. During early March they attended seminars on the due process protections required by *Wolff* and *Avant*. On March 15, 1976, the hearing officer program began at Rahway. By the end of the month the hearing officers had replaced the Adjustment Committee on courtline. At the time of the research, as well as since, the Hearing Officer Program was assigned to the Office of the Deputy Commissioner, though it was administered by a special assistant for legal affairs. The program has since been expanded to sixteen facilities and twelve hearing officers. The value of this program will be addressed later in the chapter.

29. Separate hearing procedures were authorized by the Standards for minor institutional violations. At Rahway in 1979 sergeants often conducted "unit hearings" for charges not considered serious enough to send to courtline. Unit hearings were abolished in 1980 and replaced by an even less formal procedure currently referred to as "on-the-spot correction."

30. Depending on the nature and the circumstances of the violation, an inmate could be placed in prehearing detention prior to his appearance on courtline (Standards, 255.271). According to the Standards, a prisoner could be confined in "double-lock" for the following reasons: to ensure immediate control and supervision; to protect potential victims; to ensure witnesses against intimidation; to control those whose violent emotions are out of control and to ensure their safety or the safety of others; to ensure the safety and security of the institution; and willful refusal to obey orders or demonstrated defiance of personnel acting in the line of duty.

31. At the time of the research the Internal Control Unit served as the coordinating center of the disciplinary system screening disciplinary charges, assigning "control" officers to investigate them, and processing inmates' appeals. Although it no longer functions in this role with respect to courtline, it still serves as a criminal investigative unit within the prison and it still gathers intelligence information on illicit inmate activities.

32. The Standards (254.263) required the following:

After providing the inmate with the written charge, the investigator should also read it to the inmate and obtain his statement concerning the incident. . . . He may talk to witnesses and the reporting staff member and summarize their statements as may be necessary. Comments about the inmate's attitude may be included here.

The investigator may include comments and conclusions on the inmate's prior record and behavior, his analysis of any conflicts between witnesses, and his conclusions of what in fact happened. The inmate does not receive a copy of the investigation. However, the investigation may be given to any consenting staff representative for presentation on the inmate's behalf.

33. The investigators also gathered additional material. Sometimes they spoke to the charging officer as well as other officers or staff persons who saw the incident. Occasionally they provided information on the results of lab tests or on standard operating procedures in the institution (e.g., "man should have been on tier while on restriction unless he had a pass"). It was not always the case that their remarks were directed against an inmate, as the following comment indicates: "[A]ll the officers I spoke to feel the inmate is innocent of the charge. Mrs. P. treats the inmates in Food Services very poorly."

34. Between July and September 1979, of the 534 inmates receiving courtline hearings 83 (15.5%) were in double-lock at the time. Most of them ($N = 50$) were put in prehearing detention because of an incident involving one charge, while 19 received two charges, and 14 of them three charges or more. Together, they received 134 institutional reports, or 18.7 percent of the total referred to courtline.

    Regardless of the type of charge(s) that lands an inmate in prehearing detention, placement there alters fundamentally his conditions of confinement. For this reason the Standards required that an inmate under double-lock status be given a hearing within three days, "unless there are exceptional circumstances, unavoidable delays, or reasonable postponements" (254.270).

    Of the total number of double-lock charges disposed of, 75.4 percent ($N = 101$) were decided within the necessary time frame. In 3 percent ($N = 4$) of the charges involving four different inmates the time limit was not met, and no explanation was provided on the adjudication form. Three of these inmates were found not guilty; the other was convicted. In 21.6 percent ($N = 29$) of the charges, the final hearing was held beyond the due process limit either because the third day fell on a weekend ($N = 10$) or because an initial hearing was postponed so that witnesses' statements could be gathered, a psychiatric report obtained, or the hearing officer could evaluate additional information ($N = 19$). There were no cases recorded by the hearing officer in which a charge resulted in a violation of due process for noncompliance with the three-day requirement. Although three-quarters of the double-lock charges were decided within the time limit, there was likewise no clearly demarcated point at which a reasonable postponement or unavoidable delay became a violation of due process.

35. This case later went to the New Jersey Superior Court Appellate Division where the courtline decision was upheld.

36. *Wolff*, p. 566.
37. This case was atypical in that the use of confidential reports on court-line was not common. However, when such reports are used they render the preparation of a defense very difficult for two reasons. First, the inmate has only a minimum of information from which to work, usually a summary of the report. Second, the hearing officer must assess the credibility of the inmate informant, an assessment over which the accused has very little control. In two cases (involving the same incident) the hearing officer seemed to be strongly predisposed by the information and, with little deliberation, found both inmates guilty. In Case 091, the hearing was very clearly oriented toward fact-finding and the evaluation of the inmate's innocence or guilt. Nonethe-less, when confidential reports serve as the basis for courtline adjudi-cation, their presence tends to bias the outcome unless substantial evidence is introduced that undermines their validity. In 1982 guide-lines were developed to govern the use of informant statements by the hearing officers to comply with a Third Circuit opinion in *Helms v. Hewitt*, 655 F.2d 487 (1981). In 1987 three cases were remanded by the state's Appellate Division for rehearings involving confidential inform-ant information.
38. One additional due process safeguard, use immunity, was provided to inmates charged with criminal violations. It required that the hearing officer inform the inmate that he had the right to remain silent and that anything he said would not be used against him later in a criminal proceeding. During the field work twenty charges were recommended for referral to the prosecutor. Even though the *Avant* court spent a lengthy portion of its decision addressing this protection, it was of limited value within the context of a disciplinary hearing.
39. At their most punitive, these sanctions when combined included transfer to a more secure institution, loss of privileges for 30 days, 15 days of disciplinary detention, confinement in administrative segrega-tion for one year, loss of 365 days' commutation time, reduction in custody status, and, finally, loss of contact visiting privileges for one year. A combination of such penalties was handed down infrequently, occurring in only a small percentage of cases.
40. It is important to point out that the imposition of disciplinary sanc-tions may dramatically alter either the conditions of confinement or the length of time served. The most serious collateral consequence associated with receiving charges was the negative impact this had on an inmate's prospects for parole. Both then and now parole could be denied and an established parole date rescinded. As a result of a change

in the disciplinary Standards in 1979, inmates were notified that they could restore only up to 75 percent of any commutation time forfeited, 25 percent for each of three succeeding years during which they had to remain charge-free. Prior to this, they could·restore 100 percent.

41. The category of "other" ($N = 48$) includes a hodgepodge of reasons, some examples of which drawn directly from the adjudication forms follow:

"Man used poor judgment in not trying to get wing officer to resolve problem/but he did not try to sneak into visit area or disrupt area."

"Man is given opportunity to show his intent to comply with order by suspended sentence."

"This inmate plays fast and loose with the truth."

"Inmate butted in where he is not supposed to be."

42. Elizabeth Alexander, "The New Prison Administrators and the Court: New Directions in Prison Law," *Texas Law Review* 56 (1978), 963–1008; Charles H. Jones and Edward E. Rhine, "Due Process and Prison Disciplinary Practices: From *Wolff* to *Hewitt*," *New England Journal on Criminal and Civil Confinement* 11 (1985), 44–122; Berry R. Bell, "Prisoners' Rights, Institutional Needs, and the Burger Court," *Virginia Law Review* 72 (1986), 161–93; and Thomas, *Prisoner Litigation*, pp. 246–57. Recent decisions by the Supreme Court articulate a policy of due deference to the decisions of prison administrators; these include *Jones v. North Carolina Prisoner's Labor Union, Inc.*, 433 U.S. 119 (1977); *Bell v. Wolfish*, 441 U.S. 520 (1979); *Rhodes v. Chapman*, 452 U.S. 337 (1980); *Block v. Rutherford*, 104 S.Ct. 322 (1984); *O'Lone v. Estate of Shabazz*, 107 S.Ct. 2400 (1987); and *Turner v. Safley*, 107 S.Ct. 2254 (1987). The difference between "due deference" and "hands off" is that while jurisdiction is retained, the Court refuses to grant a remedy unless prisoners are able to demonstrate that achieving their interest will not subvert prison officials' interest in maintaining institutional security and control. For a more detailed exposition of this view see Jones and Rhine, "Due Process and Prison Disciplinary Practices," pp. 109–22. For a rich empirical analysis of trends in prisoner litigation see Thomas, *Prisoner Litigation*, chapter 3.

43. On January 24, 1972, during pendency of the litigation that eventuated in *Avant*, the then Division of Corrections and Parole issued new rules covering disciplinary practices in the state's prisons and reformatories.

The Standards totaled thirteen pages and listed thirty-seven possible infractions. Substantial latitude was accorded the institutions in deciding how to implement the various provisions.

44. Comprehensive and detailed revisions were introduced after *Wolff* and during the pendency of the litigation in *Avant*. In fact, these Standards, published just three months before the latter was decided, formed the basis of the New Jersey Supreme Court's review. Additional and significant modifications were incorporated in response to *Avant*.

45. While the Standards underwent significant revisions in 1980, in 1986 the disciplinary Standards became administrative rules under New Jersey's Administrative Procedure Act (see *Department of Corrections v. McNeil*, 209 N.J. Super.Ct. 120 (1986); *Zeltner v. N.J. Department of Corrections*, 201 N.J. Super.Ct. 195 (1985). Hereafter, any amendments must comply with the rulemaking procedures prescribed by this act, a requirement that will further contribute to procedural formality relative to prison discipline. To avoid confusion, Standards rather than rules will continue to be used.

46. Mandel, "The Legalization of Prison Discipline," 84; Schafer, "Discretion, Due Process, and the Prison Discipline Committee," pp. 43–44; Thomas, *Prisoner Litigation*, 254.

47. The disciplinary report and adjudication forms, the on-the-spot correction and adjudication forms, and the appeal and disposition of appeal forms provide alleged inmate violators with sufficient information from which to prepare a defense or process an appeal.

48. In several recent instances inmates have been found not guilty when the charging officer refused to appear at the hearing to honor the inmate's request for confrontation/cross-examination or appeared with the officer's union (PBA) representative.

49. In March 1985 legislation became effective requiring the Department of Corrections to refer all disciplinary cases to an administrative law judge; a guilty finding would result in a loss of 365 days commutation time (*New Jersey Statutes Annotated* 52:14F-8). The law, which had a sunset provision attached, expired on December 31, 1987. During this time forty-one cases were referred to the Office of Administrative Law. Two cases are still pending and three were withdrawn. Of the remaining thirty-six cases, after de novo hearings, the decision of the disciplinary hearing officer was upheld in twenty-eight cases. Three cases resulted in dismissal of the charges and sanctions altogether, while in another five cases the sanctions were modified. Thus, the disciplinary hearings officers were upheld in their decisions 77 percent of the time; 14 percent of the cases received some modification in the sanction imposed; in 8 percent of the cases the hearing officer's decision and sanction were overturned.

50. Harvard Center, "Judicial Intervention," p. 223. "Flanagan, "Discretion in the Prison Justice System," pp. 230–34. Schafer, "Discretion, Due Process, and the Prison Discipline Committee," pp. 41–43.

51. The overall percentage of not guilty findings remains surprisingly high. Between 1984 and 1988 the percentage of not guilty findings relative to total charges at Rahway ranged from 17.7 to 25.5. Violations of due process (which are included in total charges but excluded from the percentage of guilty/not guilty findings) ranged from a high of 106 to a low of 32. The concern with fact-finding is also revealed in the number of charges that are returned for further investigation. These charges (which are excluded from total charges) ranged from 168 to 346. (Disciplinary Hearing Program Monthly Reports 1984–88.) The not guilty percentages at Rahway stand in marked contrast to the findings from several recent studies (e.g., Flanagan, "Discretion in the Prison Justice System"; Schafer, "Discretion, Due Process, and the Prison Discipline Committee").

52. The independence of the Hearing Officer Program and the extensive training in the law which the hearing officers undergo contribute to this outcome. It appears that the hearing officers are less vulnerable to institutional pressures to find an inmate guilty as they are assigned from the Department of Corrections and they rotate periodically between the correctional facilities. Branham ("Implementing and Ignoring the Dictates of the Supreme Court"), in a study of the prison disciplinary systems in Illinois and Michigan, also found that the independent hearing officer program associated with the latter contributed to greater fairness and compliance with the requirements of due process.

53. Harvard Center, "Judicial Intervention," pp. 225–227; Jacobs, *Stateville*, pp. 106–19; Branham, "Implementing and Ignoring the Dictates of the Supreme Court," pp. 285–316.

54. Jacobs, *Stateville*, p. 116.

55. According to statistics provided by the Hearing Officer Program, the average number of charges adjudicated monthly at Rahway varies from year to year, but it is quite high. From 1984 through 1988 the average number of monthly charges was, respectively, 340, 259, 244, 286, and 283. This compares with 237 charges per month at the time of the original research, though it should be noted that between 1979 and 1988 Rahway's population grew from 1,315 to 2,029, an increase of 54 percent.

56. Irwin, *Prisons in Turmoil*, pp. 181–213; DiIulio, *Governing Prisons*, pp. 99–118; Johnson, *Hard Time*, pp. 39–52.

57. Harvard Center, "Judicial Intervention," p. 213.

58. This is not to argue that these assumptions apply to all inmates at all times. Rather, it is to point out that with depressing frequency inmates do engage in predatory violence, they do participate in drug, extortion, and other gang-related activities within prison walls, they do put pressure on other inmates to testify for them during disciplinary hearings, and by some inmates' own admissions, they do lie during such hearings to avoid sanctioning. However, prison conditions exacerbate tendencies that may already exist toward violent and aggressive behavior on the part of the inmate population.

8

Crain: Nonreformist Prison Reform

BERT USEEM

The West Virginia Penitentiary in the state's northern panhandle was, for many years, an ancient living paradox. This artifact of Civil War–era construction was just the sort of prison thought to "breed violence." Conditions were terrible. Sewage leaked into the tiny cells, and the entire edifice was infested with rats and lice. In poorly ventilated and heated cells, inmates sweltered in the summer heat and huddled under mounds of blankets in the cold of winter. Critics, including some state legislators, said that the penitentiary must be replaced—before the inmates' anger boiled over. How could they live there peaceably?

Yet they did. During the 1970s and first half of the 1980s, the prison was surprisingly calm. Inmates grumbled about their conditions and filed dozens of lawsuits against the penitentiary. But there was little violence either among inmates or against the guard force. Inmates and guards treated each other with a degree of respect not often found in maximum security prisons. However, on New Year's

223

Day 1986 inmates seized the prison and twelve hostages and held them for three days. Three inmates were killed. Since then, the prison has continued to be a hostile, violent, and deadly place.

This breakdown in order occurred as the state courts were attempting to effect reform. In 1982 a state circuit judge had ruled that the prison violated inmates' constitutional rights against cruel and unusual punishment and other rights established in West Virginia law. Yet for seven years few of the changes mandated by the court were actually made.

To what extent, if any, did the court's intervention contribute to the disorders that began in 1986? To answer this question, we turn first to the state's economy and politics in the 1970s and 1980s.[1]

Economics and Politics in West Virginia in the 1970s and 1980s

West Virginia rises and falls with the coal industry.[2] After the turn of the century, and particularly since World War II, consumers of coal for purposes ranging from locomotive fuel to home heating switched to oil and natural gas. Ever since the Great Depression, West Virginia has been a virtual synonym for the grinding poverty of Appalachia.

The 1973 oil embargo reversed this trend; coal was plentiful and immune to OPEC threats. In consequence, the 1970s was an unusual period of economic growth and relative prosperity for West Virginia. At the start of the decade the state's per capita income was 22 percent below the national average, but by its end the gap had narrowed to 14 percent. Employment in these ten years rose from just over 500,000 to 716,000. For the first time in several dozen years, the state's unemployment rate (7.3%) was more than a percentage point below the national average.

Around 1980 the boom turned to bust. Slowed economic growth lowered the demand for energy, an oil "glut" replaced the energy "crisis," and foreign-produced coal beat out higher priced American coal in the international market. Between 1982 and 1987 the coal industry in the state let go 27,000 workers—43 percent of its labor force. The manufacturing sector, the state's second leading employer, released another 12,300 workers. The losses were felt throughout the economy.

From 1980 to 1986 the state's "gross state product" (the value of the state's goods and services) declined at an annual rate of 0.5 percent (while that of other states grew at an average annual rate of 2.6%). The state's unemployment rate hovered around 14 percent, one of the highest in the country. It would have been higher, except that 0.7 percent of the population was now emigrating from the state each year. Commentators likened the emigration to the exodus from the Oklahoma Dust Bowl of the 1930s.[3]

The swings in the economy were no more extreme than those in politics. During the 1960s and 1970s state politics became dominated by a "reform movement." The movement was strongly pro-labor, critical of nonresident corporate landholders, demanding of better schools and government services, and staunchly pro-environment. Some commentators attributed its emergence to the attention brought to the state's poverty during the 1960 presidential campaign.[4] In any case, one manifestation of this movement was the election of an activist majority in the state supreme court.

The Judiciary in West Virginia

Until the 1970s the West Virginia Supreme Court of Appeals had been among the most passive and conservative state supreme courts in the country.[5] With few exceptions, the court's five seats were filled either by uncontested reelections of incumbents or gubernatorial appointment to a vacated position. In 1976, however, three nonincumbents won contested elections, which established an "activist" majority. The most outspoken of this new majority was Darrell McGraw, a self-described "people's judge." Closely aligned with the state's labor unions, McGraw wanted to bring the "New Deal . . . to West Virginia. For years we were a little old colony. The industrial people came and took all the money away."[6] But in McGraw's view change would encounter the resistance of entrenched interests: "Traditionally, courts have represented what might be styled the power elite. . . . As the cases are decided, a new philosophy is prevailing with respect to law and this is what is unsettling to the power elite. . . . But we believe that if we have unsettled the law, and set it in a new direction, that it has been in the direction of redressing wrong and of providing a remedy where previously there was no remedy by due course [to] law."[7] The court's rulings did indeed unleash a political storm. Three cases served as lightning rods.

One was the *Mandolidis* decision, named after a worker who lost several fingers in a sawmill accident, which made it far easier for workers to sue their employers for injuries sustained on the job.[8] State business leaders were incensed. The ruling, they claimed, put businesses in West Virginia at a competitive disadvantage. There was plenty of anecdotal evidence and testimony to "prove" the point. The *Wall Street Journal* described a West Virginia clothing manufacturer who took part of his operation across the river to Kentucky because of *Mandolidis*. Another businessman was quoted as saying, "*Mandolidis* scares the bejesus out of us"; still another said that "you would have to be absolutely insane to bring a business into West Virginia right now."[9]

The reaction to the 1979 *Pauley v. Kelley* decision was just as intense though not confined to the business community.[10] The plaintiff had claimed that because she lived in a poor county, her children received an education inferior to the one received by children living in richer counties. The United States Supreme Court in 1973 had rejected the claim that equal education is a right guaranteed under the constitution.[11] The West Virginia decision was based on a clause in the state constitution which obligated the state to provide a system of "thorough and efficient" schools. As interpreted by the court, this clause required the state not only to devise a more equitable method of financing its schools but also to develop and meet high-quality educational standards.

The supreme court remanded the case to a state circuit judge, Arthur Recht, for a nonjury trial to further establish the facts of the case. In 1982 Judge Recht issued a 290-page opinion, detailing the changes the state would have to make. Recht described his order as "no less than a call to the Legislature to completely reconstruct the entire system of education in West Virginia."[12] The cost of this reconstruction was estimated as high as one and a half billion dollars.[13]

Some greeted the decision as a major breakthrough for the state. One prominent educator said that Recht's decision would help "yank West Virginia into the 20th century."[14] The *Charleston Sunday Gazette-Mail* named Judge Recht "West Virginian of the Year."[15] The critics, though, were far more vocal. The day after the decision, Senate finance chairman Ralph Williams told the press, "Judge Recht ought to get a haircut. I just thought it was a long-haired decision, and I equate it with the hippie clan. West Virginia is not in a position to afford the standards he envisioned." House Speaker Clyde See remarked, "[W]e're looking at a long, long time, and perhaps never fulfilling what Recht wants."[16] Even liberal governor Jay Rockefeller predicted consequences disastrous for the taxpayers.[17] Two years later, in November 1984, voters overwhelmingly rejected a referendum measure that would have eliminated the constitutionally objectionable method of funding schools. The ruling became known as the "Recht decision," rather than by the case's name, emphasizing the "activism" of the judge who made the ruling rather than the plaintiff's claims.

The third lightning rod was actually a set of three interrelated decisions, each concerning one of the state's three penitentiaries: the women's prison at Pence Springs, the medium security prison for men at Huttonsville, and the maximum security prison for men at Moundsville.

The first to come to trial, *Cooper v. Gwinn*, arose from a suit by women inmates who claimed that their right to rehabilitation had been violated.[18] Federal courts have rejected the claim that inmates have a right to rehabilitation. They have held that the U.S. Constitution requires only that inmates receive the "basic necessities of life," like "reasonably adequate food, clothing, shelter, sanitation, medical care, and personal safety."[19] The *Cooper* ruling was based on a state statute, interpreted by the court to mean that the "[l]egislature requires rehabilitation to be the primary goal of the West Virginia corrections system." This right could not be interfered with by the executive branch. The governor and state legislature were required to give priority in the budget to this entitlement before addressing other "societal luxuries." Thus, as it had done in the *Pauley* decision, the court interpreted the state constitution as setting a standard higher than the one mandated by the U.S. Constitution.

More surprising were some of the specific failures of "rehabilitation" that the court found, such as the prison's inadequate educational program. The prison did offer high school–level courses which led to an equivalence diploma. Since the majority of inmates had already graduated from high school, the "educational needs" of the inmate population were for college-level courses, which the prison did not provide. Thus, in a state ranking near the bottom in the percentage of college graduates, the courts had declared that inmates had a right to a college education.

The decision, in effect, forced the Department of Corrections to close the facility. In its annual report, department officials explained: "After four . . . years of trying to acquire the additional resources necessary to make meaningful program and physical plant improvement, the Department believed that it could not maintain a good faith expectation that it could comply with the *Cooper* decision within any reasonable period of time."[20] The inmates were transferred to a federal facility.

The issue at the medium security prison at Huttonsville was crowding. Although designed for four hundred inmates, the prison was housing almost seven hundred. In February 1985 a state court ruled that population had to be reduced to five hundred within a year. But the population continued to grow. In March 1985 two hundred inmates in one of the prison's dormitories voted not to admit any new inmates. The warden, Jerry Hedrick, responded by removing the inmates' radios, televisions, and coffee pots and forbidding them to leave their dormitories except for meals. After three days under these restrictions, the inmates gave in and "permitted" new inmates into their dormitory. About the incident, Warden Henrick commented, "I guess they are taking it upon themselves to implement everything right now."[21] As it developed, they were not alone in their defiance.

In May 1986 Governor Arch Moore ordered the Department of Corrections to accept no more inmates from the county jails. This, a circuit court judge ruled, was no more lawful than the inmates' protest. Governor Moore appealed the decision to the state supreme court, which found him in "willful and contumacious contempt of court."[22] Meanwhile, two former inmates sued Governor Moore and two top Department of Corrections officials in federal court. They claimed that corrections officials, under orders from Governor Moore, had simply disregarded an order from the circuit judge to give fifty-three Huttonsville inmates early releases to alle-

viate crowding. In 1988 a federal jury awarded the two inmates
$232,000.[23] (The decision is currently under appeal.)

It was the maximum security prison in Moundsville, though, that
was the object of the most controversial court decision.

Crain v. Bordenkircher

In February 1982, thirty-six petitions from inmates at the West
Virginia Penitentiary were consolidated and brought to trial in
Crain v. Bordenkircher.[24] The presiding judge was Arthur Recht,
who had ordered sweeping changes in the state's school system a
few months earlier. After a personal visit to the penitentiary and a
two-week trial, Judge Recht concluded that the penitentiary violated the U.S. Constitution's prohibition against "cruel and unusual" punishment as well as the West Virginia constitution and
statutes.

First, Recht ruled that the physical conditions of the penitentiary
and its services inflicted "wanton" and "unnecessary" pain on inmates. The plumbing was in such disrepair that toilet waste backed
up into the living areas and into the sinks. An antiquated heating
and ventilating system produced unbearably hot temperatures in
the summer and cold temperatures in the winter. Inadequate lighting in the cells made reading difficult, and insufficient recreational
facilities limited activity. The food was often poorly prepared,
served cold, contaminated with insects and hair, served on dirty
trays, and failed to meet the "minimum nutritional basic necessities
of life." The entire prison was infested with roaches, lice, fleas, rats,
and mice.

The two most serious deficiencies were the tiny cells and the
medical care. Each cell measured five feet by seven feet, 60 percent of
which was taken up by a sink, toilet, and bed. This was less than half
the floor space recommended by the American Correctional Association. The health, dental, and psychological services, Recht declared,
fell below "contemporary standards of decency" and were "grossly
inadequate." "Dental care," the judge wrote, "is either non-existent,
or delayed to such an extent to be considered non-existent."

In addition, Judge Recht ruled that the prison did not provide the
"rehabilitative" programs that the inmates were entitled to under

the *Cooper* decision. Instead, there was only "massive and pervasive idleness."

Judge Recht ordered the Department of Corrections to submit, within 180 days, a compliance plan that would bring the penitentiary up to constitutional and statutory standards conforming to the standards for rehabilitation established by the American Correctional Association. Within this framework, the department was given considerable latitude to shape its own remedy. "The Respondents," the judge wrote, "must be given the opportunity, in the first instance, to put their own house in order." Judge Recht had been stunned by the massive resistance to his earlier school decision, which had established detailed standards. Although there was no connection in law between the two cases, Judge Recht hoped that a less prescriptive approach might avoid some of these difficulties.[25]

Judge Recht, however, was firm on two matters. First, superficial change was inadequate. Given the deplorable conditions, nothing short of "massive renovation bordering on new construction" was required to make the penitentiary habitable. Second, he warned that the lack of public funds would not be accepted as an excuse for denying inmates their constitutional and statutory rights. The Department of Corrections did not appeal the order.

Judge Recht resigned from the bench in the fall of 1983. His replacement, Judge John Bronson, was considered less sympathetic to inmate concerns than Recht had been. On September 1, 1984, Judge Bronson approved the plan which the Department of Corrections submitted over the objections of the inmates' attorneys. He did, however, honor the inmates' request to appoint a special master to monitor the progress toward compliance. Bronson chose Donald Poffenberger, a professor of criminal justice, and required him to file quarterly reports on his findings.

To understand the fate of the court's orders, we need to turn back to state politics and economics.

State Politics in the 1980s

As was noted earlier, West Virginia politics in the 1970s was dominated by a reform movement. In the early 1980s, however, the political pendulum began to swing back. Oddly, an obscure report by Alexander Grant, a Chicago accounting firm, played an important role. The report ranked West Virginia last among the forty-eight contiguous states in its "business climate." Coming at a time when the state was facing a sharp economic downturn, the report became a hot issue. State Supreme Court Justice McGraw denounced it as the work of "manufacturers' associations, which are influenced by the multinational outfits guilty of greed in the Orient and Latin America. They go to foreign countries while our people . . . go hungry. They have no patriotism."[26] The electorate saw the matter differently.

In 1984 they elected Republican Arch Moore, mainly on the promise that he would improve the state's business climate and revitalize the economy. Under Moore's leadership, the legislature in 1985, and then again in 1986, sharply cut taxes on businesses.[27] This included a 90 percent tax break to companies that created one thousand jobs in the state.

Beyond this, Moore promised that the state would be governed by elected officials rather than judges. Governor Moore's press secretary explained: "We're being thrust on all sides by the judiciary. But it is the duty of the constitutional officers to determine what can be done with the money available to the state and the governor intends to fulfill that duty."[28]

Moore was facing difficult circumstances. Soon after taking office, he had to deal with a catastrophic flood, rioting inmates, and state revenues that continued to plummet. And matters grew worse. In early 1987, in response to a $63 million shortfall, Moore ordered a 20 percent cut in state spending. No agency was immune. The Department of Health, under both state and federal court orders to improve its mental health facilities, had its budget trimmed. A planned $170 million "Year of Education" package for schools gave way to a $500,000 reduction.[29] The budget for prisons was also pared down. "When the public perceives the state's economy is beginning to rev up," the governor's press secretary explained, "they will turn their attention to things like prisons. The main priority for the Governor [is] to put the state back on its feet."[30]

Even these austerity measures did not prevent the state from accumulating a huge debt. By the end of Moore's term, the state owed an estimated $250 million. This, in turn, entangled the state in another set of legal and economic problems. Contractors and vendors sued the state for more than $1 million in unpaid bills. An association representing retired public employees won a decision in the state supreme court requiring the state to repay $80 million borrowed from the state's retirement fund. State business leaders complained that the state's fiscal problems were discouraging investment.[31]

In the fall of 1988 Moore was defeated by his Democratic challenger. Claiming that the state faced "the greatest crisis in the history of West Virginia," the new governor won legislative approval of the largest tax increase in the state's history.[32] This increase and other new taxes totaled $700 million, almost half the state's budget.[33]

Court-Ordered Reform at the Penitentiary

If state legislators had balked in response to Recht's order to improve the schools, they were even more steadfast in their refusal to shoulder the cost of prison reform. Shortly after the *Crain v. Bordenkircher* ruling, the chairman of the House Judiciary Committee praised Recht "for putting the problem [of prison reform] on the agenda," but he added that given the state's other needs, "I would be unable to predict when we'd have the money to do anything about it."[34] The Department of Corrections requested $19.2 million over five years to rebuild the penitentiary. The 1984 and 1985 legislatures provided $3 million, plus a small increment to hire a few extra teachers and nurses.

The failure to achieve the court-mandated reform is reflected in the quarterly reports issued by special master Poffenberger. The message of the first quarterly report, covering the period October 1984 to January 1985, was that the Department of Corrections had worked hard to improve conditions but that many problems remained. Poffenberger noted, for example, that improvements had been made in the steam heating system but not in the ventilation system. An outdoor lighting system had been installed, but inmates still did not have adequate cleaning supplies.[35] "The Department of Corrections," Poffenberger told the press, "has indeed made a real tangible effort in terms of making physical improvements."[36] In contrast, Poffenberger's report covering the later period of July 9,

1985, to October 9, 1985, was critical and pessimistic. "No one can find the money in the Department of Corrections budget to finance fulfillment of their Plan of Compliance. Like a jilted bride, the Court is confronted by a litany of unkept promises. . . . Departmental officials spend budgeted sums as they become available, but it is not enough."[37] Poffenberger's assessment was echoed by the newly appointed commissioner of corrections, A. V. Dodrill. Testifying at a state legislative committee, Dodrill admitted, "We are not complying [with Recht's decision]. We are actually in contempt of court. We don't have the money to comply with court orders."[38] By the end of 1985 fewer than 10 percent of the court-ordered changes had been made.

Then, as the state sank into a serious fiscal crisis, the pace of reform crept to a near halt. Special master Poffenberger wrote that the 1987 spending cuts ordered by Governor Moore would "engulf what efforts have been made thus far."[39] In a January 1989 report, Poffenberger concluded that seven years of court-ordered reform had accomplished little.[40]

As the failure to achieve reform began to become apparent to the courts, they stepped in again. In March 1986 the state supreme court ruled that the department's Plan of Compliance, which had been accepted in September 1984 by Judge Bronson, did not meet the requirements set forth by Judge Recht's original ruling.[41] The court found that "health care at West Virginia Penitentiary, even assuming full implementation of the compliance plan as approved, constitutes deliberate indifference to the serious medical needs of prisons." The justices also concluded that "we cannot envision how it would be economically feasible to increase the cell size within the confines of the existing structure. It is apparent that the compliance plan must be revised by the Department of Corrections to include the development of a new facility." The court ordered the Department of Corrections to draft an "Amended Plan" in 120 days. Finally, the court appointed Patrick McManus as another special master (a position separate from the earlier appointed special master) to review the Amended Plan and to report back to the court.

In December 1988, after reviewing the Amended Plan and McManus's evaluation of it, the supreme court ordered the state to close the penitentiary by July 1992.[42] Special master McManus had told the court the state's Amended Plan had "virtually no prospect of actually remedying the unconstitutional conditions at West Virginia Penitentiary" and the only way to raise the prison to a constitutionally acceptable level would be to replace it.[43] If the state did not build a new penitentiary, the court warned, it might order the prison into receivership and empower a receiver to build a new one; or, worse, the court would order the release of all of the facility's inmates. To add teeth to the order, the court made parties to the suit twelve top state officials, including the governor, secretary of state, attorney general, president of the Senate, and Speaker of the House.

As of this writing, the new governor has proposed the building of a new penitentiary, but the state legislature has not had an opportunity to act on this recommendation.

During this protracted litigation, the penitentiary underwent profound changes, some of them the unintended consequences of the court's intervention.

The Impact of Court Reform on Order in the Penitentiary

By all accounts, the penitentiary before 1979 was minimally oppressive.[44] The rules were loosely enforced; inmates jammed their cells with as much personal property as they wanted or could afford; and there were ample leisure activities, relaxed visitation rules, and liberal rules for furloughs. The penitentiary was also easy to escape from. Between 1970 and 1979, 238 inmates escaped, an average of 3.7 percent of the population each year—this from the state's only maximum security prison. This phase in the penitentiary's history ended abruptly in 1979, after 15 inmates escaped en masse out the front door, killing an off-duty state policeman as they left. Blaming the escape and murder on lax discipline, the governor ordered prison officials to regain control of the prison and to enforce stricter discipline. A new warden was hired. Upon taking office, Donald Bordenkircher told the press that his mandate was to "tighten the place up so much, it squeaks."

Bordenkircher's personality was suited to the task. He was considered a stern though fair disciplinarian toward both inmates and guards. He had no qualms about firing corrupt guards. Soon after taking office, he told a local reporter: "We had officers stealing license plates. We've got officers involved in drugs. We fired them. Nothing thrills me more than to bust dirty cops."[45] To keep guards on their toes, he would snatch an inmate, bring him to his office, and time how long it would take for the disappearance to be reported. He commented in a 1986 interview: "I can assure you no one ever called me nice, whether staff or inmate. But I really believe in my heart that every inmate knew where he was at and so did every staff member. I never talked forked-tongue bull shit."

Beyond this, Bordenkircher often locked down the entire prison, even for relatively minor infractions by just a few. The inmates charged with the infraction could expect to spend months, if not years, in segregation. In 1986, one inmate reported: "I never like Bordenkircher, due to his egotistical mania. But he knew what he was doing when he was running this institution. He had everything in place; he had discipline; the guards' morale was up; and if they did something wrong, he'd get on their asses the same he would us. But we walked the line." The warden's most controversial policy was his tough stance toward hostage taking. He told inmates, staff, and the press that if hostages were taken, "I'll respectfully request one time that the hostages be released. There will be no debate. If they do not comply with my request, then we'll execute the hostage-taker on the spot."[46]

Throughout his tenure, Bordenkircher pleaded to the legislature for additional funds, but without success. In July 1981 the warden voiced his complaints to a legislative committee that was touring the prison: "We have not had an increase in personnel in five years. We asked for 37 new correctional officers; a dietitian and five cooks; and four medical personnel for this budget year. We received *zero*! There isn't a toilet or sink that doesn't leak. If it's 100 degrees outside, it's 116 degrees in the cell areas, and in the winter it's as cold as hell."[47] Ironically, state legislators used Bordenkircher's tough management style to justify the prison's low budget. After pleading his case for more funds to the state legislative finance committee, the warden was told by its chairman: "You don't need any money. You've got the place under control. They know if they do anything wrong you'll shoot them."[48]

Speaking in 1981, Bordenkircher offered this observation concerning the state of mind of the inmates. "We can't fix it if we don't get the money, and the Legislature's not giving us the money. . . .

The inmates believe they're being slow-walked on everything getting done. They're hearing a lot of talk but nobody's producing anything. They think the Department of Corrections is forcing them to say, 'The hell with it. Just tear it down.' The only reason that they haven't burned things down is they're waiting for their day in court."[49] An inmate agreed: "We're being squeezed as the inmate population by the Department of Corrections to tear down this place. We don't want to tear up anything. We just want what's constitutionally permitted to inmates."[50]

Despite this reported discontent, the prison *was* relatively peaceful during the Bordenkircher period. Judge Recht found that, despite the prison's other shortcomings, "[a] semblance of inmate security has been achieved by the current administration. Inmates are exposed to some risk of physical and sexual assault primarily due to the configuration and overall inadequate conditions at the Penitentiary, as well as the lack of trained correctional officers. However, there is no constant threat of violence or of sexual assault."[51] Bordenkircher boasted that officers and civilians could pass through any section of the prison without fear of molestation.[52] Never in the 114-year history had there been a year without at least one escape; there were none in Bordenkircher's first three years.

Bordenkircher resigned in 1983 to run for local office. His replacement, Manford Holland, had been groomed by Bordenkircher and pledged to continue his mentor's policies. In this he was relatively successful. However, with the election of Governor Moore in the fall of 1984, a change in administration became likely.

Bordenkircher had served as warden under an earlier Moore administration but had resigned in protest. According to Bordenkircher, Moore had ordered him to hire patronage workers and to clear all public appearances and speeches with the commissioner's office. This, in Bordenkircher's judgment, was unacceptable. "I just couldn't give up my manhood, my integrity and my word," Bordenkircher told the press. "They tried to put strings on me I couldn't accept." Moore shot back, "I shall always involve myself in the affairs of the Penitentiary. . . . I determine policy. Mr. Bordenkircher wasn't hired for that purpose."[53] After reelection in 1984, Moore wanted to put his own man in the penitentiary.

His choice was Jerry Hedrick, then warden at Huttonsville. Unlike his two predecessors, Hedrick was unable to gain the respect of inmates or correctional officers. Years earlier, Hedrick had served as deputy warden under Bordenkircher; even his old boss expressed a low opinion of his leadership abilities, describing him as a good "number-two" man, but not an effective leader.

Hedrick's three-year tenure was marked by a series of violent incidents and the mobilization of forces that pulled the prison apart. On January 1, 1986, just two months after Hedrick's appointment, inmates seized most of the penitentiary and took twelve hostages. Inmates negotiated with prison officials and the governor, finally reaching an agreement after three days. During the riot, three inmates were murdered.

Two weeks after the riot, on Moore's direct orders, eighty-six inmates were transferred to the punitive segregation unit for their suspected roles in the riot. This was the beginning of an escalating and violent series of events in that unit. Furious inmates saw the transfer as a violation of a pledge made by the governor that there would be "no retaliation." Inmates also claimed the wholesale transfer without hearings violated their due process rights. This allegation was given weight by a quarterly report issued by the special master Poffenberger: "Prison officials disregarded the rules designed to safeguard the individual's due process guarantees and the efficacy of the penitentiary's disciplinary process."[54] The governor saw it differently. In his understanding, the no-retaliation promise meant only that the inmates "would be secure in their body and mind." Also he felt that the suspension of due process hearings was justified because the prison was in a state of emergency following the riot.

Over a period of several months, attacks and counterattacks between inmates and guards in the segregation unit spiraled out of control. Inmates threw urine, feces, and boiling water on guards. On several occasions, guards were assaulted with broom handles and other makeshift weapons. The few inmates in the unit who refused to participate in the attacks, identifiable by the absence of a mess in front of their cells, became the object of attacks by other inmates. The guards retaliated, turning off the inmates' electricity for long periods, allowing the unit to remain cold, and refusing to enter the tiers unless absolutely necessary. On a visit to the unit in March, the special master observed on the floor "approximately two inches of water, urine and garbage—just floating."

Because of the violent hostilities, the unit's guards were required to wear flak jackets and helmets with face shields. In one especially violent incident, twelve inmates refused to return to their cells after taking showers. A riot squad opened fire on the inmates after one allegedly doused a guard with a flammable liquid and several others produced knives they had made.

The prison became a more hostile environment in another way. Historically, the prison had been free of gangs, at least of the more violent sort that dominate prisons in some states. A possible exception, the Avengers motorcycle gang, did not engage in routine intimidation or extortion. In early 1987 two Avengers were killed, including the gang's president, allegedly by members of the "Aryan Brotherhood." This far more violent, and racist, gang had never before existed at the penitentiary. Over the next several months, the Aryan Brotherhood crushed the Avengers in a power struggle.

The special master's reports further document the transition to a less orderly and safe prison. In comparable three-month periods at the end of 1984 and the end of 1986, the number of serious assaults against other inmates more than doubled; the number of assaults on correctional officers increased from zero to twelve; and the number of "self-mutilations" and suicide attempts increased from thirteen to thirty-five. These changes occurred despite a decrease (from the court order) in the inmate population from 670 to 620.[55]

Much to the frustration of the attorney representing the state, the courts came to consider the violence in the prison as part of the "totality of conditions" that violated inmates' rights.[56] What had been acceptable in 1982 no longer was.

Correctional officers, in their own way, became mobilized and contentious. Over the years various attempts had been made to form an active union, but they had met with limited success. Warden Bordenkircher publicly vowed that he would quit if forced to negotiate with a labor union.[57] And since under state law a union could not act as a collective bargaining unit, the guards' union that did exist was inactive.

During Hedrick's tenure, the guard union became politically

active, going so far as to directly challenge the authority of the warden. In a series of public demonstrations, the guards demanded an increase in security and "safety" in the institution. The prison officials acceded to some of the demands, including the installation of gun cages in each block, manned by guards equipped with a shotgun and a rifle. The guards also demanded the firing of Warden Hedrick and his deputy wardens, but the governor and commissioner refused this demand.

Still, by the end of his three years in office, Warden Hedrick was completely isolated. Despised by the inmates, unable to earn the respect of the guard force, and subject to calls for replacement by several state legislators, the warden could not govern. With little effective authority, the warden stayed in his office outside the walls without ever entering the prison.

In January 1989 a newly appointed commissioner of corrections fired Warden Hedrick. Bordenkircher applied for his old position but was turned down. As of this writing, the new warden, whose background is with the state police, has been on the job too short a time to evaluate changes he might institute.

The Power of the Court and Judicial Reform

Did court intervention contribute to the spiral of conflict that began with the January 1986 riot? The question is not easily answered since the increase in violence coincided with the appointment of Warden Hedrick. By the end of Hedrick's term, few disputed that he was far less capable of governing than his predecessors. Perhaps Warden Hedrick was just kept on the job too long.

Nevertheless, the evidence suggests that the task facing Warden Hedrick (or anyone else in his position) had been made more difficult by the legal environment. By "legal environment" I mean not just the status of *Crain v. Bordenkircher* but the broader context of law and order in the state.

In the period under consideration, there was a serious erosion of the power of the West Virginia courts. Political scientist Martin Shapiro has described (at the national level) the distinctive feature of the courts' power:

Legislatures may proclaim . . . interests to be rights as Congress proclaimed a right to a job in the Full Employment Act of 1946. But no one takes such proclamations very seriously, as the subsequent history of that act shows. Here the Supreme Court enjoys a comparative institutional advantage over [the] president and Congress. When it calls a social interest a right, it is taken seriously. And once elevated to the status of judicially acknowledged constitutional right, the interest is raised above the hurly-burly of political bargaining.[58]

This does *not* characterize the situation in West Virginia in the 1980s.

From the governor's chair to the halls of the state legislature to the voting booths, West Virginians did not take the rights established by the state courts seriously or consider them above political bargaining. The governor, the reader will recall, was described by the supreme court as having been in "willful and contumacious contempt of court." The state legislators refused to allocate the funds necessary for school and prison reform. Legislative leaders called the court's rulings foolish, if not the whimsical opinions of a "hippie" clan. There was little popular support and no sense of urgency for spending the money necessary to bring the prison up to constitutional standards. At Huttonsville, inmates had been punished by Warden Hedrick for refusing to allow more inmates into their dormitories; the subsequent actions of Governor Moore conceded not only that their cause was just but that violation of law to obtain that end could be justified.

Conditions at the penitentiary had been bad for many years. If we can rely on Bordenkircher's assessment of the mood of the inmates in 1982, inmates back then believed they were being "hustled." What was new in the 1980s was that public officials, from state legislators to Warden Bordenkircher, conceded that things were bad, that these bad conditions violated inmates' constitutional rights, and that inaction under these conditions was itself a violation of the law. Yet the necessary remedial actions were not taken. The state said that it could not afford to bring about the changes judged necessary by the court, but the courts had clearly stated that that excuse was unacceptable. Legitimacy is hard to establish under these conditions.

One might ask why the powers of the court eroded in this period. Obviously important were the economic conditions in the state. The cost of various court-mandated reforms began to mount while the resources to carry them out dwindled. Flood victims, the unemployed, and the general public facing a declining standard of living were not eager to foot the bill. The court could describe their preferences for public expenditures as "societal luxuries," as it did in the *Cooper* decision, but elected representatives didn't. In consequence, one project after another was put on hold.

Beyond this one can argue, as many have, that the courts in West Virginia simply overstepped their authority. In doing so, they invited the resistance they eventually encountered. One more sympathetic to the court's intent would place greater blame on the intransigence of the elected officials. From this point of view, the supreme court had made its ruling on the basis of law; the cases it ruled on were not of the judges' own choosing but had been brought before them. Public officials failed to understand that.

The electorate eventually took the view that the courts had gone too far. In a hotly contested election in 1988, Justice McGraw called his Democratic opponents "Republicans" and accused them of wanting to return the court to the pre-1976 "nowheresville." One of his opponents charged that the court had contributed to the state's economic stagnation.[59] The charge was not proven, but neither was it entirely implausible. McGraw was defeated, establishing a less "activist" majority.

Plans of Compliance and Their Failure

During the period under consideration, the Department of Corrections was caught in a political bind. It had the responsibility to implement the court's mandate to bring the prison up to constitutional standards, which meant "massive renovation bordering on new construction." At the same time, the department had to remain loyal to the governor. It could not fold its hands, declaring the task impossible with the available resources, though it may have been.

As a result, the department promised much (in the form of an original Plan of Compliance and an Amended Plan of Compliance) but delivered little. Special master McManus observed that had the department been able to make good on its original Plan of Compliance, an acceptable solution might have been achieved. But it did not.

In the end various half-baked efforts did little to improve the prison, instead wasting considerable sums of money. For example, the prison needed both a new ventilating system (at $1 million) and a new plumbing system (at $3.1 million). After the million-dollar ventilating system was installed, engineers concluded that it would have to be ripped out before a plumbing system could be installed. A new dining hall and kitchen were constructed at a cost of $2 million, but under the court's order to close the facility by 1992, this expenditure was largely wasted. The department's Amended Plan called for an increase in the cell size from thirty-five square feet to seventy square feet. The department later concluded that this was not practical but failed to develop a substitute plan—as though the issue would simply go away. The prison's operating budget increased from $5.9 million in 1983–84 to $7.9 in 1987–88, but nearly all of this 34 percent increase was absorbed by a 55 percent rise in personnel costs associated with increased security. By 1987 the ratio of guards to inmates was one to two, far above the national average of one to six. This apparent overstaffing (largely in reponse to guard union militancy) resulted in insufficient funds being available "to meet fundamental maintenance requirements."[60]

Finally, as judicial intervention appeared imminent, the governor claimed that he had a "plan" to build a new prison. No one took this "plan" very seriously—including, apparently, the governor as well as the legislature.[61] Special master McManus wrote in his report that he had "heard" about this plan, but that the Department of Corrections made no reference to it in its submissions to him.

Beyond these difficulties, there was yet another impediment to achieving the reforms mandated by the courts.[62] Even if the state legislature and governor were committed to building a new prison (and they were not), serious obstacles to financing its construction had to be overcome. Given the depressed economy and dwindling tax base, the state legislature would have found it difficult to appropriate in one or two years the fifty million to one hundred million dollars needed to build a new prison.

Alternatively, a new prison could be financed under a "lease/purchase" arrangement from a private or public corporation. But West Virginia had written into its constitution and statutes provisions designed to prevent deficit spending. One of them prohibited the state from entering long-term contracts that pledged the credit of the state. Thus any corporation that built a prison for the state would run the risk that the state could break its contract at any time. Such a venture would be especially risky since a prison (unlike, say, a football stadium) would have no alternative use, generate no revenues of its own, and might be declared obsolete by a future court.[63] State Supreme Court Justice Richard Neely suggested a legal strategy that might allow the state to get around the problem, but the suggestion was never pursued.

Conclusion

Reflecting on his experience as a special master in two states, Fritz Byers argues against the idea that prison officials can be expected to combat court intervention with every ounce of energy. More typically it is an alliance: "Prison litigation serves not so much to club persistently wicked administrators into conforming their conduct with the Constitution, as it serves to provide a lever for all interested people to use in obtaining funds, personnel, and resources required to maintain a Constitutional prison."[64] This observation is largely valid when applied to litigation at the penitentiary. The prison officials did not, for the most part, challenge the right of the court to intervene. Even Warden Bordenkircher, the named defendant, could not come to the prison's defense in the 1982 trial. "I have always said," he testified, "do not spend a nickel on that one hundred and fifteen year old facility. It is a waste of our money."

The problem at West Virginia was that the "lever"—the power of the courts—was (in the period under consideration) defective. Although it never quite broke, it could not move the forces necessary to make a timely response. This was intensely frustrating to inmates. Unsuccessful judicial reform is (in the short run) more destabilizing than no reform at all.

It also puts pressure on correctional leadership. No correctional administrator wants to be hauled into court to have his or her name etched in case law for having violated the Constitution or, even worse, to be found guilty and then not to have the resources to correct the violation. Corrections officials want to enforce the law, not break it, for both professional and personal reasons. In a 1989 interview Warden Bordenkircher reported that the publicity surrounding *Crain* had been "hard" on his wife and two children. Until prison officials have the resources needed to stay out of court, the most competent of their number will be tempted to go elsewhere.

If the penitentiary is replaced by 1992, as ordered by the supreme court, then one decade will have passed between Judge Recht's ruling and its fulfillment. The attorney representing the inmates said that one should take a long-term view of prison litigation and that a ten-year delay, regrettable as it may be, is not unexpected. Few of the inmates who initiated the suit will enjoy the fruits of their effort; most inmates are released in less than a decade—but not all of them.

Notes

1. Some of the material presented here was collected for a chapter in Bert Useem and Peter Kimball's *States of Siege: U.S. Prison Riots, 1971–1986* (New York: Oxford University Press, 1989). The present author returned to West Virginia in January 1989 to conduct an additional round of interviews.
2. The succeeding four paragraphs are based on the following sources: Bruce Boyens, "Development of Foreign Coal by American Corporations," *West Virginia Law Review* 87 (1985), 567–74; William H. Miernyk et al., *The West Virginia Economy* (prepared for the West Virginia Tax Study Commission, Charleston, W.Va., 1982); Wharton Econometric Forecasting Associates, "U.S. Regional Forecasts: State Analysis" (Bala Cynwyd, Pa.: The WEFA Group, Summer 1988); Kenneth D. Jones, "West Virginia Gross State Product," *West Virginia Business and Economic Review* 1 (Summer/Fall 1988), 1–6; and John Alexander Williams, *West Virginia: A Bicentennial History* (New York: Norton, 1976).
3. "West Virginia, Mired in Poverty, Corruption, Battles a Deep Gloom," *Wall Street Journal*, September 21, 1988.
4. Neal R. Pierce, *The Border South States: People, Politics, and Power in Five Border South States* (New York: Norton, 1975), pp. 151, 194–98; John P. Hagan, "Policy Activism in the West Virginia Supreme Court of Appeals," *West Virginia Law Review* 9 (1986), 149.
5. Hagan, "Policy Activism," pp. 149–65.
6. "West Virginia's Latest Attempts to Mine New Industry Are Hurt by Its Poor Image," *Wall Street Journal*, December 29, 1982.
7. Quoted in Hagan, "Policy Activism," p. 164.

8. *Mandolidis v. Elkins Industries, Inc.*, 246 S.E.2d 907 (W.Va. 1978).
9. "West Virginia's Latest Attempt," *Wall Street Journal*, December 29, 1982, p. 24. In a dissenting opinion, Justice Richard Neely made much the same point. The majority's opinion would "do a substantial disservice to the economy of this State by instituting frivolous suits every time a workman is injured." This would "divert needed resources from the fund available for wages, plant modernization, and stockholders' dividends." *Mandolidis v. Elkins Industries, Inc.*, 246 S.E.2d 907, pp. 922–23.
10. *Pauley v. Kelley*, 162 W.Va. 672, 255 S.E.2d 859 (1979).
11. *San Antonio Independent School District v. Rodriguez*, 411 U.S. 1 (1973).
12. "Arthur Recht: Circuit Judge and Author of the Controversial Lincoln County Schools Decision Is Sunday Gazette-Mail's West Virginian of the Year," Charleston *Sunday Gazette-Mail*, January 3, 1983.
13. Otis K. Rice, *West Virginia: A History* (Lexington: University Press of Kentucky, 1985), p. 286.
14. Quoted in Norman Oder, "Behind the Rhetoric: Philosophies Clash in Supreme Court Race," Charleston *Sunday Gazette-Mail*, April 17, 1988.
15. "Arthur Recht," Charleston *Sunday Gazette-Mail*.
16. "Senate Education Chief to Fight Recht Decision," Charleston *Daily Mail*, January 11, 1985.
17. "Recht Enjoys Role of Trial Judge, Scoffs at Publicity," Charleston *Gazette*, August 22, 1982.
18. *Cooper v. Gwinn*, 298 S.E.2d 781 (W.Va. 1982).
19. *Newman v. Alabama*, 559 F.2d at 291 (5th Cir. 1977).
20. West Virginia Department of Corrections, *Cumulative Annual Report: Fiscal Years 1981–1984* (Charleston: West Virginia Department of Corrections, 1985), p. 18.
21. "Inmates Disciplined Following Protest," Charleston *Gazette*, March 9, 1985; "Former Inmates Link Warden's Style, Revolt," Charleston *Gazette*, January 3, 1986.
22. *State ex rel. Dodrill v. Scott*, 352 S.E.2d 741 (W.Va. 1986), p. 743.
23. "Jury's Decision Against Moore May Be Landmark," Charleston *Gazette*, August 26, 1988.
24. *Crain v. Bordenkircher*, "Memorandum of Opinion, Finding of Fact, Conclusions of Law and Order" (Civil Action No. 81-C-320 R, Circ.Ct., Marshall County, W.Va., 1983). The quotes in the following five paragraphs are taken from this opinion.
25. Interview with Arthur Recht, January 1989.
26. Quoted in William P. Cheshire, "West Virginia's Rocky Road," *Policy Review* 27 (Winter 1984), 64–66.

27. Mark G. Cherry, "Tax Reform—West Virginia Style," *Journal of State Taxation* 6 (Winter 1988), 327–36; Harry Preston Henshaw III, "Analysis of Tax Incentives for Business Development in West Virginia," *West Virginia Law Review* 89 (1987), 335–56; "Economic Paralysis Could Stop Arch Moore," *Business Week*, November 30, 1987, p. 37.

28. "Judiciary and State Government Butt Heads over Funding Methods," Charleston *Gazette*, January 26, 1986.

29. "State Agencies Debate Where to Make Cuts," Charleston *Daily Mail*, April 8, 1987; "Budget Cuts May Impede Compliance with Order," Charleston *Gazette*, April 11, 1987.

30. "Governor Moore's Prison Plans Not in Concrete," Charleston *Gazette*, September 16, 1988.

31. "State Budget—Quick and Drastic Action Needed," Charleston *Daily Mail*, January 9, 1989; "Moore Paints Rosier Picture," Charleston *Daily Mail*, January 18, 1989; "Caperton to Disclose Financial Findings Today," Charleston *Gazette*, January 19, 1989; "Economic Paralysis Could Stop Arch Moore," *Business Week*, November 30, 1987.

32. "Caperton Seeks $335 Million in Taxes," Charleston *Gazette*, January 23, 1989.

33. "That's $704 Million in No New Taxes," Wheeling *Intelligencer*, February 4, 1989; "$400 Million Tax Package Passes House," Charleston *Gazette*, February 1, 1989.

34. "Economic Weight of Recht's Prison Decision Cited," Charleston *Gazette*, June 22, 1983.

35. Donald Poffenberger, "Quarterly Report: October 9, 1984, to January 9, 1985," filed in the Circuit Court of Marshall County, West Virginia, in the case of *Crain v. Bordenkircher*.

36. "Report Says Corrections Making Progress," Charleston *Daily Mail*, January 31, 1985.

37. Donald Poffenberger, "Quarterly Report: July 9, 1985, to October 9, 1985," filed in the Circuit Court of Marshall County, West Virginia, in the case of *Crain v. Bordenkircher*.

38. "West Virginia Prisons Not Complying with Standards, New Chief Says," Charleston *Daily Mail*, July 8, 1985.

39. Donald Poffenberger, "Quarterly Report: January 9, 1987, to April 9, 1987," filed in the Circuit Court of Marshall County, West Virginia, in the case of *Crain v. Bordenkircher*.

40. Interview with author, January 1989.

41. *Crain v. Bordenkircher*, No. 16646, Marshall County, Remanded, March 27, 1986.

42. *Crain v. Bordenkircher*, No. 16646, Marshall County, Writ Granted as Moulded, December 2, 1988.

43. Patrick D. McManus, "Report and Recommendations of the Special Master to the 'Revised Plan of Compliance' of the Department of Corrections," submitted to the West Virginia Supreme Court of Appeals in the case of *Crain v. Bordenkircher.*

44. This section draws on Useem and Kimball, *States of Siege.* Interviews uncited were conducted by the present author in 1986.

45. "Corrupt, Incompetent Staff Prison Problem," Wheeling *Intelligencer*, January 27, 1982.

46. "Warden Outlines 'Simple' Hostages Policy," Charleston *Gazette*, January 29, 1980.

47. "Legislators Tour 'Deplorable Pen,'" Wheeling *News Register*, July 23, 1981.

48. "Build, Don't Renovate, Say Warden, Inmate," Charleston *Gazette*, September 18, 1981.

49. Ibid.

50. Ibid.

51. "Memorandum," 20.

52. "Bordenkircher Made Presence Felt," Charleston *Gazette*, April 25, 1975. These comments were made concerning an earlier tenure as warden, though they continued to hold during the period under discussion.

53. "Former Warden Returns to Pen," Wheeling *Intelligencer*, December 26, 1979; "Bordenkircher's Career as Warden, Point by Point," Charleston *Gazette*, April 24, 1975.

54. Donald Poffenberger, "Quarterly Report: January 9, 1986, to April 9, 1986," filed in the Circuit Court of Marshall County, West Virginia, in the case of *Crain v. Bordenkircher*, p. 10.

55. Donald Poffenberger, "Quarterly Report: January 9, 1987, to April 9, 1987," filed in the Circuit Court of Marshall County, West Virginia, in the case of *Crain v. Bordenkircher*, p. 16.

56. Interview with Dana Davis, an assistant attorney general, 1989.

57. "Warden Will Quit if Forced to Parley with Union," Wheeling *News-Register*, February 11, 1982.

58. Martin Shapiro, "Judicial Activism," in *The Third Century: America as a Post-Industrial Society*, ed. Seymour Martin Lipset (Stanford: Hoover Institution Press, 1979), p. 118.

59. Oder, "Behind the Rhetoric."

60. Donald Poffenberger, "Quarterly Report: February 9, 1988, to May 30, 1988," filed in the Circuit Court of Marshall County, West Virginia, in the case of *Crain v. Bordenkircher*, p. 30; Donald Poffenberger, "Quarterly Report: July 9, 1987, to November 9, 1987," filed in the Circuit Court of Marshall County, West Virginia, in the case of *Crain v.*

Bordenkircher, p. 10; Patrick D. McManus, "Report and Recommendations of the Special Master to the 'Revised Plan of Compliance' of the Department of Corrections," submitted to the West Virginia Supreme Court of Appeals in the case of *Crain v. Bordenkircher.*

61. "Governor Moore's Prison Plans Not in Concrete," Charleston *Gazette*, September 16, 1988.

62. These two paragraphs are based on a 1989 interview with Justice Richard Neely and on a concurring in part and dissenting in part opinion to *State ex rel. Dodrill v. Scott*, 352 S.E.2d 741 (W.Va. 1986), p. 743. Also helpful was "Neely Opinion Deserves Notice," Charleston *Gazette*, July 19, 1987.

63. The latter fear—that today's court-ordered prison will be tomorrow's constitutionally forbidden one—has foundation. Nathan Glazer describes the fate of a 384-bed facility for retarded children built to comply with a 1972 federal court order. An existing facility for 5,000 had been declared unconstitutional. By the time the new facility was completed, the federal judge decided that even it was too large, because children should be treated in small, homelike settings. The new facility was never opened. Nathan Glazer, *The Limits of Social Policy* (Cambridge: Harvard University Press, 1988), p. 149.

64. Fritz Byers, "Special Masters and Prison Reform: Real and Imagined Obstacles," *Journal on Dispute Resolution* 3 (1988), 361–83.

9

Judicial Appointment and Judicial Intervention: The Issuance of Structural Reform Decrees in Correctional Litigation

ROBERT C. BRADLEY

According to a number of contemporary scholars, a new style of adjudication has developed to address certain novel and complex legal issues.[1] Traditional litigation has been supplanted in some situations by a pattern of adjudication in which the judge employs certain powers that are more commonly associated with either legislators or bureaucrats. This pattern of adjudication in which judges resolve disputes more from an administrative than from a legal perspective has been given many labels—public law, structural reform, institutional reform, extended impact, and complex enforcement. I shall use the term structural reform to describe a mode of litigation in which a judge becomes actively involved not only in providing redress for past harms but also in trying to prevent future injuries. In a structural reform lawsuit, a judge tries to prevent future injuries by restructuring the particular public bureaucracy identified as the source of the harms by the litigants. The judge acts as an administrator redirecting the provision of a public service for the benefit of a deprived segment of the populace, such as black schoolchildren, psychiatric inmates, or state prisoners.[2]

Although structural reform litigation has been handled by judges at every level of this nation's judicial system, the courts most involved with this form of litigation are the federal district courts.[3] In recent years district courts have made major policy decisions in a number of diverse legal areas.[4] The most dramatic and controversial instances of structural reform litigation, however, have occurred when federal district judges have intervened in response to alleged constitutional violations in the operation and structure of state custodial institutions, especially state prisons for adults.[5] District judges have created and supervised judicial formulations for reforms in state prisons without relying on the expertise or inclinations of possibly intransigent state officials. In numerous cases employing the totality of conditions approach, federal district judges examined state prisons in great detail and fashioned remedies that touched on every aspect of institutional life.[6]

In the last two decades, the number of state prisons operating under court decree increased dramatically. Before 1970 there were no states operating either portions or the entirety of their penal systems in accordance with decrees issued by federal judges. By July 1977, twenty-nine states were either under court order concerning conditions of confinement in prisons or were involved in litigation likely to result in court orders. By 1980 the number of states directly involved in federal litigation had risen to thirty-two.[7] By 1986 the correctional agencies or prisons in thirty-seven states were operating under federal court orders, while another eight states were embroiled in major litigation.[8] Clearly, in the 1970s the federal courts—particularly district courts—had picked up the gauntlet of prison reform and were using structural reform decrees as a major weapon to meet the challenge. Despite protests from both the legal and political communities, certain federal district judges created and used "a new jurisprudence of structural reform" to institute broad reforms in the operation and administration of state correctional institutions.[9]

The purpose of this chapter is to provide a preliminary answer to the following question: Are the appointees of Democratic presidents to the federal district courts more likely to issue structural reform decrees in state prison cases than are the appointees of Republican presidents? According to prevailing thought, one of the more influential factors affecting presidential nominations to the federal bench is the nominees' beliefs and philosophy. If a potential nominee's beliefs and philosophy are in basic agreement with the appointing president, then that nominee's chances for nomination are much better than a nominee whose beliefs and philosophy are in fundamental disagreement with the appointing president.

Recent Democratic presidents have promoted the interests of the disadvantaged and advocated federal intervention to address social ills at all levels of government. The issuance of structural reform decrees in state prisons seems to be in accordance with this general philosophy. Recent Republican presidents have advocated a less active role for government and favored a restraintist philosophy for the federal courts. The issuance of structural reform decrees appears to be antithetical to this general philosophy. Thus, one might assume that judges nominated by Democratic presidents are more likely to issue structural reform decrees than are judges nominated by Republican presidents. Given the fact that Republicans have held the White House for sixteen of the last twenty years, and will by 1992 have held it for twelve consecutive years, one might further suppose that some sort of a return to the "hands-off" doctrine is imminent.

Theoretical Framework

The method of analysis employed in this chapter is social-background analysis. Social-background analysis moves from the assumption that a judge's decisions are influenced by his or her attitudes, which in turn are shaped by social, political, and legal background factors and experiences.[10] Certain key attributes that are products of a judge's life experiences are thought to be linked to regularities in decisional behavior through the formation and development of influential attitudes and values.[11]

While cognizant of the fact that social-background attributes are not equivalent to attitudes and values, I assume that certain attributes either directly reflect or develop into deep-seated attitudes held by federal district judges. Furthermore, these attitudes are assumed to come to the forefront of a judge's decision in cases where legal precedent is either nonexistent or ambiguous and political aspects are prevalent. In legal disputes that are highly politicized where prevailing law and precedent are neither clear nor consistent, the policy preferences of judges are likely to be stimulated, and the impact of extralegal influences on those preferences will be substantially heightened.[12]

In assessing the impact of extralegal influences on federal district judges' decision-making behavior, social-background analysis has predominated previous research efforts. This predominance is due to the fact that many other methods of analysis used to study judicial decision making are predicated on a judge's involvement and interaction in a collegial court.[13] As such, these methods of analysis are inappropriate for the study of federal district judges when they are deciding cases or making policy alone.

Although social-background analysis has been used in a number of previous studies on federal district judges, the findings of these studies do not present a clear picture of the impact of social-background traits on the behavior of district judges, particularly in regard to policymaking.[14] This study will attempt to clarify this picture by addressing two issues that exist in previous literature on district judges, the impact of case contents on judicial decision making and the conceptualization of policymaking. Each of these issues will be detailed in the following section on conceptual definitions.

Conceptual Definitions

TYPE OF CASE

Each case presented to a court consists of case contents, a particular set of factors such as the type and nature of the facts, relevant statutes and precedents, and characteristics of the litigants. If a researcher is attempting to examine the influence of certain social-background traits on the decisional behavior of federal district judges, then the case contents must be adequately conceptualized and their possible effects must be controlled. Previous research on the courts has documented that both the status of the parties involved in the litigation and the type of legal issue influence judicial decision making.[15] Unfortunately, previous works on the federal district courts have paid insufficient attention to the contents of the cases under examination.[16]

To minimize variance in the case contents of selected cases, state prison cases from 1970 to 1979 will be analyzed in this study. Furthermore, the study will examine only state prison cases where the following factors are present: a state inmate is acting as the plaintiff; an official representative of a state prison and/or a state public official is named as the respondent; Section 1983 of the Civil Rights Act of 1871 is used by the inmate to gain access to a federal district court; and an official practice, policy, or regulation of a state prison or penal system is challenged in the inmate's complaint. According to the foregoing discussion, the case contents for this analysis will be conceptualized as follows:

$$CC = P + R + L + C + e$$

where CC = case stimulus for all cases to be analyzed in the 1970s

P = state inmate as petitioner

R = state official as respondent

L = Section 1983 used to bring case to federal district court

C = complaint focused on official prison policy

e = incidental fact variations

This conceptualization will control for the potential effects of the case contents by focusing on cases in a similar issue area and by holding the type of parties, form of statutory law, and format of legal complaint constant across all cases included in the analysis. If the case contents are essentially equivalent across different cases and different decisions are produced from these cases, then there is a distinct possibility that differences in the judges are causing the different decisions.

In addition, this conceptualization incorporates two dimensions that have been recently identified as being important to analyzing judicial decision making. These two dimensions are the degree of politicization in the dispute and the extent of legal leeways regarding the dispute.[17] The degree of politicization in a dispute appears to depend on two components in a case: the status differential between the litigants and the nature of the dispute.[18] In cases where there is a large difference in power between the parties, the dispute is likely to contain a high degree of politicization, particularly if the case involves an issue that directly relates to the political system.[19] In state prison litigation, there is a tremendous status differential between state prisoners and the typical respondents of such litigation, such as prison wardens and state public officials. In addition, state prison litigation involves some fundamental political issues, such as separation of powers, checks and balances, and federalism. Clearly, as conceptualized for this analysis, state prison cases are marked by a high degree of politicization.

The extent of legal leeways refers essentially to the amount of legal constraints on a judge in making a decision in a particular case.[20] If the legal constraints in a particular case are lax because of lack of precedent or the presence of a novel problem, then the range of options open to a judge in making a decision is great.[21] In state prison cases as conceptualized for this analysis, federal district judges were essentially free of significant legal constraints. During the 1970s the Burger Court could not obtain a majority position on the responsibilities of federal judges with regard to the substantial ills of state prisons. Also, state prison reform was a novel issue for district judges in the 1970s since state inmates had been routinely denied access to the federal courts prior to 1970.

As such, state prison cases appeared to fall into a category of cases where the legal constraints are minimal and the political aspects of cases are quite evident.[22] In terms of judicial decision making, this means that the discretion of judges is great in dealing with such cases. As a result, the chances of discerning appreciable differences in judicial behavior due to extralegal factors, such as social-background traits, are significantly greater than the situation where a category of cases has maximum legal constraints and minimum political aspects.

DEPENDENT VARIABLE

In previous research on federal district judges, the dependent variable was conceptualized generally to be decisions rendered by individual district judges. More specifically, the decisions are classified usually as to whether they supported the claims of the plaintiffs or the defendants in either civil or criminal cases. These decisions are obtained typically from the *Federal Supplement.* Several recent studies have used this conceptualization to study the policymaking behavior of federal district judges.[23] These studies have relied essentially on the following model:

$$PD = PM \text{ for all cases}$$

where PD = a published decision in the *Federal Supplement*
PM = a policy made by a federal district judge

According to this model, if a district judge's decision is published in the *Federal Supplement*, then that decision is assumed to be making policy. The inclusion of a decision in the *Federal Supplement* without any other considerations is sufficient to define it as a policymaking decision.

There is a significant problem with accepting this model as a valid indicator of policymaking behavior. The problem is the inclusion of decisions that clearly do not make policy. As pointed out in one of the studies, 10 to 15 percent of the decisions published in the *Federal Supplement* deal with legal issues that border on the trivial.[24] This suggests, as the study notes, that these cases do not reflect policy decisions. But do the remaining 85 to 90 percent of the cases contain policy decisions? The answer is not clear because the study does not empirically or substantively demonstrate that these cases all made policy.

To address this problem and answer the posed research question, the following model will serve as the basis for the conceptualization of policymaking behavior as the dependent variable:

$$PD = D$$
$$D \neq PM$$

where PD = a published decision by a federal district judge in the *Federal Supplement*

D = a quantifiable decision by a federal district judge

PM = a policy made by a federal district judge

This model states that published decisions of federal district judges in the *Federal Supplement* represent quantifiable or empirical decisions because they can be accessed by researchers from available source material. This model also states that a decision of a federal district judge does not automatically qualify for designation as a policymaking decision because it is published in the *Federal Supplement*. In other words, not every decision made by a district judge that is published in the *Federal Supplement* makes policy. For this study, policymaking behavior will be conceptualized to consist of a set of decisions by federal district judges that incorporate, to borrow from a previous study, a policy-change option.[25] A policy-change option is present in a case where a district judge is confronted with the choice of either changing an established governmental policy or leaving the policy intact.[26] For a decision to be included in this study, a district judge must be confronted with the choice of either directly intervening or not intervening in a state prison to deal with its alleged problems. The direct involvement of a federal district judge is indicated by the presence of a structural reform order in the decision. As previously discussed, a structural reform order is essentially a court-mandated change in an existing public policy. Lack of direct court involvement will be indicated by the absence of a structural reform order. While structural reform decrees do not constitute the entire universe of judicial policymaking, such decrees are easily identifiable and have been the major impetus in achieving reforms in our nation's state prisons.

The discretion to either issue or not issue a structural reform decree that is designed to remedy state prison problems is present only in decisions that are made in the favor of state inmates. This conceptualization of policymaking behavior is based on the knowledge that structural reform orders are used exclusively to ameliorate the dismal conditions affecting inmates in state prisons. When issued, structural reform decrees always strive to enact remedial policies that would benefit state inmates. Thus, if a district judge decides against the claims of a state inmate, then logically no structural reform order will be issued which would alter the policies of the state prison for no apparent reason.

INDEPENDENT VARIABLE

It is impractical—perhaps impossible—to identify and examine all the possible background attributes of every federal district judge who served from 1970 to 1979. For this study, one social-background trait will be treated as an independent variable: appointing president. This trait has been used frequently in previous research on federal district judges. The trait will be defined as it is incorporated into the forthcoming conceptual hypothesis.

Conceptual Hypothesis

APPOINTING PRESIDENT

In recent years, several studies have documented empirically that the variable of appointing president has a significant impact on the behavor of federal district judges.[27] According to these studies, appointing president is an important predictor of a district judge's policy choices in a variety of legal areas, such as criminal justice, civil rights and liberties, and labor and economic regulation. Specifically, several studies found that the party affiliation of the appointing president has a substantial effect on district judges' policymaking behavior.[28] Discernible differences were found in the policymaking behavior of the appointees of Republican presidents as opposed to the behavior of appointees of Democratic presidents.[29] In addition, discernible differences in policy choices were observed between the appointees of different individual presidents by all the studies. These findings, however, must be examined with some reservations. The primary reservation comes from the conceptual definition of policymaking behavior that is used in these studies. As indicated earlier, these studies do not adequately isolate the policymaking cases rendered by federal district judges.

The purpose of the conceptual hypothesis is to determine if the observed relationship between party affiliation of appointing president and policymaking behavior by federal district judges in previous studies either is statistically significant or even remains in existence when the impact of case contents is controlled and a more precise conceptualization of policymaking behavior is used in the analysis. The hypothesis is: In state prisoner suits, there is a relationship between the policymaking behavior of federal district judges and the party of their appointing president. For this hypothesis, the independent variable is the party of the appointing president. This variable consists of district judges who were successfully appointed by either Republican or Democratic presidents. The dependent variable is the policymaking behavior by federal district judges. Policymaking behavior will be defined by the presence or absence of a structural reform decree in a decision on the merits by a federal district judge.

Characterizing federal district judges who were appointed by Democratic presidents as Feddapps and federal district judges who were appointed by Republican presidents as Fedrapps, the hypothesis may be stated as follows:

H(1): In cases in which state inmates are plaintiffs and state prison officials are defendants, a significantly greater percentage of decisions containing structural reform decrees will be provided by Feddapps than by Fedrapps.

Confirmation of the hypothesis will be indicated by a level of significance of 0.05 or lower.

Data Collection

Data were gathered on all the active, nonsenior federal district judges who served on the district courts in the 1970s and on any active district judge who served for any length of time during the 1970s. Several sources were used to collect these data, including the *Biographical Dictionary*, *Who's Who in America*, *Who's Who in American Law*, and *Judges of the United States*.

For this study, a subset of all the federal district judges who presided in the 1970s will be used for data analysis. This subset will include only those district judges who decided state prison cases that meet the requirements for inclusion in this study. The subset totaled 147 federal district judges. A summary of the pertinent social-background traits of this subset of district judges is presented in table 9.1. In table 9.1, the number of district judges per social-background trait does not total 147 because some of the judges could not be classified in terms of the categories provided for the traits.

Several steps were taken to collect the data on the decisions that fulfilled the requirements in the prior conceptualization of policy-

TABLE 9.1. Summary of Pertinent Social-Background
Characteristic of the Subset of Federal District Judges

Social-Background Trait: Party of Appointing President	Number of District Judges Who Possess Trait
Democrat	79
Republican	65

making behavior. The first step was to identify all the published district court decisions dealing with state inmates' complaints which were rendered during the 1970s. LEXIS, a computer-assisted legal research system, was used to identify the initial body of applicable cases in the appropriate time frame. Using certain programmed key words and phrases, LEXIS found approximately five hundred decisions in the *Federal Supplement* from 1970 through 1979 that included inmates and Section 1983.

The second step in collecting data was to filter out those cases that did not meet all the requirements established in the conceptualization of the case contents from the LEXIS-identified body of cases. Cases were excluded from the data set for the following reasons: cases were brought by a federal inmate; case was against a mental hospital or institution; case involved a challenge to inmate's sentencing or some other facet of trial; case was a challenge to the actions of a guard or other staff member who was not acting in accordance with official policies or practices; case was resolved on the grounds of jurisdiction or standing; and case was a challenge by an inmate to a government regulation that was entirely unrelated to prison practices and procedures.

After this screening stage was completed, there were 328 decisions in the data set that were appropriate for analysis. Detailed information on each of these decisions was collected. This information included the case citation, the date of the decision, the name of the presiding district judge, the complaints cited in the case, and various details about the decision of the judge. The details about the decision involved whether the plaintiff or defendant won the case and whether the decision contained a structural reform decree.

Findings

As presented earlier, the hypothesis postulates that there is a relationship between party of the appointing president and policymaking behavior by federal district judges. According to this hypothesis, party of the appointing president has a discernible impact on the tendency of federal district judges to issue structural reform decrees in state prison cases.

Table 9.2 demonstrates that **H**(1) is rejected. The high level of significance reported in table 9.2 clearly exceeds the 0.05 level that is generally sufficient to confirm a hypothesis. This high level of significance indicates that the observed difference in the policymaking behavior of Feddapps and Fedrapps is not significant and is most likely due to chance. The measure of association reported in table 9.2 indicates only a minimal association between the independent variable (party affiliation of appointing president) and policymaking behavior. These findings indicate an absence of a relationship between the social-background trait and the policymaking tendencies of federal district judges in state prison cases.

In table 9.2, the reader should note the relatively high percentage of decisions that contained structural reform decrees regardless of the values of the independent variable. For each of the values of the independent variable, approximately 60 percent of the decisions contained structural reform decrees. This means that if a state inmate wins a case, his chances for generating court-ordered re-

TABLE 9.2.   Findings in Respect to **H**(1)

Independent Variable: Party of Appointing President	Percentage of Decisions that Contain a Structural Reform Decree	Total Number of Decisions
Feddapps	58.8	80
Fedrapps	60.0	35

Statistic	Value
Chi-square	0.03
	Level of significance = 0.90
Phi	0.01

forms in response to state prison problems are good. Still, the number of structural reform decrees is low in comparison to the total number of decisions on state inmates' complaints because of the small percentage of cases that are won by state inmates.

Also in reference to table 9.2, the discrepancy in the total number of decisions for the values of each of the independent variables is a reflection of the fact that district judges who are the appointees of Democratic presidents (Feddapps) decided a higher percentage of cases in the favor of state inmates than did the appointees of Republican presidents (Fedrapps). As a result, Feddapps have a higher total number of cases in table 9.2 than do Fedrapps.

One possible explanation of the findings in table 9.2 is that the problems of state prisons probably do not weigh very heavily on a president's determination of suitable candidates for the federal district courts. A president is more likely to be concerned with a potential nominee's handling of more visible and politically divisive social issues, such as racial discrimination in education and housing or state-supported religious practices. This would be particularly true in the decades prior to the 1970s when state prison problems received minimal attention from the public and the government. Even in the 1970s, when the lower federal courts began to address the concerns of state inmates, the other branches of the national government continued to treat state prison problems as nonpriority items.

Although it is clear that there is no significant relationship between party of the appointing president and policymaking behavior, there remains a possibility of differences in the policymaking behavior of appointees of different presidents from the same party. Table 9.3 shows that the appointees of the different presidents rendered a fairly consistent percentage of decisions containing structural reform decrees. The chi-square value of 0.20 indicates an absence of significant differences in table 9.3. The appointees of Republican presidents Eisenhower and Nixon had about the same percentages as did the appointees of Kennedy and Johnson, who were Democratic presidents. This finding provides additional support for table 9.2, which demonstrated no significant relationship between party of the appointing president and policymaking behavior.

The potential of direct court intervention in state prisons would not appear to be foremost among the criteria used by the presidents

TABLE 9.3.   Decisions That Contain Structural Reform Decrees
by Appointees of Various Presidents

Appointing President	Percentage of Decisions that Contain a Structural Reform Decree	Total Number of Decisions
Eisenhower	55.6	9
Kennedy	57.9	19
Johnson	62.0	50
Nixon	61.5	26

Statistic	Value	
Chi-square	0.20	Level of significance = 0.98
Cramer's V	0.04	
Lambda	0.00	
Number of missing cases = 224		

Note: The appointees of Roosevelt, Truman, Ford, and Carter are not included in the table because of the small number of applicable cases that they decided.

selecting the appointees included in this study. In the selection of nominees to the district courts, a variety of factors, such as party affiliation, law school attended, prior political and legal offices held, and general ideological beliefs, would be more influential on presidents than the possibility of active policymaking in an area that had received little, if any, attention from the private and public sectors. Thus, the finding of a lack of a significant relationship between appointing president and policymaking behavior, as conceptualized for this study, should not be surprising.

Conclusion

In recent years, the policymaking responsibilities of federal district judges have clearly expanded with the emergence of structural reform litigation. In making structural reform decrees, certain federal district judges have been established as key policymakers who directly affect the operation and structure of public programs and institutions. The policymaking propensity of federal district judges is particularly evident in the issuance of structural reform decrees in regard to state prison problems.

This area of policymaking by federal district judges became the focal point of my study for several reasons. First, the presence of a structural reform decree in a decision by a district judge provided a clear and empirically identifiable indicator of policymaking. Moreover, state prison cases are a good focal point because these cases possess the values of two dimensions—the degree of politicization and the extent of legal leeways—that are important in enhancing the discretion of judges to respond to extralegal factors. If a legal area is marked by a high degree of politicization and an absence of legal constraints, then the discretion of judges will be increased in handling cases in that particular area. State prison cases, as conceptualized for this study, certainly possess a high degree of politicization and a lack of legal constraints.

In the context of the social-background model, one conceptual hypothesis was formulated. By controlling for the impact of case contents and providing a more precise conceptualization of policymaking, this hypothesis was argued to present a valid test of the relationship between a specific social-background trait and the policymaking behavior of federal district judges. In the conceptual hypothesis, the social-background trait that was selected as an independent variable was appointing president. Based on the presented findings, appointing president had little if any impact on the decision of federal district judges to issue structural reform decrees in state prison cases. A significant relationship was not found between the trait and policymaking. Also, the degree of association between the trait and policymaking was minimal.

These results should not be taken to mean that social-background analysis has little to offer in providing an explanation of the policymaking actions of federal district judges. The issuance of structural reform decrees represents one dimension of the broad range of activity that can be deemed judicial policymaking. Although this dimension is significant and worthy of scholarly attention, there are certainly other aspects of policymaking where a relationship might exist between appointing president and the actions of district judges.

Further, appointing president represents a single variable and is not inclusive of all the social-background traits that could possibly be analyzed. There are other social-background traits, such as age, tenure in office, gender, experience, local ties, and race, that might be related to judicial policymaking. Certainly studies can be conducted to assess the impact of any other social-background traits either specifically on the issuance of structural reform decrees or on any other dimension of judicial policymaking.

Other theoretical approaches could also be utilized in future research to study district judges' issuance of structural reform decrees. One approach would be a focus on the personality traits of district court judges. Future research could combine the best elements of Kitchin's study and Ducat and Flango's work to assess whether "maverick" district judges are responsible for the issuance of structural reform decrees.[30]

A second approach could examine the judicial track record of federal district judges. More specifically, are the district judges who are making structural reform decrees in state prison cases the same judges who made earlier structural reform decrees that were aimed at eliminating segregation in public schools? Has the experience of becoming directly involved in developing and implementing detailed public school integration plans made certain federal district judges more receptive to using structural reform decrees to resolve other problems? Although the research would be quite time consuming, these questions can be addressed through empirical analysis.

A third approach would be to analyze the form and presentation of inmates' complaints as possible determinants of the discretion by district judges to issue structural reform decrees. For instance, does the type of targeted policy in an inmate's complaint have an impact on the policymaking of federal district judges? Do interest groups play a role in increasing the probability of certain cases being the targets of structural reform decrees?

Clearly, there are alternative approaches for studying the issuance of structural reform decrees. This study selected social-background analysis because of its frequency of use in previous literature. In addition, I wanted to determine why previous studies that used fundamentally the same form of analysis found contradictory results. Based on my analysis, the basic reason for the contradictory results rests on the lack of precise and valid conceptualizations of both the independent and dependent variables that were examined in prior studies. Particularly, the vague and inconsistent notions of policymaking that were prevalent in previous studies of the district courts were primarily responsible for the contradictory results generated from those studies.

In regard to the issuance of structural reform decrees in state prisons, the party affiliation of the appointing president bears little weight on the policymaking behavior of federal district judges. Thus, those who hope that the "Republicanization" of the federal bench will spell the end of judicial intervention into prisons and jails are likely to be disappointed.

Notes

1. Ralph Cavanagh and Austin Sarat, "Thinking About Courts: Toward and Beyond a Jurisprudence of Judicial Competence," 14 *Law and Society Review* 371 (1980); Abram Chayes, "The Role of the Judge in Public Law Litigation," 89 *Harvard Law Review* 1281 (1976); Colin S. Diver, "The Judge as Political Powerbroker: Superintending Structural Change in Institutions," 65 *Virginia Law Review* 43 (1979); Owen W. Fiss, *The Civil Rights Injunction* (Bloomington: Indiana University Press, 1978); and Fiss, "The Supreme Court—Forward," 93 *Harvard Law Review* 1 (1979); Gerald E. Frug, "The Judicial Power of the Purse," 126 *University of Pennsylvania Law Review* 715 (1978).
2. For a more detailed description of the characteristics of structural reform litigation, see Robert C. Bradley, "Structural Reform in State Custodial Institutions: An Analysis of Federal District Judge Policy Making" (doctoral diss., University of Kentucky, 1987).
3. Robert A. Carp and C. K. Rowland, *Policymaking and Politics in the Federal Courts* (Knoxville: University of Tennessee Press, 1983), p. 4.
4. Ibid.
5. Cavanagh and Sarat, "Thinking About Courts," pp. 403–4; Diver, "The Judge as Political Powerbroker," p. 49; Frug, "The Judicial Power of the Purse," p. 715.
6. Comment, "Confronting the Conditions of Confinement: An Expanded Role for Courts in Prison Reform," 12 *Harvard Civil Rights–Civil Liberties Review* 370 (1977), p. 370.
7. Stephen D. Gottfredson and Ralph B. Taylor, "Public Policy and Prison Populations: Measuring Opinions About Reform," 68 *Judicature* 400 (1981).

8. Samuel J. Brakel, Prison Reform Litigation: Has the Revolution Gone Too Far?" 70 *Judicature* 5 (1986), p. 5.

9. Diver, "The Judge as Political Powerbroker," p. 43.

10. Sheldon Goldman and Thomas P. Jahnige, *The Federal Courts as a Political System*, 3rd ed. (New York: Harper & Row, 1985), p. 147.

11. Sheldon Goldman and Austin Sarat, *American Court Systems*, 2nd ed. (New York: Longman, 1989), p. 381.

12. Carp and Rowland, *Policymaking and Politics*, pp. 8–11; Charles A. Johnson, "Behavioral Jurisprudence: Notes Toward a Theory," paper presented in Chicago at the 1985 meeting of the Midwest Political Science Association, pp. 15–16.

13. C. K. Rowland and Robert A. Carp, "The Relative Effects of Maturation, Time Period, and Appointing President on District Judges' Policy Choices: A Cohort Analysis," 5 *Political Behavior* 109 (1983), p. 111.

14. For a detailed discussion of previous literature on federal district judges, see Carp and Rowland, *Policymaking and Politics*, pp. 25–144, and Bradley, *Structural Reform*, chapter 3.

15. Carp and Rowland, *Policymaking and Politics*, pp. 14–24, and S. Sidney Ulmer, "Are Social Background Models Time-Bound?" 80 *American Political Science Review* 957 (1986).

16. Bradley, *Structural Reform*, pp. 88–92.

17. Johnson, "Behavioral Jurisprudence," p. 11.

18. Ibid., p. 12.

19. Ibid.

20. Ibid., p. 13

21. Ibid.

22. Ibid., p. 15.

23. Carp and Rowland, *Policymaking and Politics*, pp. 17–18, and Rowland and Carp, "The Relative Effects of Maturation."

24. Carp and Rowland, *Policymaking and Politics*, p. 18.

25. Kenneth M. Dolbeare, "The Federal District Courts and Urban Public Policy: An Exploratory Study (1960–1967)," in *Frontiers of Judicial Research*, ed. J. Grossman and J. Tanenhaus (New York: Wiley, 1969), p. 388.

26. Ibid.

27. Carp and Rowland, *Policymaking and Politics*, Rowland and Carp, "The Relative Effects of Maturation," pp. 64–81, and C. K. Rowland, Robert A. Carp, and Ronald A. Stidham, "Judges' Policy Choices and the Value Basis of Judicial Appointments: A Comparison of Support for Criminal Defendants Among Nixon, Johnson, and Kennedy Appointees to the Federal District Courts," 46 *Journal of Politics* 886 (1984).

28. Rowland and Carp, "The Relative Effects of Maturation," and Carp and Rowland, *Policymaking and Politics*, pp. 51–83.
29. Carp and Rowland, *Policymaking and Politics*, p. 81.
30. William Kitchin, *Federal District Judges: An Analysis of Judicial Perceptions* (Baltimore: Collage, 1978); Craig R. Ducat and Victor E. Flango, "The Outsider on the Court," 47 *Journal of Politics* 282 (1985).

10

Courts, Corrections, and the Constitution: A Practitioner's View

CLAIR A. CRIPE

It is widely accepted that there are two approaches for federal courts in institutional or public law litigation: the traditional approach, which sees the function of the courts as concentrating on dispute resolution; and the activist or reform approach, which uses litigation and its remedies as a means to accomplish needed change, usually for the protection of individuals' rights, and usually based on constitutional guarantees for the protection of those rights.

To examine litigation involving this country's prisons and jails is to explore these two approaches. It is a comparatively recent body of law, barely twenty-five years old. Its recency gives us ready access to the parties and to the backup materials which facilitate

The views expressed by the author of this chapter do not necessarily reflect those of the U.S. Department of Justice or of the Federal Bureau of Prisons.

research and analysis, but it thrusts us into the midst of a heated and ongoing public policy debate. It might be better to wait some years before attempting to assess the overall benefits and detriments of this massive body of litigation. But here I will draw on some three decades' worth of reading and experience to provide a general review, leaving it to later analysts to devise a better historical perspective.

Overview

The intersection between courts, corrections, and the Constitution was first paved in 1962. The rise of judicial activism in this area can be pinpointed pretty closely at the litigation brought by inmates who were members of the group then called Black Muslims.[1] At that time, I recall, the position of prison administrators was that allowing Black Muslim activities would be extremely dangerous in their prisons, and the government's position was that the Black Muslims were not in fact a religious group. The first inquiry which must be made in such a First Amendment case, where individuals claim the "free exercise" protections of that amendment, is whether a group such as the Black Muslims is in fact a religion. This particular inquiry is one of the most difficult for the courts to tackle. Definition of what constitutes a religion did occur in the Black Muslim litigation. The courts in several cases established criteria and found that this group met them, concluding that it was in fact a religion, entitling it to First Amendment protections.[2]

In the *Fullwood* case (1962), the District of Columbia Department of Corrections lost its argument about the religious nature of the Muslims and consequently was ordered to allow certain activities such as holding meetings inside the prison. This was not the end, however. Scores of additional suits by Black Muslims were brought in the ensuing year or two, in the District of Columbia alone. The litigation floodgates were opened. Vast numbers of First Amendment cases were filed, in this and many other jurisdictions. These involved not only religious claims but other rights asserted under that amendment, such as freedom of speech, press, and association. Other constitutional protections were also claimed by prison and jail inmates, under the Eighth (cruel and unusual punishment), Fourteenth and Fifth (due process protections), Fourth (searches and seizures), and Sixth (access to counsel) amendments.

A perusal of the federal reporters (those books which contain published federal court opinions) from the 1960s to the 1980s will show the large volume of federal court involvement in prison matters. Federal court involvement in civil rights cases brought by black citizens and school desegregation cases may well be areas of public policy reform and activity with greater social impact, but in sheer number of cases in the last two decades, I know of no area of the law that has involved the judges more than prison and jail litigation.[3]

This area of published cases on prison litigation—the most basic reference point for reporting what has gone on in the prisoner rights reform movement—is itself indicative of an underlying problem, namely, exaggeration of the words and actions of the reform jurist. This happens because only a small fraction of federal court decisions are in fact reported in these official publications. This is most true at the district court level, where judicial activism has occurred most frequently. Even at the appeals court level, only the most potentially influential opinions (judged generally in terms of those cases which will have the greatest precedential value for future cases to be considered in that jurisdiction) are published.[4]

Here, we encounter a sensitive and really unmeasurable phenomenon—the factor of prestige seeking, or "showboating," which may occur among judges. Judges are human, and they display the personality quirks or foibles that may show up in any human endeavor. That is, judges (particularly at the district court level, where publication of court opinions is less common) may enjoy the notoriety to be gained by having a published opinion, especially a major one which is going to gain widespread attention in the profession. This notoriety, of course, supplements that which may already be gained by media or other public attention to the court's actions.

On the other side, there are judges who do not seek such notoriety, who handle cases in many areas, including prisoners' rights, which raise difficult constitutional issues, and do not obtain special attention, either in the media or in the court reporters by sending their opinions to be published. Thus, there have been many court decisions which have been decided in favor of the government, on major issues, which have not been published. The same cases, heard by more activist judges, not only would have been decided differently, but almost certainly would end up being published.[5] This phenomenon of legal practice is pointed out primarily as a caution: One should not assume that the cases in print reflect accurately the whole body of litigation in this field, or that published cases are indeed representative of thinking in the federal judiciary, at the lower levels.

My initial premise, then, is that there are two approaches in the federal judiciary to handling prison and jail cases: the traditionalist, more conservative approach, and the activist, or interventionist approach. Further, the attention gained by the latter group of jurists (who, indeed, may be a minority among federal judges, even in the booming activist years of the 1960s and 1970s) both in the media and in legal publications is not balanced by attention to the actions of those judges who feel very differently about the same issues. Of course, the matter is much more complex than a philosophical division between two sets of jurists; there is a continuum of judicial activism, and judges fall at different points along that measurement line (and, indeed, may be at different points on that line on different issues). What I hope to present here is one individual's (albeit a veteran, calloused litigator's) perspective on the issue.

Judicial Activism and Distorted Interpretation

Let me also give some examples of how, even in the reported court cases, there are some views on this issue which may differ from those that are usually presented. It is widely commented on (in this volume, for instance) that the most notable cases of court intervention occurred when courts received evidence across many areas of treatment of prisoners in an institution, or even across a whole system, which led the court to a conclusion of overall mismanagement of the prison. This was usually based on an analysis that the conditions, in totality, shocked the court's conscience (the court here considering itself a pulse reader, a thermometer of society's views).

This "shock to the conscience" is a definition often used in measuring whether the conditions amount to a violation of the Eighth Amendment's proscription of "cruel and unusual punishment." As a result, the court orders massive corrective action, often inserting a court master into the litigation, to achieve corrective measures in the prison system. It is widely quoted that some thirty-seven state systems are under court order for such broad-scale relief.

In these cases, typically, a federal judge finds that the totality of conditions reveals a systematically unconstitutional government agency or facility. To correct that situation, only massive intervention, to substitute constitutional policies, practices, and conditions, will suffice. Quite an opposite approach is shown in one appeals court decision in the Ninth Circuit (the West Coast Circuit).[6] There, the court noted that the lower district court had used the "totality of conditions" approach in its review of challenged prison conditions in four California state prisons (Deuel, Folsom, San Quentin, and Soledad). As a result, the trial court entered an injunction, requiring extensive changes in the prisons.

In this *Rushen* opinion, the appeals court found that the standard used by the district court was wrong, and that "totality of conditions" cannot be used as a key to open the door of massive intervention in the operations of the state prisons. Rather, the court concluded that the proper approach is for the court to look at each challenged condition of confinement. If any such condition, such as medical care or food, is found to be incompatible with "the evolving standards of decency that mark the progress of a maturing society" (another one of the equations frequently used to measure Eighth Amendment "cruel and unusual" violations), then the court may intervene. Any individual condition found to be violative of the Constitution warrants corrective measures as to that condition alone. The court emphasizes that any condition which passes the Eighth Amendment test is immune from intervention.

The *Rushen* opinion, of course, reflects the analysis of a panel of judges who are in the traditionalist, nonactivist mold. It is indeed a model of this approach for prison litigation. Interestingly, it is hardly cited in the literature, even though it deals with a major suit in a major jurisdiction.

What the *Rushen* court calls into question is that issue so rarely addressed in federal opinions: What is the authority, and where is the justification, for individual judges to intervene, so as to take over the management of prison facilities? It is not my intent to enter into a detailed analysis of the legal authority of courts to intervene on a systemwide, or even a prisonwide basis. That, especially with respect to the authority to use masters or comparable judicially blessed intervenors in the carrying out of broad court orders, has been done expertly in other publications.[7] My personal conclusion, as the reader by now might suspect, comes down emphatically on the side of concluding that the federal courts have vastly overstepped their authority to use special masters, as provided by statute or by the Federal Rules. Apart from the technical legal authority (or, more properly, the lack of it) to so act in remedial decrees or in long-term oversight capacity, I question the practical justification to do so. This is based on several concerns: (1) lack of experience or expertise in the courts to manage; (2) similar lack of experience in the master, along with other deficits in the very nature of a master's office; (3) deleterious effects of massive intervention; and (4) doubt about the practical advantages of heavy court intervention, including the use of masters.

Judges as Intervenors/Managers

The courts, I would argue, have little capacity to intervene widely into institutional management. Judges, by nature of their appointment and background, are not equipped to take over the management of prisons. A cynic would ask whether judges manage their own business well. (Throughout this discussion I am, of course, focusing on federal judges—those who have been the leaders in judicial intervention into prison matters, and also those who are generally looked to as some of the best jurists in the country.) From my own observation, and from the little I have seen published in this area, I would say that the answer pretty clearly is that in the most essential parts of their business, such as management of court dockets, of staff and resource support to the courts, and of priority goal accomplishment, they have a pretty sorry record of success.

But this may be quibbling, for I think the underlying fact is that judges are in no way placed into their positions because of any expertise to manage. Federal judges—even if they are the best of the judicial lot—are appointed to their offices because of political connections, if not cronyism. Although they are carefully scrutinized in the appointment process and generally have outstanding experience as lawyers, this experience is to my knowledge seldom evaluated as to managerial ability. This, of course, is a very tangential, and almost crass support of Fuller's thesis: that judges should limit themselves to doing that which they are trained and equipped to do, namely, to gather and weigh evidence, to analyze factual and legal issues, and to apply precedent standards in resolving disputes between parties.[8]

The persons judges use as proxies in the management fight are not much more formidable in their credentials as prison managers—or managers of anything, for that matter. I want to avoid any reference to specific individuals used as masters in prison cases. However, even casual examination of the background of the masters who have been used in the leading prison cases raises substantial doubts about whether they have managerial skills or significant correctional knowledge. A few have had some corrections experience, but even these have generally lacked experience in running the very types of facilities they have been called on to "master." I know that other skills, such as the basic political skills of conciliation, mediation, and personnel management, are extremely useful. Some would say that these are the vital skills, and that the technical aspects of prison management can be learned by those who come to the job with other priority skills. Ideally, a master would bring all these abilities as well as experience to the post. What I am arguing for is acknowledgment that the master, as well as the judge, may need special skills, which, judging from the record, seem to have been in short supply.

Another factor that limits the capacity of judges to intervene as prison managers is their lack of legal or political responsibility to do so. For any exercise of significant authority over others, and particularly for the power to direct policies and programs which affect broad and intimate aspects of the jobs, lives, and freedoms of others, there should be a system of checks on the exercise of that authority and opportunity for review of the decisions made and of their impact.

These elements of checks, review, and restraint, I believe, are notably missing in the approach of the activist judges and their master helpers. Seldom are these decisions or orders set up with any built-in protections. Even the most basic legal review, the appellate process, is often avoided because of the entry into the order by consent of the parties (always coerced by the weight of the litigation), and specifically by consent of the corrections department.[9] Consent orders, or remedial orders designed by the district judges, seldom have had built-in means for amendment with the passage of time and the changing of circumstances. Thus, they have hung over the heads of state officials for indeterminate periods of enforcement.

The indeterminate nature of many decrees and the fact that consent decrees have been entered into by directors of corrections who thought the provisions advantageous (or perhaps the best that could be obtained under the circumstances) are definitely adverse factors. The sad fact is that the directors or commissioners who approved the settlement often depart soon after, in the perpetual musical chairs operation which besets most corrections systems in this country.

This constant turnover of commissioners in many states, tied to the governor by his appointment authority or otherwise politically affected, is an element outside the focus of my analysis. But it is a fact of life that must be taken into account when assessing the role of the courts in the troubled and turbulent recent history of prison management in this country.

The Disruption of Change

Let us assume that a prison facility has a longstanding problem in a particular area; for example, its problem is occasional but recurring instances of physical mistreatment of inmates by some of that prison's guards. Or there may be a combination of deficiencies; for example, there may be inadequate health care, food that is not sufficiently nutritious, poor conditions in the segregation portion of the prison, and interference with the correspondence of inmates— with their families, with their attorneys, and even with the courts. Any of these four areas may be of such a deteriorated or "shocking" nature that most courts in the country would find the condition violative of constitutional requirements.

Another point—and one that is often forgotten—is that the prison administrators themselves find these same conditions to be undesirable and professionally "shocking." The prison warden or commissioner of corrections who believes a segregation unit should be filthy, unlighted, unventilated, and lacking bedding is hard to find. More to the point, these conditions are directly violative of the standards of the profession, which have been adopted by the members of the American Correctional Association and published and monitored by the Commission on Accreditation for Corrections.[10] Other broad guidelines, adopted officially by the association for the use of its members, are the public policies for corrections.[11] The accreditation standards and the public policies go into far more detail and cover far more areas of prison and jail management than are constitutionally required.

It is safe to say that all areas that have been described as constitutionally mandated—at least those so defined by the Supreme Court along with those agreed upon by at least two or three courts of appeals—are covered by the standards and policies. In other words, if a facility is accredited under the association's standards, it can face with optimism any court challenge to its treatment of inmates. The worst that should be expected in such a lawsuit is a finding that a particular practice or policy fell short in some detail, probably because that detail by itself, though noted as deficient in the accreditation process, did not require denying accreditation for the whole facility. The leaders in corrections, state and federal, with whom I associate constantly in my work are supportive of the contents of the standards and policies, and they strive to achieve them.

To return to the facility which falls short of constitutional norms, let us assume that the State Penitentiary in the State of Adams has a terrible, long-entrenched practice of guard brutality, of physical punishment including whippings and beatings of those placed in disciplinary detention. This situation clearly needs to be changed. It violates current Eighth Amendment standards of decent treatment, and it is a violation of a mandatory professional standard of accreditation. There are two ways to accomplish the change: by court action or by administrative action within the corrections department. In my view, the latter is always the preferable course.

Change is disruptive. Accomplishing change is the most challenging assignment, in my view, for any manager, whether in prisons or in any other agency or organization. It is perhaps particularly

troubleso   se the prison has very complex
interactio   evels of authority: administrators,
line staff,   assumed that in prison, as in any
large com   policy, direction, and programs
should be   by the first group, the administrators, but in   sometimes lies more strongly with
the other   aff and the inmates. The relative
strength o   reatly from one place to another,
and may e   tution according to the particular
practice in   ront line officers may have strong
control of   is and in enforcing discipline by
meting ou   unning a "tight" disciplinary housing unit.   mates may exercise more control
than an   r in deciding what goes on in the
housing   sleep (cell assignments), who gets to
do the be   ly or clerk), and what goes on in the
recreation   unit (such as what TV programs are
watched—a decision that may seem trivial to an outsider, but one
which produces tension and even violence in the prison setting).

These are merely examples; the same kind of analysis may apply
in myriad other areas of the prison, such as work assignments and
working conditions; special benefits including visits, phone calls,
and trips outside the institution; access to programs such as education, chapel, and counseling; and the most basic provision of
clothes, food, and health care. Inmate authority may be exercised,
in varying degrees, over any of these areas, or strong line staff
control may exist. The point is, these may exist despite the presence
of standards of prison policy, issued by the administrators, which
say just the contrary.

Who Should Rule the Prison?

The ongoing, and thus solidified, placement of practical authority
in the hands of line staff or inmates has been, I would assert, the
most intransigent and obstructive element of prison operation. This
is because a fundamental premise—and I would say it may be *the*
fundamental premise—of sound prison management is that the

more authority one finds at the bottom of the prison pyramid, the worse its operation and conditions. The pyramid referred to here is the one with the largest group, the inmates, on the bottom; the middle of the pyramid occupied by staff, particularly those who work on the front lines, in direct contact with inmates; and the top of the pyramid being the managers, the wardens and their immediate staff, and the headquarters officials above them.

It is a truism in the corrections field that if one looks closely at a prison and finds that many activities and decisions—or some of the most vital ones—are controlled by the inmates themselves, that is a poorly run prison. (By poorly run, I mean not just removing authority from those with whom we think it should be placed, but in terms of the basics upon which we all agree—the provision of safe living conditions, where inmates do not need to fear constantly for their safety or fear going to sleep at night, and of basic shelter, sanitary living quarters; decent food, and access to medical care.) Some of our prisons, and these are the ones which I would say are in the very worst shape, are those which allow many of the basics to be controlled by inmates. The next step (going up the pyramid of authority) is the one where line staff and inmates have a "working understanding" of some type of shared authority in these areas. And the next step is that where the line officers themselves wield most of the authority.

All of these conditions lead frequently, if not inevitably, to evil results, such as abuse of individual inmates or favoritism toward others, and the entrenchment of those conditions that require drastic change. Why is this? Certain observations have led to this conclusion, for example, the finding that in the New York State system just before the Attica uprising, a reform-minded commissioner issued needed changes in policy, leading to expectations among the inmates that things would soon get better, but these policies in many respects were ignored by staff, who continued the entrenched practices, greatly exacerbating tensions. There are also those reasons for which I criticized the entry of courts into the management of prisons: lack of professional expertise, lack of political responsibility, lack of checks, and no review of their actions.

I wish to emphasize strongly that although those types of misplaced authority existed, and unfortunately still exist, in many prisons, the situation is not universal. Regrettably, we hear of all the systems which are in poor shape, focusing our attention on those that receive heavy play in the media and from the writers who concentrate on those court decisions in "totality" cases, referred to earlier. This leads to distorted conclusions, like the one that says that all prisons in the South are cesspools of constitutional violations (a conclusion which is inaccurate in assuming that all systems in the South are poorly run and that prisons in the North, or Midwest, or West are in far better shape). In fact, there are many systems which are well run (I am not immodestly bragging about my own federal prison system but am talking about Minnesota, South Carolina, Washington, Wisconsin, Florida, and many others), which have authority at the top of the pyramid, where it belongs, and which have a history of providing good prison conditions and programs. Indeed, there are some, such as Ohio and Alabama and perhaps some of those just named, which have pulled off—if not completely, at least to a notable extent—that hardest of tasks, reasserting authority at the top of the pyramid and concomitantly improving greatly the prison system, even in the midst of court intervention.

Practical experience indicates that the prison system with authority placed where it belongs—at the top, with necessary filter-down authority delegated as needed to line staff—operates well and can accomplish needed improvements if it receives the necessary support in dollars and staff from the legislature. Moreover, prison administrators, not judges, are the source of the best thinking about how prisons can be humanely and decently run. Indeed, those who concentrate too greatly on the prison litigation history have wrongly concluded that the courts have done the reforming and have come up with all the great ideas, based on their constitutional analysis. That is inane. Where does the Constitution say anything about prisons, and the standards for running them? Nowhere. What federal judge has *any* knowledge about how a prison should be run? Not a single one that I know of. (Sadly, many federal judges, including those who issue massive, strongly worded opinions about prisons, have never even set foot in the very places that they end up micromanaging.)

The Real Reformers: Judges or Prison Administrators?

Where then do the judges get their ideas about how to run a prison, or a particular aspect of a prison? To some extent, from the literature, but mainly from expert witnesses or consultants, who testify about the unacceptable nature of conditions, and who then provide guidance as to what conditions should be mandated by the courts. Again, I do not want to get into any personal references, but I contend that a review of the list of "expert" witnesses who have appeared for plaintiffs in these cases will not reflect those persons who are the best qualified and most successful administrators of prisons, or of particular departments of programs within prisons. That is to say, their qualifications as experts are suspect, and in some cases gravely suspect, in that an expert who is extremely supportive of the plaintiffs' (the inmates') position is one who can be shown to have been an unmitigated failure in running prisons; unfortunately, this witness establishes his "expert" reputation and by some kind of bootstrap operation becomes a lead expert witness in one case after another.

Many courts (most of them in the "totality," systemwide cases) used such experts, used standards set by diverse groups (such as the ABA, certainly a well-known corrections body, with loads of expertise among its members!), and also looked to published academic writings for their guidance. Reliance on these elements was soundly criticized and rejected by the Supreme Court in *Rhodes*.[12]

Rather than giving the courts so much credit for being the innovators of reform, I argue that most of the credit should go to the prison leaders themselves. It was they who came up with the reforming ideas and who accomplished changes in policies, anticipating court-ordered requirements years before they were handed down. To take one example, in 1965 several central office Bureau of Prisons staff members, including me, were called into the office of the director, Myrl Alexander. Mr. Alexander had a group discussion of the process we were then using for the disciplining of federal inmates who broke the rules in our institutions. He gave us the specific assignment to come up with a new policy, one which would give procedural protections to inmates, depending on the level of action taken. As an aside, this policy was also to anticipate any court requirements of due process which we might think would be forthcoming from the courts. A new policy was adopted; it provided basics of procedural protection in disciplinary hearings, which were later referred to in court opinions, and which essentially met the due process requirements described by the Supreme Court nearly ten years later.[13]

As Edward E. Rhine suggests in chapter 7 of this volume, there is probably no area of prison administration which is more essential to good control over the institution, and to providing safe living and working conditions, than the disciplinary policy. It must be fair, and fairly administered, to foster respect for authority among the inmates and to satisfy constitutional procedural expectations. In many other areas, such as correspondence, access to courts, sanitation, provision of medical care, and good food, the standards were set by good administrators and were implemented by a well-managed, well-trained staff, who were professionally committed to the policies because of their experience and training.

What, then, of the courts as reformers? They have been credited with a lot; in my view, they deserve some of the credit, but not nearly the sanctified position to which some have elevated them. I believe that insertion of court authority, even if it avoids the pitfall of taking over the prison by the court itself or by a special master, undermines the proper pyramidal authority structure that is essential for safe and humane prisons. Other authors, including some in this volume, analyze this problem in some detail. Suffice it to say here, I think the evidence is clear that achieving drastic change by massive court intervention often produces bad morale among staff, stripping top management of much or all of its status and leadership authority and creating among inmates greatly elevated, and probably exaggerated, expectations of change. On an even more practical matter, the research that is reported raises serious questions about whether the conditions which are targeted for improvements in the courts' orders are in fact improved in any reasonable amount of time.

Let us return then to the hypothetical State of Adams, with its need for change in its physical mistreatment of prisoners. How can the change be accomplished? The preferred means, I would argue, is to give authority, and opportunity, to the corrections commissioner. This will require time (under any scenario), because the situation is probably based on a long-time placement of too much authority in the line staff, with possible support even by a portion of the inmate population. The overextended staff authority may be strongly supported by the union if this is a unionized facility. Steps to accomplish the change by the commissioner require firming up of political support (from the attorney general, in case of litigation, from the governor, and from the legislative leaders) and careful development of steps for change with staff, starting with midmanagement leaders and working down. Training steps are essential. Careful attention to new hires and to their training may help greatly. In other words, directives may be issued, and may be necessary, but the support needed to carry out those directives must be carefully planned, nurtured, and implemented.

What if the staff do not buy the changes and continue, even in a reduced degree, the old practices? The next desirable step is for the state system to have a mechanism for inmate grievances to be filed. Virtually all states have such grievance programs, even though they may not meet the federally mandated standards administered by the Department of Justice.[14]

If the condition complained about is not taken care of satisfactorily by the grievance mechanism, then the court must review it, in light of constitutional standards. This is a proper role for the federal court, and I do not quarrel with it. However, if a violation is found, and the court believes it must be corrected, I argue that correction must be accomplished by the court ordering action by the state officials who have control, and who must maintain control, of the condition. Here, in our State of Adams example, the court would require the Adams commissioner to correct the practice. There are several coercive measures which can be taken. In no case should the court use an outsider, whether master or othertitled person, to carry out any management function or direction inside the corrections system. Corrections leaders in the state should be encouraged and supported in their attempts to effect change, never undermined by outside or alternative authority.

Conclusions

Lest it be thought that my view of the role of the federal courts is totally negative, let me sum up my views. Federal courts have made a difference in the state of correctional practice in this country. Without them, without the prisoners' rights litigation which has flooded the federal judicial system since the early 1960s, we would not be as far down the road as we are toward that goal of decent and humane prisons and jails, a goal upon which I assume we all agree.

In many cases, and on balance in the current posture of court involvement, the courts do not reflect the public's attitudes on what should be happening to inmates; they are far out in front of where the public, American society, believes they should be. That is perhaps as it must be. This still presents a largely unconfronted challege—finding a way to educate the American public about the conditions, the purposes, the needs of our prisons and jails. For the most part, Americans agree with the hands-off attitude of the courts and are surprised whenever they hear that a court has required changes in the prison system. Once the public is informed, and comes to expect basic decency in the jails and prisons, the legislative support in funding will not be far behind.

Further, what we need is more academic involvement in the corrections field, in both research and instruction. Expanding and improving our schools of criminal justice, criminology, and social work, with specialization on entry into corrections professions, will enhance the quality of workers in this field and thus the type of career commitments we can expect. The human support to a facility or a department—the staff who run the prison—is just as important to achieving a high-quality result as the budget resources obtained from the legislature.

So I greatly applaud the work done, examining closely the work of the federal courts and of the masters who help implement the courts' orders. More follow-up work is needed to measure the impact of litigation on prison policy and to assess the implementation of court orders. Do the things which need changing really get changed by court intervention, and do they stay changed? Is it possible to show that one type of court intervention, or remedial approach, is more successful than another?

What I am seeking, too, is the attribution of some credit to those who most deserve it, the corrections people, who, day in and day out, fought the fight with their bosses in the executive branch, with their oversight and appropriations committees in the legislature, and then with the courts, who lambasted them for doing nothing. All too frequent are the complaints I have heard from wardens and commissioners, who have had to spend 20, 50, even 80 percent of their time during some years in court or in litigation-connected work. What is needed is some degree of restraint by those reform-minded judges, especially by those who have just been waiting for the opportunity to get their hands on the jail or prison system, to whip it into shape. If a court gets a case where the evidence shows reform is needed, the court should examine all ways of letting the legally appointed administrators solve their own problems. Of course, if an administrator is adamantly resistive, steps to have him replaced or to order changes despite his resistance will have to be taken. In no case should his authority be supplanted by a court adjunct, whether special master or other person. The court is entitled to have any order reported on, by the parties or by independent monitors. These monitors are fact-finding reporters and should be so limited.

The courts will best fulfill their judicial role when they pursue those functions for which they are well trained: development of facts, analysis of competing claims and legal arguments, and application of constitutional or statutory standards to actions taken, or not taken, by the parties. Nothing in their experience, or in ours in assessing their corrections involvement, recommends them as managers of any prisons or jails.

Notes

1. Clair A. Cripe, "Religious Freedom in Prisons," *Federal Probation* (March 1977).
2. *Fullwood v. Clemmer*, 206 F. Supp. 370 (D.D.C., 1962), for example. For an interesting companion case dealing with Black Muslims in the District of Columbia Department of Corrections, see *Sewell v. Pegelow*, 304 F.2d 670 (4th Cir. 1962).
3. One of the problems in this area is to get an exact handle on the volume of prison litigation. In the federal courts, the best measure we have is the annual statistical report on case filings published by the Administrative Office of the U.S. Courts. From the late 1960s to the present, several thousand prisoner petitions have been filed each year. This is the largest volume of civil case filings among those categories used by

the Administrative Office. On this same point, some may think that the impact of litigation has been on the states; the federal government (i.e., the Federal Bureau of Prisons) is not much involved. This is certainly not true. Federal prisoners have filed in excess of twenty-five hundred lawsuits per year for over fifteen years.

4. The sets of books used by lawyers, and other researchers, are these: (1) decisions of the federal trial courts, called U.S. district courts, are published in the *Federal Supplement*; (2) decisions of the appellate courts, the U.S. courts of appeals (also called circuit courts), are published in the *Federal Reporter* series of books; (3) decisions by the Supreme Court are published in different sets, the official set printed by the government being called the *U.S. Reports*. Sets 1 and 2 are published by the West Publishing Company of St. Paul, a private publishing company. An opinion by a district court judge is sent by the judge to West Publishing with a request that it be printed. This is not binding, though cases submitted by the courts are usually published. The final decision to publish is made by editors at West. A "to be published" request by an appeals court is almost always followed, but many decisions are not sent to West for publication. Only the Supreme Court has all of its opinions, and other actions, reported.

5. When the government wins such a case, we of course have the option of asking the judge to submit the opinion to West Publishing so that it may be published. This may or may not be done by the judge; it is totally in her or his discretion. We of course may cite the opinion later, as an unpublished opinion which we maintain in our files. But it is generally unknown and unavailable to lawyers (and others) doing research, since the complex legal research system is largely based on those cases which are in the officially reported sets of books.

6. *Wright v. Rushen*, 642 F.2d 1129 (9th Cir. 1981).

7. For example, David Kirp and Gary Babcock, "Judge and Company: Court Appointed Masters, School Desegregation and Institutional Reform," 32 *Alabama Law Review* 313 (1981); Note, "Mastering Intervention in Prisons," 88 *Yale Law Journal* 1062 (1979); Donald Horowitz, *The Courts and Social Policy* (Washington, D.C.: Brookings Institution, 1977).

8. Lon Fuller, "The Forms and Limits of Adjudication," 92 *Harvard Law Review* 353 (1978).

9. A district judge's massive remedial actions were closely reviewed in one of the most notorious of the systemwide conditions cases, that involving prisons in the state of Alabama. There, in *Newman v. Alabama*, 559 F.2d 283 (1977), the Fifth Circuit Court of Appeals noted that it was basically approving the steps taken by the highly complimented

federal judge in trying to make the prison system constitutional. However, the appellate court concludes that he overstepped his authority in many areas of his remedial order, and less intrusive measures should have been taken. For example, to ensure compliance with the court's orders, a "Human Rights Committee" of thirty-nine persons was appointed to inspect facilities and services, to interview inmates, and to review plans and implementation steps. These were found by the appeals court to have been excessive steps, and the committee was dissolved. Similarly, a "Prison Classification Project" at the University of Alabama, originally part of the district court's remedial package, was disapproved, as were other remedial steps addressing different programs and practices in the prisons.

10. The published standards adopted for the association's adult prisons, for example, are called *Manual of Standards for Adult Correctional Institutions*. Similar sets of standards are published for juvenile facilities and for jail or detention facilities. The Commission on Accreditation has accreditation monitors, or inspectors, who visit and closely inspect prison facilities to see whether the level of compliance with standards warrants accreditation by the commission.

11. *Public Policy for Corrections: A Handbook for Decision-Makers* is the title of the current set of public policies. ("Corrections" here, and in the title of the association, encompasses juvenile care facilities, probation, parole, and community facilities such as halfway houses, as well as adult prisons and jails.) Sample policies are in the areas of education and training, services for female offenders, prison design, use of force, and classification of offenders.

12. *Rhodes v. Chapman*, 452 U.S. 337 (1981).

13. *Wolff v. McDonnell*, 418 U.S. 539 (1974).

14. In the Civil Rights of Institutionalized Persons Act of 1980 (CRIPA), Congress provided two new federal procedures: opportunity for the federal government (through the U.S. attorney general) to file suit against state systems for constitutional violations flowing from their treatment of institutionalized (in prison or mental institutions) persons; and standards for certifying state inmate grievance systems, so that a state with a certified system may obtain from federal court a postponement of proceeding with an inmate's civil rights suit (under 42 U.S.C. 1983, the most common means for state inmates to enter federal court), to allow the state to try to solve the matter administratively. Only a few states have sought this certification from the Justice Department, and fewer yet have been successful in achieving certification. Discussion of this phenomenon, the disuse of the two major sections of CRIPA, would be an appropriate subject for another essay.

11

Conclusion: What Judges Can Do to Improve Prisons and Jails

JOHN J. DiIULIO, JR.

In 1971 an Alabama inmate filed a lawsuit charging that six inmates had died in the state prison hospital because of improper treatment. The following year, Federal District Judge Frank M. Johnson, Jr., ordered major changes in Alabama's prison health system. As a result of Judge Johnson's intervention, the state's prison health system improved somewhat.

But Alabama's prisons remained filthy, violence-ridden, and overcrowded. In 1976 Judge Johnson assumed control of the entire Alabama prison system. In 1979 Judge Johnson moved to the appellate court, and Federal District Judge Robert E. Varner took the reins. In the same year, Governor George C. Wallace, who had strongly opposed Judge Johnson's intervention, left office and was replaced by Fob James.

287

Governor James worked with rather than against Judge Varner. In turn, Judge Varner appointed Governor James temporary receiver for the Alabama prison system, and the governor appointed a new, reform-minded corrections commissioner, Robert Britton. In 1983, when Governor James left office, Judge Varner established a four-member expert committee to oversee the system. In an interesting twist of courts and corrections history, one member of the committee was Dr. George Beto, the former director of the Texas Department of Corrections (TDC), whose administrative legacy was challenged in the *Ruiz* litigation in Texas (see chapters 2, 3, and 4). Britton had worked in TDC under Beto.

Britton set in motion a number of changes in the way that Alabama ran its prisons. Gradually, things began to improve. In December 1988 the committee recommended that Judge Varner dismiss the seventeen-year-old suit. The judge did so, but he warned that prison overcrowding, caused in large part by Alabama's stiff mandatory sentencing laws, might result in constitutional violations that would necessitate a new round of court intervention. And committee members stressed that although conditions inside Alabama's prisons were generally far better at the end of 1988 than they had been at the start of 1972, conditions remained far from ideal.

Judicial Intervention: More to Come?

Alabama was the first state to be placed under a comprehensive court order mandating changes in its penal system. It was also the first state to have such a comprehensive court order lifted. Since 1970, major prison litigation and judicial intervention has occurred in forty-four states, the District of Columbia, Puerto Rico, and the Virgin Islands. There is little reason to suppose that the era of judicial intervention into prisons and jails is coming to an end. The days of sweeping Alabama- or Texas-style intervention may be behind us, but that will depend largely on two factors: the federal judiciary's disposition toward prison and jail overcrowding, and the disposition of the United States Congress toward judicial intervention.

Demographic and sentencing trends make it likely that institutional overcrowding will worsen over the next decade. If that happens, and if prison and jail officials prove unable to maintain any semblance of safe and humane conditions behind bars, then sweeping judicial intervention into prisons and jails may be more of a growing prospect than a fading memory. Overcrowding has figured in most instances of judicial intervention into prisons and jails, and as overcrowding becomes more severe, judicial intervention may well become more frequent and extensive.

The hope of some (and fear of others) that the "Republicanization" of the federal judiciary will soon render the courts inactive in this area is contradicted by Robert Bradley's interesting statistical analysis (chapter 9). It is also contradicted by the simple fact, apparent to even casual observers, that regardless of their political or ideological background, few contemporary judges seem willing to reject evidence of unsafe and inhumane conditions behind bars, to reflexively pronounce such conditions legally, constitutionally, and morally acceptable, or to consistently adopt anything like a "hands-off" approach.

The Congress, however, can act to delimit the scope of judicial involvement if it so chooses. Though constitutional theorists may differ over the propriety of any such congressional action, most would agree that Congress has significant power to act. To be reminded of the full extent of latent congressional authority to regulate the federal judiciary, one need only read Section 1 of Article 3 of the United States Constitution, wherein the "inferior Courts" (all federal courts save "the one Supreme Court") are made to exist at the pleasure of Congress, and Section 2 of the same article wherein the "appellate Jurisdiction" of the Supreme Court itself is bounded by "such Exceptions, and under such Regulations as the Congress shall make."

Until recently, congresspersons interested in asserting and exercising this latent authority over the federal judiciary have not concentrated much on the courts' role in prison and jail cases. Instead, they have focused on such things as stripping the courts of their appellate jurisdiction in school prayer and school desegregation cases. In mid-1989, however, a number of senators drafted an omnibus National Crime Emergency Act. The draft bill included a section headed "Appropriate Judicial Remedies for Prison Overcrowding." The explicit purpose of this section of the proposal was to delimit judicial intervention into prisons and jails:

The Congress finds that the Federal courts are unreasonably endangering the community by sweeping equitable prison and jail cap orders as a remedy for State detention conditions. . . . The purpose of this section is to provide for reasonable and proper enforcement of the Eighth Amendment, as applicable to the States by incorporation under the due process clause of the Fourteenth Amendment. . . . A Federal court shall not hold prison or jail crowding unconstitutional under the Eighth Amendment. . . . Federal judicial power to issue other equitable relief, including improved medical or health care or civil contempt fines, or damages where appropriate, shall not be affected by this subsection.[1]

Whether this language transcends the bounds of congressional authority to delimit the role of the judiciary in prison and jail cases, and whether this or other language restricting judicial involvement could win majority approval in both houses and become law, remains to be seen. For our purposes, however, the important point is that, in the 1990s, the Congress may, for better or worse, make the courts, corrections, and the Constitution a ménage à quatre.

Judicial Intervention: The Net Is Positive

As a rule, since the 1970s interventionist judges have had wide latitude in fashioning and enforcing prison and jail decrees. It is the fact of this wide judicial latitude that has upset proponents of judicial restraint and triggered legislative proposals to limit judicial discretion in deciding whether, and how broadly, to intervene in prison and jail cases.

On philosophical grounds, as an advocate of judicial restraint, I support such proposals; so do a few other authors of this volume. But most of the authors of this volume do not support such measures, and all of us agree that, on strictly empirical grounds, it is foolish to believe that judicial intervention into prisons and jails has yielded nothing but increased violence, soaring costs, and other negative consequences.

It is equally foolish, of course, to deny that, in many cases, including several discussed in this volume, judicial intervention has been associated with such ills. The authors of the "Three Faces of *Ruiz*" (chapters 2, 3, and 4) differ over how much, if any, blame to assign to the court for the upturn in violence that occurred in Texas prisons in 1984 and 1985. But they are as one in recognizing that the intervention changed formal prison operations and informal "guard culture" in ways that rendered traditional means of control ineffective. And they are as one in seeing the postintervention regime, which would never have come about but for the court's involvement, as potentially more conducive to safe, humane, and lawful conditions behind bars than anything that went before it.

Thus, if the question is one of net assessment, then the impact of judicial intervention into prisons and jails over the last two decades has been positive—a qualified success, but a success just the same. For proponents of judicial restraint, there is no use denying that in most cases levels of order, amenity, and service in prisons and jails have improved as a result of judicial intervention. And in most cases it is equally futile to assert that such improvements would have been made, or made as quickly, in the absence of judicial intervention.

This is not to argue that the ends (improved prisons and jails) justify the means (judicial intervention), or that there is no good constitutional or moral case to be made that some or all prisoners simply do not deserve safe and humane living conditions. Nor is it to deny that, as Clair A. Cripe argued forcefully (chapter 10), corrections officials in many jurisdictions have initiated improvements independent of any judicial pressure or guidance; clearly they have. But if the question is whether, in most cases, judicial intervention has been associated with improvements in cellblock living conditions, the answer is clearly yes.

Granted, the financial bill for the improvements has often been steep; and, I would argue, the human toll of the transition to what Ben M. Crouch and James W. Marquart (chapter 4) termed "bureaucratic order" has been an increase in vicious and deadly violence directed against both inmates and staff and the destruction of a traditional way of administrative life that, whatever its vices, was not without its virtues. But in Texas and most other cases, these human and financial costs were not paid in vain, and a more astute exercise of judicial powers might make it possible to achieve the same (or better) effects for less money and less human suffering in the future.

Judges: Key Decision Makers

If there is a single message that can be taken from the foregoing chapters of this volume, it is that judges can and do exert enormous control over prisons and jails. In the first place, the decision to intervene or not is theirs and theirs alone. Despite the recent history of judicial activism in this field, a judge who wishes to steer clear of intervention will find no shortage of law and precedent to justify his or her decision; and a judge who wishes to intervene will find few, if any, well-established legal, procedural, or other limitations on the scope of his or her intervention.

Of course, as Bert Useem indicated in his penetrating account of the *Crain* litigation in West Virginia (chapter 8), the political and economic context in which orders are issued can render them moot, practically if not legally. And, as Bradley S. Chilton and Susette M. Talarico powerfully illustrated through their discussion of the *Guthrie* case in Georgia (chapter 5), judges are not the only influential actors in the intervention process. Over the course of the litigation, key actors, including judges, may come and go, creating what Chilton and Talarico termed "generational effects" on the intervention process. Though one judge (Morris E. Lasker) steered most of the intervention, Ted S. Storey's detailed account of judicial involvement in New York City's jail system (chapter 6) provided a look into certain types of bureaucratic arrangements that have been devised to cope with the complex interactions among the key actors—elected officials, commissioners, defendants' attorneys, plaintiffs' attorneys, prisoners' rights representatives—and across "generations" of them.

But nobody doubts, and nothing in this volume denies, that judges are generally the most influential of all the actors who shape an intervention. To be sure, most significant instances of judicial intervention into prisons and jails present us with what political theorist Dennis Thompson has termed "the problem of many hands," that is, the problem of sorting out and assigning practical and moral responsibility for the consequences of actions involving complex interactions among many actors and many organizations, public and private.[2] But this problem is simplified where only one set of hands at a time holds the gavel, dons the robes, and writes the orders. Where judicial intervention into prisons and jails is concerned, many actors matter, but judges are almost always "first among unequals."

Judges: Making and Implementing Public Policy

"Policy," wrote political scientist Herbert Kaufman, "is enunciated in rhetoric; it is realized in action."[3] When judges issue remedial orders, especially "totality of conditions" decrees, they are making public policy. Some analysts have argued that judges are inherently less capable than legislators and other government officials, elected and appointed, of making and implementing sound public policies. As Malcolm M. Feeley and Roger A. Hanson noted in their probing review of the literature on judicial intervention (chapter 1), one of the most capable exponents of this view is Nathan Glazer, "who in a series of articles has argued that court orders aimed at restructuring public institutions" normally result in "a decline in staff morale, an increase in staff turnover, and an increase in the unruliness of clientele groups." As Feeley and Hanson observed, Glazer "developed his arguments with public schools and welfare agencies in mind, [but] he could as easily have directed them at prison and jail conditions suits."

One need not reject Glazer's argument to observe that there has been, and continues to be, variation in the impact of judicial intervention on prisons and jails, and that this variation often seems to have been related to the intervening judge's modus operandi. Glazer may be correct in contending that, by virtue of their formal position within government and other relevant characteristics, the modal legislator is more likely than the modal judge to succeed in making and implementing (or overseeing the making and implementation) of sound public policies, meaning policies that, at a minimum, do more to help than to hurt the citizens at whom they are directed, and that have few if any negative consequences, intended or unintended.

Indeed, many interventionist judges themselves have recognized as much. For example, in a speech delivered before the American Correctional Association, Judge William Wayne Justice, who presided over the *Ruiz* litigation (see chapters 2, 3, and 4), observed that "the courtroom is a less than ideal setting for the development of correctional policy" and acknowledged that it is ultimately corrections administrators who are responsible for "maintaining prisons that are safe, lawful, and humane."[4] And as is suggested by my own interpretation of the impact of judicial intervention on Texas prisons (chapter 2), and to a lesser but still significant extent by Sheldon Ekland-Olson and Steve J. Martin in their more sympathetic portrait of the judge's actions and their impact on Texas prisons (chapter 3), Glazer's point about the potential administrative and other mischief wrought by intervening judges is not groundless.

But at least where prisons and jails are concerned, the overall track record of judges is not demonstrably worse (and is arguably much better) than that of relevant legislators and legislative committees, federal, state, and local. More to the point, variations in success among judges and by given judges at different points in the course of an intervention suggest that certain intervention approaches may work better than others and that judges who follow these approaches will, under most conditions, do more to foster sound policies than those who do not. Rather than worrying about the real or perceived comparative disadvantages of judges versus other officials qua policymakers and administrators, the better part of wisdom here may be to recognize that, whether emanating from the halls of the legislature, the office of the executive, the bowels of the relevant bureaucracy, or the chambers of the court, policies can be framed and implemented well, badly, or not at all.

How, or whether, a given policy will be framed and implemented depends, of course, on many things. There is, alas, no shortage of academic theories about how best to make and implement public policies, and there is no shortage of disagreement over which theories are best.

Based on the foregoing chapters of this volume, however, there is one approach to making and implementing sound prison and jail policy from the bench that seems to work better under most conditions than certain frequently practiced alternatives. We do not claim that this approach represents a sure-fire way of enhancing judicial capacity in this area. For one thing, as noted in the introduction, our efforts here are exploratory and we await more and better research on the subject; for another, each of the authors of this volume recognizes irreducible elements of contingency in human affairs that, in the case at hand, may affect how a judge intervenes and how his or her manner of intervening affects staff, inmates, and others (including taxpayers) over time. Rather, we claim only that the recommended approach represents simple strategic rules of thumb practiced with varying degrees of intensity and consistency by judges who have presided over our more successful interventions, rules that can, we think, be applied to some good effect by just about any interventionist judge regardless of his or her particular temperament and talents.

Enhancing Judicial Capacity: Proceed Incrementally

The main strategic rule of thumb is to proceed incrementally. There is a large general literature on the pros and cons of making and implementing policies in an incremental fashion, and there is a small but interesting literature on the pluses and minuses of incrementalism as an approach to judicial intervention in areas outside of criminal justice, especially school desegregration and environmental protection.

Incrementalism

In a classic public administration essay published in 1959, Charles Lindblom distinguished between two approaches to administrative decision making, the "rational-comprehensive or root method," and "the successive limited comparisons or branch technique."[5] In the former approach, the official identifies and clearly defines an objective, rationally ranks the benefits and costs associated with achieving the objective, formulates several alternative ways of achieving the objective, and then selects the best option, defined as that which maximizes goal attainment at the lowest possible human and financial cost.

Generations of public administration scholars had advocated this logical, synoptic decision-making method, and it is still favored by some policy analysts, especially urban planners. Lindblom, however, criticized the approach as both unrealistic and unintelligent;

most real-world policymakers and administrators, he argued, do not operate by "root," nor should they.

Basically, Lindblom offered three sets of criticisms. First, the rational-comprehensive approach assumes "intellectual capacities and sources of information that men simply do not possess, and it is even more absurd as an approach to policy when the time and money that can be allocated to a problem is limited, as is always the case."[6] Second, in a democratic society, the public arena is home to multiple, competing, and contradictory values (e.g., punish, deter, incapacitate, and rehabilitate incarcerated criminals); people disagree, often fundamentally, over what ends to pursue and how best to pursue them; public administration is thus an inherently political process that normally makes the "rational" pursuit of one objective both impossible (because interests and views conflict) and undesirable (because competing interests and views should be democratically represented and registered by public officials). Third, it naturally follows that the proper test of any policy is not whether it "maximizes" some objective but whether it represents "a compromise" that all affected parties can accept without undue recriminations, which might range from outright violence directed against the policy's promoters or beneficiaries to more subtle forms of policy subversion (e.g., bureaucratic "footdragging").

Lindblom thus advocated the branch technique of decision making, the key feature of which is incrementalism. Policymakers and administrators take a series of small steps to achieve their (often shifting, contradictory, and ill-defined) aims, avoiding leaps and bounds wherever possible. By proceeding "through a succession of small incremental changes," advised Lindblom, the administrator has the advantage of avoiding "serious lasting mistakes" and can alter his or her course should that seem necessary.[7]

This incremental approach relieves the decision maker of the impossible burden of omniscience about the full range of actual policy options available at any given moment, the likely consequences of each option if pursued, and so on. Furthermore, the incremental approach prepares the decision maker to expect—and grapple creatively with—the unexpected. "A wise policy maker," observed Lindblom, "expects that his policies will achieve only part of what he hopes and at the same time will produce unanticipated consequences he would have preferred to avoid."[8] Finally, the incremental approach moves from a "pluralist" conception of politics in a democratic society. In that conception, the role of the official decision maker is not to articulate and impose a singular vision of how things ought to be on others. Rather, it is to accommodate, within broadly defined normative boundaries, the interests and aspirations of as many parties that will be affected by the policy as possible.

In short, when confronted with a public dilemma in which the interests and views of different citizens are at stake, and not all of those interests and views can be fully accommodated, the incrementalist searches for viable compromises, not final solutions; in effect, he or she moves in inches even when the aim is to go miles. The incremental approach is favored not for intellectual reasons (logic rebels against it) or for ideological reasons (why go slow when your cause is clear?), but for practical ones, chief among them that, at least in our particular constitutional system of government, public ends are best and most surely achieved via incremental means. "Fiery" politicians, neophyte social reformers, and "maverick" administrators tend to equate incrementalism with defeatism, "doing nothing," or "selling out." But those politicians, activists, and administrators who ply their trade long enough learn that incrementalism is often the best, or the only, approach to effecting and sustaining needed changes.[9]

It is not surprising that interventionist judges seem not to learn this lesson as well, or as quickly, as most other public officials and policy activists. Even as they intervene widely in highly controversial areas of public policy, judges can remain largely insulated from the conflicting pressures that drive legislators toward an incremental approach; and even after they have issued a sweeping order, judges can remain largely insulated from the conflicting pressures that swirl about the implementation process. If you are intervening to "uphold the law of the land" or "the Constitution," then "half-measures" will not do. If a "totality of conditions" order has been "issued" to remedy systemic violations of inmates' civil rights, then the immediate or potential unavailability of the human and financial resources necessary to implement and sustain all or part of the order—including the time necessary to change long-established administrative cultures and customs to make them more consonant with the new requirements—furnish "no excuse" for "noncompliance." Judges "do justice," not "make compromises"; their opinions are moderated in light of competing legal principles, not in light of conflicting political and administrative pressures; they think mainly in terms of jurisprudence, not political economy or organization theory.

Judicial intervention qua policy incrementalism thus seems "unjudicial"—and it is. But so, alas, is interventionism itself. Therein lies the practical and moral dilemma. The professional ethos of a bench that confined itself to interpreting laws is inappropriate, even perverse, for judges who make and oversee the implementation of laws. As I shall suggest later, to increase their likelihood of success, interventionist judges should leave the serenity of their chambers physically and venture behind bars in order to get firsthand, detailed knowledge about the objects and subjects of their policies. Here, however, I am suggesting that they must first leave the serenity of their chambers *conceptually.* They must not think like J.D.s but like J.D.-M.P.A.s; they must intervene not as judges, but as judge administrators. The first step in this conceptual transformation is to grasp the first general principle of sound policymaking and implementation: whenever you can, proceed incrementally.

Incremental Intervention and School Desegregation

The wisdom of an incremental approach to judicial intervention has been explored by some prominent students of the subject, most notably political scientist Jennifer Hochschild in her masterful 1984 study of school desegregation cases. Essentially, Hochschild argues that incrementalism in the making and enforcing of controversial public policies leads to inaction or to changes that are even less desirable than the status quo. But Hochschild's powerfully argued cautions against incrementalism (and certain forms of popular control) should not blind one to the implicit thesis she offers regarding the best strategy for effecting controversial policy changes via judicial intervention; namely, that while the incremental approach leads to stalemate or faulty action in normal policy situations, it may often be the best available strategy for issuing and implementing controversial policy *from the bench.*

According to Hochschild, the evidence on judicial capacity in the area of school reform was "mixed and murky," since there were "few systematic and no statistical analyses of how or how well courts design and oversee" desegregation orders.[10] But in her highly informed judgment, most "of the several hundred districts that have desegregated under court order or prodding have done so without generating horror stories."[11] And through the development of special masters, monitoring bodies, "desegregation administrators," and other devices, she argued, interventionist judges were getting progressively "better at handling institutional reform litigation" and often produced "better policies than do other institutions."[12]

In Hochschild's moving analysis, it is strongly implied that the chief reason judges often do better is that they are better able to effect major changes via a quasi-incremental approach than are other officials, elected and appointed, federal, state, and local. She offers the by now well-known example of Judge W. Arthur Garrity's intervention into Boston schools. Like most judges, observed Hochschild, Garrity was not eager to intervene massively. But Boston school officials, with the full support of key federal, state, and local politicians, refused to submit school desegregation plans of their own, refused to implement plans fashioned by Judge Garrity, and, when the judge's orders were finally being implemented, refused to address problems caused by their earlier refusals.[13] From the bench, Judge Garrity was able to break through the logjam of such "popular control" by taking a series of small but decisive steps, bringing about a measure of school desegregation in Boston over and against the wishes of many officials and citizens.[14]

Historically, incremental policymaking by elected and appointed officials spelled either no school desegregation or more harm than no desegregative change at all would cause.[15] Interestingly, however, Hochschild found a species of incremental judicial intervention to be a necessary (and in some cases sufficient) remedy that, given her admirably explicit statement of her personal value preferences, she was glad to embrace as a way of achieving school desegregation: "Incrementalism makes good sense, but it is not the stuff of Fourth of July speeches. 'Democracy' is. Nevertheless, if most citizens choose not to grant the rest of the citizens their full rights, then perhaps democracy must give way to liberalism."[16]

With Kenneth Clark, who years earlier (indeed, before the famous *Brown* decision of 1954) had criticized incremental approaches to school desegregation, Hochschild found that court-

ordered desegregation was "as effective, if not more so, than
desegregation due to other causes" and even worked better than
"voluntary desegregation."[17] Where school desegregation was concerned, Hochschild concluded, the appropriate maxim was "full
speed ahead," often with an interventionist judge working the throt-
tle of social change in a decisive but incremental fashion.[18] One cure
for the diseases of incremental popular control, she hinted, was
incremental but unyielding judicial intervention.

From the shadows of Hochschild's analysis, therefore, the ideal
typical incremental interventionist judge emerges as someone who
differs from his or her incremental-minded counterparts among
politicians and other officials in at least one crucial respect: The
judge *does* have a clear sense of mission, a clear objective or set of
objectives that he or she wants to achieve, actively pursues, and will
not cashier or "compromise away" as a result of political pressures,
bureaucratic resistance, or popular dissatisfaction. The judge may
be willing and able to let his or her actions (or simply the pace of his
or her actions) be modified and moderated by such pressures and
controversies, if only because he or she recognizes that no policy,
however wise and just (or dumb and unfair), is self-executing, and
that some measure of political, administrative, and popular support
will be necessary to implement and sustain any but the most trivial
court orders. But though he or she may steer left, steer right, and
coast along the way in order to avoid political and other whirlpools,
the incremental interventionist judge stays on course and will see
the situation remedied "or bust."

In an in-depth and methodologically sophisticated study of the
Boston case published in 1986, D. Garth Taylor suggested that
Judge Garrity's intervention was less successful than many others
had concluded; the Boston case, he concluded, supported not advocates of judicial intervention but the proponents of "incremental,
voluntary action."[19]

More important for our purposes, however, Taylor's account
indicated that Garrity's intervention succeeded to the extent that it
did because Garrity behaved in the sort of decisive but incremental
fashion sketched here. Even after Garrity and his desegregation
plan had been denounced by opponents from President Ford to
Mayor Kevin White of Boston, and even after his orders had been
blatantly bucked by local school board members and others, the

judge did not try to settle the issue in one sweeping move. He was extremely sensitive to the political, bureaucratic, and popular resistance to his plan. Though his enforcement rhetoric was sometimes harsh, and though he never blinked at his own enforcement aims, his approach throughout was gradual and flexible yet clear and steady—in short, incremental but decisive.

Indeed, Garrity's incremental approach encouraged opponents of his desegregation plans to believe that the "court might be lax and forgiving. Federal and state aid to the schools had more than once been withdrawn then restored by court order in spite of few tangible signs of cooperation by the school board."[20] For months Garrity threatened to find the school board in contempt of court for willful noncompliance with his orders. He enforced the threat but lifted it within a month, even though the school board had yet to move toward compliance.[21] Though clearly far from wholly sympathetic to the intervention, Taylor concluded: "Judge Garrity's intervention forced self-examination and public accountability on a school system that was not functioning well. . . . Those who stayed in the public school system received a better education than would have been the case without the court order."[22]

Judge Garrity's intervention achieved this measure of success largely because his approach was primarily incremental, or, as J. Anthony Lukas described it in his monumental account of school desegregation in Boston, "cautious."[23] In this connection, it is worth noting that Garrity's incremental approach was tested first in a jail case. When called upon in 1971 to remedy conditions inside Boston's dungeonlike Charles Street Jail, Garrity took his time, studying the matter and visiting the institution before opening the trial, and then letting discrete bits and pieces of his remedial order take shape over the course of a year.[24]

Of course, no one can say for sure whether things would have gone better (or worse) in Boston if Garrity had intervened in a less (or more) incremental fashion than he did. But the bulk of the evidence respecting judicial intervention into schools suggests that the incremental modus operandi exemplified by Garrity works best overall. A good complementary example is offered by Philip J. Cooper in his account of judicial intervention into Detroit's school system.

In the 1971 case of *Milken v. Bradley*, Judge Stephen Roth found Michigan officials and the Detroit School Board "guilty of fostering, operating, and maintaining segregated schools."[25] He fashioned a remedy that included large-scale busing to desegregate the city's schools, busing schoolchildren across school district boundary lines when necessary. The plan was controversial and generated widespread state and local opposition. Shortly after Roth died in 1974, the United State Supreme Court reviewed his decisions and remedial orders. The Supreme Court held that Roth had erred in ordering the busing of schoolchildren across boundary lines to achieve racial integration. Such action, the Court ruled, could be justified only if each school district affected had been found to practice racial discrimination or if it could be proven that the school district lines had been deliberately drawn to create racially segregated schools.

In giving strong support to the concept of the "neighborhood school," the Supreme Court's 1974 *Milken* decision was viewed by many as a major step away from the injunction the Court had issued twenty years earlier in its famous *Brown* II decision, namely, to desegregate the nation's public schools "with all deliberate speed." In Detroit, however, the *Milken* drama unfolded immediately as the question of what to put in place of Judge Roth's remedial plan. That question was left to Judge Robert DeMascio, who presided over the case after Roth's death.

In 1977 DeMascio's substitute plan was able to withstand the scrutiny of the United States Supreme Court. More important for our purposes, however, DeMascio succeeded in actually implementing the plan. Unlike Roth, who "found himself in trouble for having exceeded his discretion with respect" to the scope of his plan, DeMascio acted incrementally but decisively within the limits established for him by the Supreme Court's 1974 decision.[26] As Cooper concluded:

> DeMascio's second remedy established a set of remedial premises and then linked the elements of the decree to those keystones. He was able to connect the program elements to the violation rather easily even though his actions were more intrusive into local decision making in some respects than Roth's. . . . DeMascio found himself issuing a number of orders concerning faculty reassignment, changes in program requirements, and other rulings that did not substantially alter the core remedy but sought to resolve problems encountered during implementation. . . . DeMascio's use of a variety of specified particular steps virtually guar-

anteed that his office would play a major ongoing role in the implementation process.[27]

DeMascio thus intervened in small but decisive steps toward a clear goal (school desegregation), in tune to the administrative and other "practicalities of the situation"[28] but intent on finishing what Judge Roth had started. Cooper finds parallels between DeMascio's incremental interventionist approach to desegregating schools and Judge Frank M. Johnson's approach to bringing decent mental health services to Alabama's prisons.[29] By proceeding incrementally but decisively, both judges achieved most of what they set out to achieve, apparently with lasting effects.

Incremental Intervention and Environmental Protection

The popular and scholarly literature on judicial intervention in environmental protection cases is tiny by comparison to the parallel literature on school desegregation cases. R. Shep Melnick, however, has written a major study of judicial capacity in this area that focuses in part on the question of how judges, by their own manner of approaching an intervention, can enhance judicial capacity. As I read his fascinating 1983 work, the approach he recommends is quite similar to what we have been discussing: proceed incrementally but decisively.

In general, Melnick found that judicial intervention had not improved either the performance of the Environmental Protection Agency (EPA) or, in turn, the quality of the nation's air. "Taken as a whole," he concluded, "the consequences of court action under the Clean Air Act have been neither random nor beneficial. . . . The courts have formed an integral part of a policymaking system that has bred cynicism, muddled debate, created serious inequities and inefficiencies, has made rational debate and conscious political choice difficult, and kept pollution levels high in the most heavily populated parts of the country."[30]

But Melnick's persuasive negative net assessment of the impact of judicial intervention on environmental protection did not keep him from recognizing that judges would continue to shape environmental policy and that it would be beneficial to explore ways in which they might enhance their effectiveness despite "the limits of their knowledge and control."[31]

The "case studies in this book," Melnick argued, "show that what the courts need most is a better understanding of *administrative* issues, not technical ones. . . . To perform competently the tasks they have taken on, judges must learn more about the nature of the problems they seek to cure, the policy options open to administrators, and the constraints on those who must carry out their orders."[32] The proposals Melnick offered to facilitate such judicial learning are, in effect, a recipe for an approach to intervention that is incremental but decisive.

For example, Melnick recommended that intervening judges start thinking "about specific remedies as soon as they consider possible interpretations of the law."[33] On the one hand, and as Melnick was quick to point out, greater specificity in remedial orders would reduce the discretion of EPA officials. But on the other hand, and as he also observed, to fashion specific remedies at an early stage judges would need to "put themselves in closer touch" with the views of agency officials and line workers (not just agency attorneys) "*before* the decision is carved in stone. This diminishes the likelihood that courts and agency attorneys will set goals that other agency officials know cannot be achieved," or achieved in accordance with a given timetable.[34]

Thus Melnick suggested that, at the very outset of the remedial phase of an intervention, judges should take pains (and time) to gather information and perspectives from a wide variety of actors, including some who might be hostile or highly skeptical about the need for any changes. They should allow the information and perspectives thus gathered to shape their orders. But the orders, once fashioned, should be specific and rigorously enforced. To increase the chances for success in environmental policy directed from the bench, Melnick, in effect, recommended that remedies be fashioned and enforced incrementally but decisively.

For our purposes, another especially relevant aspect of Melnick's powerful analysis is his discussion of judges' variance-granting behavior in relation to judicial capacity. When Congress passed the Clean Air Act of 1970, most states responded by issuing hastily drawn up pollution control plans. Many states made their plans effective immediately and used variances to give polluters time to achieve compliance. Both the EPA and the states "found it necessary to use enforcement orders—which differed from variances in name only—to negotiate deals with polluters."[35] But fearing "that the administrative leniency would undermine the Clean Air Act's rigid deadlines, several circuit courts prohibited EPA from allowing states to grant polluters variances after 1975."[36] As Melnick observed, these prohibitions proved extremely counterproductive, doing much to create legal and administrative turmoil, controversy, and confusion but nothing to clean the air. The Supreme Court eventually reversed the prohibitions, but by that time the damage had already been done.

Incremental Intervention and Correctional Institutions

How judges handle variances is an acid test both of whether they are willing, and how adeptly they are able, to initiate and sustain an incremental but decisive approach to intervention. As should be obvious, at the core of this approach is a dialectical tension between being cautious and being firm, being flexible and being resolute, being gradual and being determined. A judge who almost never grants variances is probably "too decisive"; a judge who almost always grants them is probably "too incremental." Somewhat paradoxically, it may be that to successfully perform what many consider to be the least judicial of acts—making and implementing laws—a judge may need an even greater measure of intellectual balance and restraint than he or she does when successfully performing the traditional task of interpreting laws.

With respect to judicial intervention in prisons and jails, probably our best single illustration of the importance of balanced variance-granting behavior, and of the general capacity-enhancing value of proceeding incrementally but decisively, is Storey's account of Judge Morris E. Lasker's role in reforming New York City's jails (chapter 6).

The Rhem *Case in New York City*

As Storey recounts, Judge Lasker's approach to the litigation was "pragmatic." Lasker would have agreed with Glazer's argument that judges are not in the best possible position to effect good public policies. "The legislature and the executive," Lasker reflected, "are without question better equipped to handle these matters. They have more power, funds, and experience." In the case before him, however, most of the relevant elected and appointed officials seemed indifferent at best to the constitutional status of living conditions and operations inside the old Tombs jail. There was no shortage of written materials, from legal documents entered in evidence to newspaper stories, indicating that the old Tombs, a place where pretrial detainees were routinely handled as maximum security felons, was filthy, dilapidated, and otherwise unfit for human habitation. Lasker read these materials, but he also visited the Tombs to examine things for himself. He concluded that the plaintiffs' allegations were correct. His *Rhem* decree left no doubt about either the necessity of changes at the Tombs or his resolve to see that these changes were made.

Led by Mayor Abraham Beame, however, New York City officials, resentful of the judge's "interference" and harboring other budgetary priorities, stonewalled Lasker's decree to improve the jail. Lasker understood that the changes he was ordering at the Tombs, and those that he might yet have to order at other city jails, probably could not be sustained if he effected them through any sort of judicial blitzkrieg. He understood enough about jail administration, the complicated politics of New York City, and the opposition that correctional officers and their unions could generate to sense that such an approach could result only in a Pyrrhic victory for reform. So he moved slowly but firmly, building up a measure of goodwill within the corrections department and beyond it.

For example, the city's corrections commissioner, Benjamin Malcolm, recognized that Lasker could have issued contempt citations against him and other officials, "but being the compassionate person he is, he did not." The Beame administration, however, remained uncooperative, and Lasker gradually turned up the heat. Finally, the judge ordered the Tombs closed within thirty days unless the city produced a detailed plan to remedy the unconstitutional conditions at the jail. The city appealed, but the Second Circuit upheld Lasker's gutsy improve-it-or-close-it decision.

Lasker thought the city would comply; he was surprised when Beame opted to close the Tombs rather than implement his orders to improve the dungeonlike jail. But manifesting his incrementalism as a form of judicial jujitsu, Lasker turned the city's decision against it by holding that inmates transferred from the Tombs to another institution were entitled to the living conditions specified in *Rhem*. The Second Circuit Court agreed.

Thereafter, inmates at the House of Detention for Men (HDM) claimed on behalf of all HDM detainees the protections spelled out in *Rhem*. The city kept a temporary injunction for relief at HDM tied up on appeal. Then, in the heat of the summer of 1975, HDM experienced a major riot that included the taking of hostages. The rioters requested that Lasker come to the facility; he did so. The riot ended, but the city's stalling tactics continued.

Naturally, Lasker was frustrated. But, as Storey observes, "Lasker hesitated to push the city too quickly toward reform" and normally proceeded "as if the parties were operating in good faith." Never, however, was there any doubt in the minds of city officials that Lasker intended to see the intervention through to the operational and other changes specified in *Rhem*.

One significant overall effect of Lasker's incremental but decisive approach was to make converts out of both zealous reformers and skeptical administrators. For example, in the aftermath of the HDM riot, Joel Berger, a project director for the Prisoners' Rights Project of the Legal Aid Society, felt that "Lasker made some mistakes in allowing the city's delays." Years later, however, Berger observed: "Lasker was going slow in the way he was implementing things, but he wasn't cutting back on substance. . . . Today, I realize he steered us through the budget crisis very successfully." Coming from the opposite side, Commissioner Malcolm observed that, over the course of the intervention, his "early view of Lasker as a judge overstepping his boundary changed to that of a judge who had the guts and courage to stand up and keep the system in line."

Storey's rich account provides evidence aplenty that Lasker's intervention was not an unqualified success. And, of course, one can always wonder how much better (or worse) things would have gone had Lasker behaved less (or more) incrementally than he did. Lasker never envisioned the intricate web of organizations and personalities that would eventually prove necessary to move the city into only partial compliance or the twists and turns in city politics that would define the Koch years and profoundly affect the post-1978 course of the intervention. But today "parties on both sides of the litigation agree that, absent the court's intervention and the firm stewardship of Judge Lasker, pretrial detainees in New York City would still be suffering inhumane conditions."

As is hinted in Storey's analysis, and as I myself learned when I served as a consultant to the New York City Board of Corrections in 1986, Lasker's incremental but decisive approach was displayed clearly in his variance-granting behavior. Lasker did not suppose that he or his aides had any special correctional expertise or that either the substance or the timetables established around his remedial orders were beyond the reproach of experience. He thus remained genuinely open to requests for variances with his orders, including those pertaining to jail population limits.

City officials, however, understood that they could not expect judicial grace from Lasker at every turn; good-faith efforts to comply, coupled with good reasons for temporary nonperformance, were required before Lasker would grant a variance. As one city Board of Corrections official told me: "Lasker set the tone back in 1974. The tone was 'You play fair with me, and I'll respect your legitimate limits and needs.' He would take two steps forward and one step back to give the department and the City administration time to get the job done, and to prepare the line staff psychologically; but everyone understood that his patience could be exhausted. He was cautious and liked to operate by consensus, but he never sent mixed signals."

The Crain Case in West Virginia

As Storey's account makes clear, the political and budgetary context in which Lasker's intervention occurred was by no means favorable to the intervention. And as Bert Useem's account of the *Crain* case in West Virginia (chapter 8) makes equally clear, no political brass band greeted Judge Arthur Recht's intervention into the West Virginia Penitentiary. Just months before handing down his decision on the prison case, Judge Recht had issued a 290-page opinion ordering "the Legislature to completely reconstruct the entire system of education in West Virginia." This opinion caused a firestorm of protest, including this comment from the chairman of the state senate's Finance Committee: "Judge Recht ought to get a haircut. I just thought it was a long-haired decision, and I equate it with the hippie clan. West Virginia is not in a position to afford the standards he envisioned."

Recht was "stunned by the unexpected outcry" and determined resistance triggered by his sweeping school decision. He thus proceeded a bit more carefully in the prison case. The West Virginia Penitentiary was physically dilapidated and overcrowded. Food and medical services were clearly substandard. And the prison did not offer the "rehabilitative" programs mandated by an earlier ruling, based on a state statute, and interpreted by the court to mean that "rehabilitation" was the "primary goal of the West Virginia corrections system." Recht, who toured the facility, found the prison in violation of constitutional and statutory standards. But his decree gave corrections officials nearly five months to submit a compliance plan, stating that the "[r]espondents must be given the opportunity, in the first instance, to put their own house in order." At the same time, however, he made clear that massive renovations of the prison's physical plant would be required, and he warned that "the lack of public funds would not be accepted as an excuse" for failures to comply with this or any other part of his order.

Unfortunately for our purposes, and possibly for the cause of penal reform in West Virginia, the experiment of Recht's tentative embrace of an incremental but decisive approach to intervention ended prematurely. Recht resigned from the bench in the fall of 1983. The corrections department's compliance plan was reviewed and approved by Recht's replacement, Judge John Bronson. In Useem's account, Bronson emerges as a judge whose approach to the intervention is best characterized as weak and halfhearted. In 1986 the compliance plan accepted by Bronson was declared inadequate by the West Virginia Supreme Court. In 1988 that court ordered the penitentiary closed by 1992.

This process of "nonreformist reform," as Useem characterizes it, "was intensely frustrating to inmates" and probably figured in the 1986 riot that occurred at the penitentiary. The court proclaimed the penitentiary to be in need of basic changes. It thereby legitimized inmate grievances about conditions inside the penitentiary. It promised to improve these conditions despite the contrary wishes and priorities of many state and local officials. But in this instance, the "lever" of court power, as Useem phrases it, was not exercised in

an incremental but decisive manner. After 1983 elected and appointed officials defied Recht's rulings on both prisons and schools
with impunity, calling the rulings "foolish, if not the whimsical
opinions of a 'hippie' clan." "Unsuccessful judicial reform," concludes Useem, "is (in the short run) more destabilizing than no
reform at all." Or, one might add, weak and stunted intervention is
worse than no intervention at all.

Often, the only type of experiments open to one interested in
"what if" questions as they relate to such complex real-world
dramas as judicial intervention are so-called thought experiments.
What if "a Lasker" had presided over the entire intervention in
West Virginia? Although they did not tell him to "get a haircut" or
charge him with being part of a "hippie clan," the officials who
resisted Lasker's intervention into New York City's jail system were
arguably every bit as determined, and even more politically re-
sourceful, than those who bucked Recht in West Virginia. And,
arguably, a bankrupt New York City in 1974 furnished an economic
environment no more conducive to potentially costly penal reforms
than that furnished by a recession-ridden West Virginia in 1982. At
a minimum, it may be safe to say that had "a Lasker" (or a
succession of "Laskers") presided in West Virginia, the political and
economic factors that eroded the court's capacity there would probably have proven less fatal to the cause of reform.

The Guthrie Case in Georgia

We need not speculate, however, about the effects of an incremental
but decisive approach to intervention in the *Guthrie* case in Georgia. As Bradley S. Chilton and Susette M. Talarico stress (chapter
5), Judge Anthony A. Alaimo was but one of thirty-six key decision
makers who affected the course and consequences of the intervention. At certain points, Alaimo "did play a pivotal role in leading
the case toward resolution," but these occasions were rare, and the
judge left many crucial decisions to his court-appointed personnel.
From Chilton and Talarico's account, however, it seems clear that
Alaimo's delegational style of handling the litigation did not keep
him from steering the intervention in a slow but firm fashion. Other
actors, especially the special master and court monitors whom

Alaimo selected, were influential, but most of them followed the judge's incremental but decisive tempo.

As Chilton and Talarico report, Alaimo "used the contempt citation once to enforce remedial decrees and threatened to use receivership or other punitive measures if compliance was not achieved quickly." At the same time, however, Alaimo apparently cut a deal with the state's governor that gave the state "more input in the formulation of the remedial decrees in the case." In return, the state agreed to settle the case rather than litigate to appeal. Many of those involved in the litigation believe that the "case took far too long to settle." But Alaimo's approach embodied a recognition that "settlement of the case by court-approved consent decrees and stipulations might not have been possible had the state pursued full civil trial and appeal." "It may be," Chilton and Talarico observe, "that Judge Alaimo foresaw that the state would not have made long-lasting changes had he mandated them by judicial order alone."

The *Guthrie* settlement proved quite costly in financial terms. Also, Alaimo kept his court aides on a rather long chain, and resentment of his special master was widespread among corrections staff. And the transparent lunacy of letting a case that began with a complaint concerning seven basic quality of life issues end in over twenty-five hundred remedial decrees, covering everything including the temperature of various hot food items served in the inmate dining hall, raises some serious questions about Alaimo's approach. Nevertheless, after over a decade of court involvement, "all parties to the *Guthrie* case appeared satisfied with Judge Alaimo and the results." The key result, of course, was that the Georgia State Penitentiary (GSP) was safer and more humane at the close of the intervention than it had been the first day that Alaimo intervened. If Alaimo had not intervened, or if he had intervened in a less incremental but decisive fashion, conditions at GSP would almost certainly be less decent than they are today.

The *Ruiz* Case in Texas

Much the same, agree the authors of our "Three Faces of *Ruiz*" (chapters 2, 3, and 4), can be said of Judge William Wayne Justice's intervention into the Texas Department of Corrections (TDC). Though my own interpretation of that instance of judicial intervention gives the court very low marks for several aspects of how it proceeded (chapter 2), I was still able to write that "there was absolutely nothing about the court's ruling, least of all in Judge Justice's order to abolish the corruptive building tender system, that made good prison government in Texas impossible. . . . While parts of the court's order . . . wrested important carrots and sticks from the hands of Texas keepers, nothing in the letter of the court's decree gutted TDC's basic custodial controls or made tight, security-conscious institutional management illegal."

Substantively, Judge Justice did proceed in an incremental but decisive fashion. Sheldon Ekland-Olson and Steve J. Martin (chapter 3) highlight many instances in which Justice showed restraint, moved in small steps, and gave TDC the time he believed it needed to comply with key provisions of his decree. Ben M. Crouch and James W. Marquart (chapter 4) reinforce this image of a patient, pragmatic Justice who, at least in some instances, tolerated TDC's "footdragging" in the interests of its eventual, and sustainable, compliance with his specific orders.

From each of our three interpretations of *Ruiz*, however, it seems clear that Justice's intervention would probably have succeeded better, in the sense of reducing somewhat the overall human and financial toll for the improvements finally rendered, had it been as consistently incremental but decisive in tone as it was in content. The authors of these interpretations cannot agree on whether, or to what extent, the judge's actions were indirectly responsible for the violence that racked TDC in 1984 and 1985. Nor can we agree on whether the huge financial bill for the intervention, the modus operandi of the judge's special master, and other controversial aspects of the litigation were justified. And, at bottom, our respective interpretations move from fundamentally different conceptions of the proper role of the judiciary, the proper way to treat incarcerated citizens, and the nature of moral responsibility. But we can and do agree that there were certain symbolic things that the judge could have done, but did not do, that might have made his intervention somewhat less costly in human and financial terms, things that would have made his approach more consistently incremental but decisive in style as well as in substance.

First, we suggest that Judge Justice's intervention might have been helped had he personally set foot inside of the prisons he was trying to reform. Other intervening judges in other cases have personally toured the objects of their intervention—Johnson in Alabama, Lasker in New York City, Recht in West Virginia, Alaimo in Georgia, and many more. As every serious student of correctional institutions knows, one can read all of the books, essays, operational manuals, post orders, and neatly typed depositions in the world and still have a less clear sense of how, and how well, a prison or jail operates than someone who has read none of this material but has spent a day or two observing operations and talking to inmates and staff, behind the walls. If you want to know whether cells are cramped, enter them; if you want to know whether food is decent, eat it; if you want to know whether the staff-to-inmate ratio is too low, sit in a cellblock and see how it runs; and so on.

Of course, there are limits to how detailed and frequent a judge's on-site visits can be; and we recognize that, in any complex intervention, judges must use special masters, monitors, and other aids to be the "eyes and ears" of the court out in the field. But there is a large indirect benefit that may accrue to judges who "personalize" the intervention by visiting the institutions, talking to staff as well as inmates, and taking the time to observe things for themselves, a benefit that goes beyond firsthand fact-finding or merely informational visits; namely, it may help them to better understand and to harness the organizational culture of the institutions they are trying to change.

As James Q. Wilson has defined it, organizational culture is "a persistent, patterned way of thinking about the central tasks of human relationships within an organization. Culture is to organization what personality is to individual. Like human culture generally, it is passed on from one generation to the next."[37] The "personality" of TDC was proud, self-confident, and insular to the point that, as Ekland-Olson and Martin phrase it, many TDC staff felt that the agency was properly "a law unto itself." This strong organizational culture was not solicitous of "outsiders" or "know-nothing critics."

For example, in my own research on the Texas case, I kept files of interviews with TDC staff, each of them labeled with an epitomizing quote taken from one of the interviews contained therein. One of these files was headed "Sonofabitch judge never even bothered to come in here"; it contained several pages of comments by scores of TDC workers at all levels who felt that Judge Justice's failure to visit the prisons bespoke his bias, contempt, and lack of appreciation for the "redneck guards" who were the backbone of TDC's operation. The judge's perceived "anti-TDC" sentiments, these same TDC staff felt, were amplified in the "attitude" of the judge's special master and other court aids. As Ekland-Olson and Martin make clear, TDC staff believed deeply in the legitimacy of their way of running prisons, which for many included the "skilled" use of physical intimidation against troublesome inmates by officers and by their quasi-official inmate assistants, the so-called building tenders. And as Crouch and Marquart stress, TDC was an enormously complex organization in which the informal and formal aspects of "guard subculture" formed a seamless administrative web. Thus, even those TDC veterans who eschewed any use of illegal force against inmates bitterly resented the judge's "attack on TDC."

Clearly, as Ekland-Olson and Martin perceptively write, where "the court saw brutality, administrators saw order, safety, and cleanliness. It is in this unbalanced view of the same reality that the seeds of mutual distrust were sewn"; and, one might add, it was because of this mutual distrust that the rocky road of the intervention was set in stone. The "mistrust of Judge Justice by prison administrators," they observe, "was grounded in perceptions of fairness and bias."

For our purposes, whether these perceptions matched the reality (as I think is partially true) or were groundless (as Ekland-Olson and Martin persuasively argue) is largely irrelevant. Instead, the question is whether the judge could have done a bit more than he did to effectively manage these perceptions in a way that would have short-circuited the reflexive hostility of bureaucrats in a position to subvert his orders and to otherwise raise the human and financial costs of the intervention. Though to varying degrees, we think that in addition to visiting the institutions, he could have done more, if only in stylistic and symbolic terms.

Read with a dispassionate eye, the judge's statements on TDC quoted by Ekland-Olson and Martin do not automatically strike one as unqualified, all-out attacks on the personal character, professional integrity, and agency achievements of each and every TDC worker, past and present. But as Ekland-Olson and Martin indicate, the TDC officials who read these statements were far from dispassionate. Thus did TDC leader W. J. Estelle denounce one of the judge's statements as having "vilified one of the finest prison staffs in the U.S."; and thus did I record a typical veteran TDC line worker complaining that the judge "was all over us like stink on a skunk," and another lamenting that the "judge gave us no credit."[38]

These sentiments of wounded organizational pride deepened the resistance of a demoralized TDC staff to the court's intervention, empowered inmates to assert themselves, and may have contributed to the relatively weak staff response to the violence that mounted in 1984 and 1985. As Ekland-Olson and Martin conclude, certain "messages coming from the court" struck TDC staff as "insulting and uncalled for. They appeared, as DiIulio notes, as an unkind preoccupation with the failings of TDC. As such they further symbolized the illegitimacy of the court's findings. This denial of legitimacy and perception of insult had very real consequences for the constraints on and opportunities for violence within the cellblocks."

So far as the Texas case is concerned, our main point is certainly not that all would have been calm in TDC had Judge Justice toured the facilities, shaken hands with officers in the cellblocks, spent hours in private, philosophical discussions with Estelle and other TDC leaders, patted TDC workers on the back in public statements, or merely qualified his rhetoric and actions (and that of his special master and other aids) to make unmistakably clear that the intervention was not an indictment of everything that TDC and its staff had ever done and ever stood for. Rather, our main point is threefold: first, organizational cultures cannot be changed by fiat; second, as Ekland-Olson and Martin phrase it, "strong loyalties to a long-established way of life die slowly"; and third, an intervening judge can, by the way in which the spirit of his or her actions is perceived by staff, either hasten the death of the "old ways" or galvanize the resistance of those who cling to them.

In this regard, the penetrating account of TDC's guard subculture provided by Crouch and Marquart makes clear that some, though by no means all of the court's orders threatened the organizational life of TDC staff in ways that they were bound to resist. "Even when consent decrees on some issues were signed by state officials," Crouch and Marquart observe, "unit staff and even central office administrators in TDC continued to operate in the old ways. . . . [But] not all points of Judge Justice's decree were equally resisted." TDC staff agreed that poor medical care, overcrowding, and sanitation were problems, and they did not resist the judge's efforts to remedy these defects. "The resistance came instead on those points in the decree that directly questioned the dominance of officers and their discretion to maintain control in ways they deemed effective."

If the judge had moved from the reading of TDC's organizational culture implied by our three faces of *Ruiz*, and if he were attuned to the full range of implementation problems that might occur if that culture were activated in general opposition to his decree, then he might have opted to move in the less controversial areas first, personally visit the institutions, court and coax TDC officials a bit more than he did, and restrain his rhetoric without raising any doubts about either his extreme displeasure with the agency or his firm intention to change it. In short, he might have tried to make his intervention as incremental but decisive in style as it was in substance.

What, if any, other lessons (or, better, "hypotheses") about the relationship between judicial approach and judicial capacity can be drawn from the *Ruiz* case we leave to our readers, and to whichever interpretation of the case they favor. But this much, we think, is clear: The *Ruiz* case suggests that, especially in a far-reaching intervention, it is not enough to proceed incrementally but decisively in substance; like any good change-inducing administrator working with a large, complex organization, the judge must manage the symbols and the perceptions of legitimacy surrounding his or her organizationally disruptive actions.

Conclusion

The impact of judicial intervention on prisons and jails has varied from instance to instance, jurisdiction to jurisdiction, and within given jurisdictions over time. Overall, however, the impact of judicial intervention in this area has been positive. Generally, levels of safety, services, and basic life amenities have improved where judges have intervened. The human and financial costs of judicial intervention, however, have rarely been trivial. Many factors, it seems, determine the net impact of an intervention. One powerful influence on the course and consequences of an intervention is the modus operandi of the intervening judge. Since there is a fair probability that judges will continue to intervene in prisons and jails, it is vital that they proceed in ways that stand the greatest probability of maximizing improvements at the lowest possible human and financial costs.

The costs of an intervention are increased where the judge's actions stir popular and bureaucratic resistance. Based on the instances of judicial intervention analyzed in this book, and the broader knowledge of the field brought to bear by the volume's authors, it seems that one thing that judges can do to reduce such resistance and the costs it entails is to proceed incrementally but decisively. This suggestion implies many things. It implies that "totality of conditions" interventions are to be avoided whenever possible in favor of specific remedies aimed at specific institutional problems. It also implies the need to frame the substance, tone, and timing of an intervention in light of whatever popular and bureaucratic pressures may arise, and to physically go "where the action is," meaning into the prisons and jails where the problems exist and where the people who will be most directly affected by the intervention live and work.

Despite the illustrations offered here, and despite whatever further evidence one may add in support of the approach advocated, we recognize that the injunction to proceed incrementally is little more than a "proverb of administration" offered up to enhance judicial capacity. The practical value of such administrative proverbs has long been questioned by academic theorists, and we recognize that its value to judges, even as a rule of thumb or a mere reminder of the complex events that an intervention may set in motion, may be limited at best.[39] Given the exploratory level at which we have been working, however, we think that this recommendation points in the right direction, and we doubt that any more precise or prudent strategy can be formulated before more systematic empirical research on this topic is produced; we happily await that day.

Earlier I mentioned that Storey's account of Judge Lasker's intervention into the New York City jail system is perhaps our most clear-cut success story and the best single illustration of the merits of an incremental but decisive approach to intervention. But if there is one chapter in this book that is evocative of our more general conclusions about judicial intervention into prisons and jails, it is Edward E. Rhine's detailed examination of how the U.S. Supreme Court's *Wolff* decision and the New Jersey Supreme Court's *Avant* decision played themselves out in the disciplinary process at New Jersey's Rahway State Prison (chapter 7). Let me conclude, therefore, by highlighting three key points suggested by this chapter.

First, any reader of Rhine's analysis should be struck by the level of detail it contains. But the detailed medium in this case is part of the broader message. Rhine's account of the process of implementing court-ordered changes in disciplinary practices at Rahway is a vivid testimony to the fact that public policies, including those enunciated from the bench, do not "trickle down" into implementation; the implementation process is often long, tangled, painstakingly staged, and the source of good and bad effects that no one, including the policy's architects, intended. Where operational changes in large, complex bureaucracies are concerned, God is truly in the details; policymakers, including interventionist judges, who ignore this administrative reality, and who thus assume that every instance of policy "noncompliance" is due to willful bureaucratic neglect or subversion and react accordingly, do so at their peril. Especially for the judges who may be among our readers, therefore, the details of Rhine's analysis should be not mind-numbing but mind-liberating.

Second, Rhine's account leaves the unmistakable impression that, prior to the court decisions, conditions and key operational practices inside Rahway were sorely in need of reform, and that, absent those decisions, no such reforms would have been made, or made as quickly. At the same time, however, Rhine takes us inside a corrections department and inside one particular prison, in which most managers and line workers were well motivated, cared about the inmates, and wanted to fulfill not only their legal obligations to the court but their professional obligations as persons in charge of the care and custody of incarcerated citizens.

In this respect, Rhine hints at what Clair A. Cripe argues force-fully (chapter 10); namely, that neither judges nor others with an interest in improving the quality of life behind bars should ever forget that contemporary corrections workers are public servants who conscientiously perform a tough, often thankless job. We should not judge them by unseemly conditions or practices born through generations of neglect by others—conditions and practices that, given the necessary resources, corrections workers would be the first to correct and improve. "At Rahway," Rhine observes, "there was a discernible—if matter of fact—recognition that in-mates were entitled to fairness [in disciplinary proceedings], that they could not be treated as they had been prior to *Wolff* and *Avant*. This recognition was extended from the superintendent down to prison staff and even to some of the officers. The hearing officers themselves seemed to be committed, at least in most instances, to giving a prisoner a fair shake."

Third, Rhine's study highlights the competing moral values and practical tensions that surround not only the question of how to structure a prison disciplinary process but the broader question of the proper way to run prisons and jails. In *Wolff* and *Avant*, judges forced correctional administrators to temper their natural desire to discipline unruly inmates with a concern for treating alleged viola-tors fairly. The judges set in motion a process of administrative changes in which disciplinary hearing officers at Rahway, and perhaps at other prisons as well, "usually provided an inmate [formally charged with a rule violation] with an opportunity to establish his innocence . . . within the context of taken-for-granted assumptions [about the inmate's veracity and character] that render his efforts to do so difficult but by no means impossible." In effect, in the place of a situation in which corrections officials could dole out punishment if they informally "sized up the convict" and thought "he had it coming," the judges fostered a situation in which corrections officials were expected to follow a pale but recognizable version of the due process procedures that the criminally accused citizen in the "free world" is normally granted.

Finally, there are many Americans, including the editor, who do not feel that inmates have any clear moral or constitutional entitle-ment to such protections, and who further believe that, as a general rule, it is improper for the judiciary to engineer changes in public policy and administrative practice. And there are many Americans who, while harboring no particular opinion on such issues one way or the other, care little if at all about the quality of life behind bars. Both groups should know that judges have intervened, and may well continue to intervene, to effect improvements in the nation's prisons and jails and to protect inmates' legally established rights to safe and humane confinement. Philosophical differences (or uninformed apathy) to one side, it is in everyone's best interest that judicial capacity in this area be enhanced, and that the intersection of courts, corrections, and the Constitution be further analyzed to see how, if at all, this can be achieved.

Notes

1. Draft of National Crime Emergency Act, April 18, 1989.
2. Dennis J. Thompson, "The Moral Responsibility of Public Officials: The Problem of Many Hands," *The American Political Science Review* 74, no. 4 (December 1980), 905–16.
3. Herbert Kaufman, *The Forest Ranger: A Study in Administrative Behavior* (Baltimore, MD: The Johns Hopkins University Press, 1960).
4. Address of the Honorable William Wayne Justice presented to the 114th Congress of the American Correctional Association, San Antonio, Texas, August 20, 1984.
5. Charles E. Lindblom, "The Science of 'Muddling Through,'" in *Public Administration: Concepts and Cases*, ed. Richard J. Stillman II (Boston: Houghton Mifflin, 1976), pp. 151–61.
6. Ibid., p. 152.
7. Ibid., p. 159.
8. Ibid., pp. 158–59.
9. There are exceptions to this rule, but both the scholarly and the popular literature on American public sector careers tend to support it. For one reflective account, see Stimson Bullitt, *To Be a Politician*, rev. ed. (New Haven: Yale University Press, 1977).
10. Jennifer L. Hochschild, *The New American Dilemma: Liberal Democracy and School Desegregation* (New Haven: Yale University Press, 1984), p. 136.
11. Ibid.
12. Ibid., p. 138.
13. Ibid., p. 137.

14. Hochschild points out that Garrity allowed for "extensive citizen control of desegregation implementation" in Boston; the results were mixed (*The New American Dilemma*, pp. 111–12). For our purposes, however, the point is that Garrity structured his intervention in a way that permitted some delays and compromises but did not derail implementation of his major orders.

15. Hochschild, *The New American Dilemma*, especially chapters 4 and 5.

16. Ibid., p. 145.

17. Ibid., p. 147.

18. Ibid., pp. 177–98.

19. D. Garth Taylor, *Public Opinion and Collective Action: The Boston School Desegregation Conflict* (Chicago: University of Chicago Press, 1986), pp. 203–4.

20. Ibid., pp. 185–86.

21. Ibid., p. 186.

22. Ibid., p. 198.

23. J. Anthony Lukas, *Common Ground: A Turbulent Decade in the Lives of Three American Families* (New York: Knopf, 1985), p. 230.

24. Ibid., pp. 230–31.

25. Phillip J. Cooper, *Hard Judicial Choices: Federal District Court Judges and State and Local Officials* (New York: Oxford University Press, 1988), p. 110.

26. Ibid., p. 346.

27. Ibid., pp. 346–48.

28. Ibid., p. 346.

29. Ibid., p. 347.

30. R. Shep Melnick, *Regulation and the Courts: The Case of the Clean Air Act* (Washington, D.C.: Brookings Institution, 1983), pp. 344, 387.

31. Ibid., p. 387.

32. Ibid., p. 388.

33. Ibid.

34. Ibid., pp. 388–89.

35. Ibid., p. 351.

36. Ibid.

37. James Q. Wilson, *Bureaucracy: What Government Agencies Do and Why They Do It* (New York: Basic Books, 1989), p. 91.

38. It is worth noting that few of the line staff ever read or heard any of the judge's statements. Word of what "Willie Wayne" had said or penned trickle down from the central office; as the "news" passed down the line, translations of what the judge had written or said grew more negative. At one point in the intervention, for example, a number of

TDC line officers told me, in the words of one, "The judge calls us no-good bastards right there in the court papers, right there in black and white." Of course, the judge never wrote any such thing.

39. For a classic critique of such administrative proverbs, see Herbert Simon, *Administrative Behavior* (New York: Macmillan, 1945), chapter 2. Simon, however, did not put anything of practical value to practitioners in place of the proverbs he criticized so forcefully; neither have subsequent "administrative scientists." For a brief defense of one whose "proverbs" Simon challenged, see Steven Blumberg, "A Tribute to Luther Gulick," *Public Administration Review* 41 (1981), 245–48.

Index